ACTS OF NARRATIVE:
TEXTUAL STRATEGIES IN
MODERN GERMAN FICTION

THEORY / CULTURE

Editors: Linda Hutcheon, Gary Leonard, Jill Matus, Janet Paterson, and Paul Perron

PATRICK O'NEILL

Acts of Narrative:
Textual Strategies in
Modern German Fiction

UNIVERSITY OF TORONTO PRESS
Toronto Buffalo London

ISBN 0-8020-0982-4

Printed on acid-free paper

Canadian Cataloguing in Publication Data

O'Neill, Patrick, 1945–
  Acts of narrative

  (Theory/culture)
  Includes bibliographical references and index.
  ISBN 0-8020-0982-4

  1. German fiction – 20th century – History and
  criticism.   2. Narration (Rhetoric).   I. Title.
  II. Series.

  PT772.054 1996   833'.910923   C96-931035-8

University of Toronto Press acknowledges the financial assistance to its publishing program of the Canada Council and the Ontario Arts Council.

This book has been published with the help of a grant from the Canadian Federation for the Humanities, using funds provided by the Social Sciences and Humanities Research Council of Canada.

For Trudi,
as always;

Conor, Owen, Brian, and Siobhán,
whose stories continue;

and Archimedes,
for a place to stand.

Contents

Conclusion 175

Acknowledgments

Earlier versions of certain chapters and parts of chapters in this book, here comprehensively reworked, have already appeared in print. Chapter 2, chronologically the oldest layer of the project as a whole, reshapes and combines two earlier pieces on Kafka that first appeared in *Franz Kafka (1883–1983): His Craft and Thought*, ed. Roman Struc and J.C. Yardley (Waterloo: Wilfrid Laurier University Press, 1986), and in my book *The Comedy of Entropy: Humour, Narrative, Reading* (Toronto: University of Toronto Press, 1990) respectively. Chapter 5 develops work that first appeared in *Analogon Rationis: Festschrift für Gerwin Marahrens*, ed. Marianne Henn and Christoph Lorey (Edmonton: University of Alberta Press, 1994). Versions of chapters 6 and 7 first appeared in *German Quarterly* (1991) and *Seminar* (1991) respectively, and a version of chapter 8 first appeared in *Hinter dem schwarzen Vorhang: Die Katastrophe und die epische Tradition. Festschrift für Anthony W. Riley*, ed. Friedrich Gaede, Patrick O'Neill, and Ulrich Scheck (Tübingen: Francke, 1994). My thanks are due to the respective editors and publishers for permission to make further use of the relevant material. My particular thanks are due to the Social Sciences and Humanities Research Council of Canada for a generous three-year research grant that finally enabled me to bring together the different strands of a complex of ideas I had been mulling over in various formats and contexts, interrupted and accompanied by several other more or less related projects, for twenty years and more. Several generations of graduate and undergraduate students of modern German narrative at the University of British Columbia and at Queen's University assisted me materially over those years in clarifying and testing my overall critical approach. Three anonymous readers at the University of Toronto Press rendered valuable assistance in eliminating further blind spots. My thanks are also due to Queen's University for initial research support for the project that emerged from all of this and especially for an invaluable year of sabbatical leave during which much of the present book took shape.

ACTS OF NARRATIVE:
TEXTUAL STRATEGIES IN
MODERN GERMAN FICTION

Introduction

every telling has a taling and that's the he and the she of it

James Joyce, *Finnegans Wake* 213.14–15

This book has a straightforward aim: to apply the principles of modern narratology to a selection of twentieth-century German narratives, with a view to generating readings that will have something to say both to those whose primary interest is in the intersection of narrative theory and critical practice and to those whose primary interest is in modern German (or comparative) literature. The approach adopted rests on three assumptions: first, that all stories are stories *told* in particular ways; second, that these particular ways of telling stories are interesting objects of study in and for themselves; and third, that modern German fiction includes a number of narratives that allow us to indulge that interest in ways that are themselves interesting. Why German? First, and most obviously, because it is a body of narrative texts with which I have been professionally involved for many years as a university teacher of German literature; second, because this particular approach, for various reasons, is relatively rare among critics who specialize in the study of German literature; and third, because modern (and postmodern) German narrative constitutes a body of important and often fascinating texts with which international narrative theorists and critics, regrettably, are for the most part relatively unfamiliar.

The book is thus aimed at a double audience, for, on the one hand, international currents of poststructuralist criticism of this kind remain still largely unapplied to German literary texts, and, on the other, modern German narrative, unlike French or Latin American or Italian, is still relatively little known in the English-speaking world. My aim is therefore twofold and bidirectional: to bring a major international current of criticism that has hitherto been largely neglected in the criticism of German literary texts to bear on a group of key twentieth-century German narratives and, conversely, to bring those key texts to the attention of an international audience in this particular tradition. To accommodate the double audience envisaged here, the texts, though consistently referred to for simplicity's sake by their German titles, will therefore be cited throughout both in German and in translation.

This book, finally, is centrally concerned with the systemic capacity for *play* that is structurally inherent in literary narrative texts, and although it is certainly intended to be readable purely in its own terms – and should obviously stand or fall entirely on its own merits – it is also conceived of as the final volume in a 'ludic' trilogy that has occupied my energies for the better part of the past two decades. The trilogy began with *The Comedy of Entropy* (1990), which investigated in the overall framework of general cultural studies the intersection of ludic and entropic discourses in the cultural fabric of modernism and postmodernism; it continued with *Fictions of Discourse* (1994), which examined in the framework of contemporary narratological theory the degree to which ludicity – the capacity for play – can be read as an inherent and indeed inescapable component of narrativity; and it concludes with *Acts of Narrative*, which examines in the framework of poststructuralist narrative semiotics the degree to which the critical exploitation of this ludicity of narrative discourse can lead to what I hope are productive and interesting readings of a more or less canonic body of modern and postmodern texts, specifically German.

I

What we see as readers always depends on what we are looking for and where we are looking from. The particular theoretical context in which the present project is situated is that of structuralist and poststructuralist narratology.[1] While the term *narratology* may be used in a broad sense as a synonym for narrative theory of all theoretical persuasions, in a more restricted sense (as here) it refers specifically to the theory (or theories) of narrative structure. This centrally important current of modern narrative theory first came to prominence in France in the 1960s, and it continues to flourish in France as well as (especially) in North America, Israel, and Holland. The term *narratology* itself (or, at any rate, its French original, *narratologie*) was coined by Tzvetan Todorov only in 1969 to designate a systematic study of narrative structure anchored in the common intellectual tradition of the Russian and Czech formalism of the early twentieth century and the French structuralism and semiotics of the sixties.[2] There is already an overwhelming mass of specialized studies in a variety of languages on various aspects of narrative structure, written from a wide variety of theoretical orientations within the field of narratology itself. There are also several excellent general introductions to the field as a whole, including especially Gérard Genette's *Narrative Discourse: An Essay in Method* (1980, originally published in French in 1972), Seymour Chatman's *Story and Discourse: Narrative Structure in Fiction and Film* (1978), Shlomith Rimmon-Kenan's *Narrative Fiction: Contemporary Poetics* (1983), and Mieke Bal's *Narratology: Introduction to the Theory of Narrative* (1985).[3]

The single most important distinction espoused by all narratologists in the narrower sense is that between what Seymour Chatman has programmatically called *story* and *discourse*: 'In simple terms, the story is the *what* in a narrative that is depicted, discourse the *how*' (1980: 19). Deceptively 'obvious,' the differentiation of story (*das Erzählte*, the content plane of narrative, 'what really happened') and discourse (*das Erzählen*, the expression plane, or how 'what really happened' is presented to the reader) is the most fundamental and most powerful distinction of contemporary narratological theory.

The distinction between story and discourse is by no means a recent invention, of course. As a theoretical concept, it has a tradition extending all the way back to Aristotle's differentiation in the *Poetics* between *logos* (the events represented, the 'story') and *mythos* (the plot, rearrangement, or 'discourse').[4] Cervantes in the early 1600s, Sterne in the 1760s, and the Romantics throughout the first half of the nineteenth century all made extensive use of its ironic and parodic possibilities. With the rise of international Realism in the mid-nineteenth century, however, the favoured central strategy of narrative discourse essentially came to be the powerful (and in practice widely variable) fiction that there *was* no narrative discourse, only the story that was told. (Ironically, this was often achieved by way of the entirely fictional notion of an 'omniscient' narrator, whose assumed omniscience guaranteed the reality, authenticity, and truth of the story related.) As Realism itself began to wane towards the end of the nineteenth century, the relativizing power of discourse (voluntarily subdued for half a century) came to the fore once again, and Henry James in the English-speaking world established it as centrally emblematic of the concerns of literary modernism almost a century ago when he wrote that in modern narrative such as his own later work there are always two stories involved: 'There is the story of one's hero and then, thanks to the intimate connection of things, the story of one's story itself' (quoted in Bradbury 1993: 31–2).

The relationship of story and discourse (which because it is so obvious is also frequently ignored) is the central point of the present book, which might perhaps best be described as an exercise (or a series of exercises) in semiotic narratology, exploring, on the basis of the particular texts selected for analysis, a variety of aspects of the semiotics of narrative as a discursive system. Semiotics, originally defined as the study of signs, has, as Robert Scholes observes, in modern practice become 'the study of codes: the systems that enable human beings to perceive certain events or entities *as* signs, bearing meaning' (1982: ix). One of the most powerful cultural codes throughout human history has been that of narrative – while semiotics is essentially a particular and specialized form of *reading*, the term having been coined on the Greek *sēma, sēmeion*, both meaning 'sign,' and *sēmeiōtikos*, 'one who interprets signs.'

The single most significant innovation of semiotic narratology is to see the narrative text as essentially a matter for negotiation, positioned *between* an author who writes and a reader who reads. In this it is fundamentally different from the almost exclusively author-centred approach that has long dominated German (and German-inspired) literary criticism – systematized some half a century ago in the theoretical work of Franz Stanzel and Eberhard Lämmert – in which the role of the reader is in essence merely to consume an artefact that is presented to him or her already complete (and thus closed) in every significant aspect. Literary texts, however, as opposed to other and more purely pragmatic acts of communication, are texts that demand by definition to be read in as interesting a way as possible. The present book is thus fundamentally about the role of the reader in the narrative transaction – for every reading is also an act of narrative, and no authorial act of narrative is complete without a reader who transforms it also into his or her own act of narrative.

In the end, *each* of the texts under analysis here, as read in this particular context of investigation, continually foregrounds the active role of the reader, which foregrounding may itself be read as the single most significant formal feature of modern and postmodern narrative as a semiotic structure. Where the discourse of realist narrative essentially (if entirely duplicitously) invites the reader to ignore it, in other words, modern and postmodern narratives insist alike on the centrality of due attention to the semiotic functioning of narrative in terms of its particular strategies of discourse. The term 'strategies of discourse,' however, has a threefold connotation in this context, including not only particular authorial strategies and particular readerly or critical strategies but also the (involuntary) strategies exercised by literary discourse itself in shaping both of these. Writer and reader alike are not outside but rather part of the textual discourse, not only controllers but controlled as well.[5] By the same token, the ludicity or capacity for play both of the literary text and of the necessary readerly strategies it demands for its appropriate realization is firmly foregrounded. The play of the text, in other words, *includes* both the play of writing and the play of reading, for literary texts are texts that are both written *and* *read* in special ways. This is, in principle, true of all literary texts, but most particularly of texts designated as 'modern(ist)' or 'postmodern(ist).'

The term *modern*, as Malcolm Bradbury observes in *The Modern British Novel*, has both a weak and a strong meaning, 'referring both to an overall period, the "modern" century, ours, and to a distinctive tradition of *avant-garde* literary and artistic experiment' (1993: ix). The term *modern*, in the German-speaking countries no less than in Britain, may also be limited more specifically in yet a third sense to the chronologically earlier products of this experimental tradition, the artistic products of international high Modernism, as opposed to those of a later international 'postmodernism,' which may be (and has been) variously interpreted as either a rejection or an extension of its predecessor (or a combination of the two) but whose existence at any rate is hardly conceivable without that of its mighty predecessor.

There are many ways of distinguishing between these three predominant discourse formations – realism, modernism, and postmodernism – in the literary history of the past hundred years.[6] One of the most productive for the purposes specifically of narrative criticism, however, is to invoke the shifting relationship between story and discourse. The realist text, in these terms, presents itself in principle as largely concerned with the evocation of a believable story, focusing our attention as readers primarily on the ostensibly real world of its characters and duplicitously directing our attention away from the literary artifice that has gone into the production of that world. The modernist text, admitting to a greater degree of interest in its own workings, directs our attention also to the discursive processes involved in the narrative production of that world. The postmodern text, fascinated by its own workings, challenges us to concentrate primarily on discursive processes per se, on the nature of its constitution *as* text in the first place. To oversimplify: realist texts focus on the story, modernist texts focus on the relationship between story and discourse, postmodernist texts treat the discourse *as* the story. In consequence, the realist text aims at directing its reader towards a particular central meaning; the modernist text aims at complicating the discursive possibilities of that meaning; while the postmodernist text aims at the multiplication of possible discursive meanings per se. In these terms, what distinguishes the three literary mastermodes is evidently a matter of degree rather than kind. The final location of the text on this sliding scale, moreover, is by no means for its author alone to determine: since the literary transaction is always a matter of negotiated settlement between author and reader, any reader, to the best of his or her abilities, may elect (with greater or lesser success) to read a text conventionally assigned to any one of these three modes in the terms of either one of the other two.

II

As opposed to any other form of discourse, literary discourse, especially in its modern and postmodern manifestations, systemically draws attention to its own rhetoricity, its own fictionality, its own status as discourse – and its own essential incompleteness without a reader to bring it to life. The aim here is therefore to treat each one of the chosen texts, individually, as a *writerly* text in Barthes's sense, which is to say, by engaging as a reader in a sustained dialogic engagement with it: 'The writerly text is *ourselves* writing' (1974: 5). The aim, in other words, is an unabashedly formalist one, namely, to focus on the specifically *literary* qualities of the texts considered – not, however, in the essentialist terms of New Criticism or Russian Formalism (for both of which the literary text was characterized a priori by particular qualities of language, texture, and thought) but rather, as already indicated, in terms of the interactivity of a semiotic narratology. The distinction warrants some further comment.

Narrative as a semiotic system is characterized by what we might call the Archimedes Effect. 'Give me a place to stand, and I will move the world,' the Greek philosopher is traditionally supposed to have claimed some twenty-two centuries ago – though the alleged context was the mechanical uses of levers rather than any possible narratological application. As far as narratology is concerned, however, Archimedes' legacy is precisely that principle of leverage: *what* is said is always dependent on *how* it is said. Authentic or not, his alleged utterance is splendidly emblematic of the essential situation of narrative as a system of discourse: the narrative 'voice' is always in a position to move, revoke, and/or replace completely the constructed worlds inhabited by the characters it evokes. The present work focuses on this discursive provisionality of narrative and its creation of narrative worlds that are always retractable – in other words, it focuses on narrative discourse and its semiotics rather than on the stories narrated by that discourse. The Archimedes Effect thus names the fact that in a *literary* narrative, much traditional reading to the contrary, discourse is always necessarily primary, story always necessarily secondary. Necessarily, because that is exactly what makes literary texts literary. To read literary texts *as* literary texts is therefore always necessarily to engage in critical analysis of the semiotics of discourse.

The approach favoured in this book, narratological in the narrower sense, evidently falls into the general tradition of formalism and 'close reading.' Formalism in a wider sense – what we might call 'small-*f* formalism' – has two quite separate orientations, however. The formalism of the Anglo-American New Critics and the German *werkimmanente Kritiker* may be called an aesthetic formalism, in that it adhered to a closed and a priori conception of the literary text as an organic artistic whole and directed its analytic attention to demonstrating that already assumed wholeness, which was deemed to be independent of either authorial or readerly intentionality. The quite different formalism that inspires the narratological approach to fiction espoused here sees the literary text as a semiotic structure – or rather as a series of interrelated structures – and attempts to explore the workings of the particular process(es) of structuration involved. Here we may thus speak of a *semiotic* rather than an *aesthetic* formalism, whose essential role is to attempt to open up rather than to close down the literary text. Aesthetic formalism is concerned with the already-guaranteed presence of literary meaning and its wholly autotelic, self-sufficient modes of aesthetic operation; semiotic formalism is concerned with the operation of the discursive processes by which meaning (literary or otherwise) is constituted at the ever-shifting intersection of authorial production and readerly reception.

The semiotic formalism of the structuralist tradition ranges from the approach of the Russian Formalists of the twenties to the very different poststructuralist neoformalism of French and American deconstruction half a century later. To simplify rather drastically, structuralist formalism from the twenties to the sixties saw itself as a science rather than an art and tended to look for immutable rules underlying the workings of texts, rules that would eventually constitute a universal grammar, for example, of narrative as a semiotic system. Poststructuralist formalism, which may conveniently be dated from Roland Barthes's ground-breaking essay *S/Z* in 1970, saw itself as being just as much a form of art as a form of science, and demonstrated a pronounced interest not only in how texts worked but also, and with considerably greater emphasis, in how texts *played*. The poststructuralist brand of semiotic formalism – in which overall context the present work sees itself as situated – generates readings that function, like the writings with which they engage, primarily as exploratory fictions rather than as explanatory statements. The results, it will be evident, are therefore not so much about what the texts under analysis *are* as about what they can productively be *read* as being.

There is an indefinitely large number of possible contexts in which literary texts may be situated as an object of theoretical and critical scrutiny. One means (among many) of sorting the entropic proliferation of currently available approaches is to see them in terms of the relationship of the literary text and society as a whole. We may thus construct an ideational scale on which the text is regarded at one extreme as existing completely independently of society and at the other as being entirely contingent upon the society that produces it. The extreme formalism of the New Critics, for example, theoretically naïve for all its institutional success, belongs at one end of this scale: the literary text is completely independent of its author, its reader, and all other extratextual reality, existing essentially only in and for itself. At the other end of the scale we find both the (likewise theoretically naïve and institutionally very successful) historicism of the traditional philological approach – for which the literary text was essentially less itself than something *else*, namely, attractively packaged social discourse of a primarily historical or biographical or philosophical or sociological kind – *and* the theoretically sophisticated New Historicism of contemporary cultural studies, for which literary discourse is likewise, however much more complexly theorized, only one competing or complementary form of social discourse among many.

The course of literary critical history over the last century, in fact, may be seen in terms of two intersecting pairs of paradigms, historicism versus formalism on the one hand, essentialism versus semioticism on the other. A continuing intellectual power-struggle between adherents of formalism and of historicism results chronologically in a movement from historicism to formalism and back again, but under a very different sign. Two very different expressions of formalism are sandwiched in the process between two very different articulations of historicism: what we might call the essentialist *old historicism* of the philological tradition followed by the equally essentialist *old formalism* of the New Critics yielding to a semiotic *new formalism* currently succeeded (but by no means replaced) by a semiotic *new historicism*.

It is important to realize that both formalism and historicism are entirely valid analytical and interpretive paradigms, that the tension between them is a highly productive one, and that their strengths and weaknesses are not just opposed but complementary. The 'cultural studies' approach based on the New Historicism that is currently in vigorous ascendancy among academic critics is indeed an entirely legitimate – and exciting – way in which to read texts as far as the global hermeneutic context of the human sciences is concerned – but all too frequently it drastically neglects the specifically *literary* quality of those texts, the very factor that by definition differentiates literary discourse from other forms of social discourse such as history, philosophy, psychology, sociology, and political studies. Because of its theoretical presuppositions, traditional aesthetic formalism, producing readings that are closed (even though frequently highly complex), no longer offers a convincing intellectual alternative to the powerful new historicism of transdisciplinary cultural studies. Semiotic formalism, on the other hand, because of its focus on the interdiscursivity of all communication, points by its nature to the potential openness and debatability of all meaning, an openness that is realized most especially, most systemically, and most provocatively precisely in the literary text.

III

Although this book deals with a selection of modern and postmodern narratives written in German and spanning much of the twentieth century, it is by no means a would-be historical survey of twentieth-century German fiction. Its intended contribution to German studies is much more narrowly and much more specifically focused, consisting namely in the detailed analysis of discursive strategies in some centrally important narratives of our time. To this extent its place in German studies is most obviously in a tradition of close reading exemplified by Roy Pascal's study of Kafka's narrators or John Ellis's study of narration in the German *Novelle*. It differs from such studies, however, in drawing on a radically different tradition of narrative analysis and criticism, that of poststructuralist semiotics.

In the eight individual analyses that make up this book I consciously deviate from the mainstream of German (and German-inspired) literary criticism, which has been heavily historicist in character, whether of the traditional historical or biographical variety or, more recently, of the cultural studies variety. German literary scholarship during the nineteenth and early twentieth centuries developed a massive and highly successful critical establishment that depended largely on biographical and historical criticism. Even after the Second World War, the prestige of this scholarly and critical orientation remained almost unassailable. One result was that neither structuralist- nor poststructuralist-inspired criticism in a semiotic vein made anything like the impact in German-language criticism that it made in criticism written in French or English.[7] What I am calling semiotic formalism here is therefore something of a 'lost generation' in German literary history – prevented from establishing itself by the prestige of historical scholarship in the first place, and essentially leapfrogged, overtaken before it had a chance to happen, by the growing hegemony of a new generation of sociocritically oriented cultural studies.

A semiotic reading, as we have seen, pays particular attention to the discursive strategies employed in and by the text under consideration. The selection of texts to be dealt with here is to some extent arbitrary, of course, since the same basic relationship of story and discourse evidently holds in all narrative texts. Certain narratives, however, lend themselves particularly rewardingly to being read in terms of their discursive strategies. In what follows, we shall look at a selection of German-language narratives written during the twentieth century, some of them already well known outside German-speaking Europe, others considerably less so, but all characterized by the fact that in one way or another they each very markedly privilege narrative discourse over the story it tells – or at any rate can productively be read as so doing.

Each of the texts chosen demonstrates its own particular strategies of discourse – and in the process, of course, also allows me to develop my own particular strategies of (critical) discourse. Thomas Mann's *Der Tod in Venedig* (1912; *Death in Venice*) develops the concept of an ironically distanced narrator in an exemplary fashion, and thus can be seen as a foundational example of that primacy of discourse that marks both modern and postmodern narrative. It does so especially by means of an interesting exploitation of the possibilities of a doubled narrative setting, which is to say, in terms both of story-setting (most obviously Venice) and of discourse-setting (the distance that is ironically evoked between the story presented and the discourse that presents it). In the process, the theoretical distinction between the syntagmatic (or linear) thrust that is natural to all stories and the paradigmatic (or presentational) thrust that is fundamental to all narrative discourse is systemically and ironically blurred. Franz Kafka's *Der Prozeß* (1925; *The Trial*) exploits the same distinction to entirely different ends by powerfully combining it with a radically indeterminate focalization, creating in the process that effect of hermeneutic indecision that obsessively pervades the worlds of all Kafka's characters. Hermann Hesse's *Der Steppenwolf* (1927; *Steppenwolf*), an overtly ludic text, raises and exploits fundamental questions about the nature of the narrative voice itself and about the 'ventriloquist' strategies by which the location both of that voice and of narrative focalization may be disguised by narrative discourse. All three of these texts make considerable demands on their readers, a demand that is itself thematized in Elias Canetti's *Die Blendung* (1935; *Auto da fé*), which focuses both thematically and discursively on what Harold Bloom has called misprision or misreading, the fallibility of reading strategies (1973: 19). Canetti's characters all live in solipsistic fictional worlds almost entirely of their own creation; the overt challenge to the reader is 'simply' to distinguish between these explanatory fictions and the (also fictional) 'real' world entirely obliquely presented /created by the highly self-effacing narrator.

Though the distinction is not a crucial one for our current concerns, since the chosen focus is individual analysis rather than literary historical development, the first four of the eight texts discussed (Mann, Kafka, Hesse, Canetti) may be read as primarily modernist, the second four (Grass, Johnson, Handke, Bernhard) as primarily postmodernist. Of all the texts examined, Günter Grass's *Die Blechtrommel* (1959; *The Tin Drum*), treating the horrors of two world wars in an ostentatiously inappropriate fashion, most overtly exemplifies the possibilities of a totally unreliable narrator – and thus implicitly invites or impels the reader, in narratological terms, to construct an alternative locus of narrative authority, an implied author who (or which) will allow the narrator's inventions to be measured against a putative (implied or inferred) discourse whose reliability is (putatively) beyond question. Uwe Johnson's very different *Zwei Ansichten* (1965; *Two Views*) is none the less concerned with similar questions of narrative authority, presenting two parallel stories recounting the politically charged course of a relationship between a young West German man and a young East German woman from their respective points of view. Superimposed on this simple plot, however, a third parallel narrative, that of the reader, takes gradual shape, inducing the reader increasingly to question the system of the text in much the same way as its characters come to question the nature of the political reality in which they find themselves. Those individual realities, moreover, are presented by Johnson's text as sufficiently different to warrant the further argument that the three narratives are most appropriately read as operating in three quite separate typological modes, classifiable respectively as realism, modernism, and postmodernism. Peter Handke's *Die Angst des Tormanns beim Elfmeter* (1970; *The Goalie's Anxiety at the Penalty Kick*) presents the story of a man who abruptly loses the ability to function in a semiotic system whose rules of operation he is no longer capable of recognizing. Josef Bloch's multiple resulting confusions concerning signs and semiosis on the level of story are reflected in the multiple possibilities for confusion that are put in the way of the reader on the level of discourse. Handke's narrative is the most overtly postmodernist of the texts examined, in that it constitutes first and foremost an interrogation of the act of reading itself – whether of the literary text at hand or of the textual world we live in. Thomas Bernhard's *Das Kalkwerk* (1970; *The Lime Works*), finally, tells the story of another reader, a would-be scholar who spends his entire life in a futile attempt to write a scientific monograph that will impose at least a limited degree of local order on a world presented as almost wholly entropic. Not only does the monomaniacal Konrad fail spectacularly in his endeavour, however, finally putting not a single word on paper; the narrator who attempts to tell the story of that failure fails almost equally spectacularly, though himself producing in the process a lengthy and remarkable text that systemically invites its readers to re-examine once again the relationship that is fundamental to each of the texts examined here – and indeed to *all* literary narratives – that between story and discourse, between meaningful narrative and meaningless noise.

Why, finally, these particular texts rather than others? The eventual choice was partly the result of a desire, within the parameters of my principal theoretical concern, to gesture at least to some extent towards a 'representative' selection of major writers of German narrative since 1900 – though with no ambition to write anything like a history of modern German fiction, and inevitably with glaring omissions, such as Broch, Musil, Döblin, Böll, Frisch, and Lenz, not to mention the entire canon of women's writing. Partly, too, however, the choice was frankly and unapologetically arbitrary: I *like* these texts, I can work with them – or rather, *play* with them, and the importance of play as a factor in the reading of literary texts is crucial to my endeavour throughout. This attitude should certainly not be misconstrued as advocating an uncontrolled relativism.[8] What it *is* advocating (other than the importance of personal taste) is, above all, the importance of the pleasure principle in our encounters with literature: if reading literature, however else it may be understood, is not also understood as being itself (like its object of study) a form of disinterested play, then we are reading literature not as literature but as something else altogether.

IV

Since the foundational relationship of story and discourse is at the heart of our investigation, each chapter begins with a very brief outline of the story and continues with an analysis of the discursive means by which that story is conveyed to the reader. The innocence of this procedure, however, is of course only ostensible, for *any* retelling of the story (including mine) is itself precisely a form of discourse. I also wish to disclaim any inferred suggestion that the particular method of exploring narrative texts pursued here is being argued for as the only or even the most important way to read literary narratives. Nor should it be understood that these particular texts are the only ones to demonstrate particular discursive strategies in an interesting way. There is an indefinitely large number of other ways of reading each of the texts dealt with here, and there is likewise an indefinitely large number of other texts in which similar discursive strategies could be analysed to varying degrees.

Perhaps the crucial characteristic of the present undertaking is simply that it is a way of reading that privileges the ludic element in the texts explored, for the ludic moment is central both to all narrative and to all literature – and, at least potentially, to all reading as well.[9] Read in this context of investigation, literary texts (and their readings) are always more importantly about generating provocative questions than about providing conclusive and comforting answers. That is not by any means to suggest, however, that literature is somehow beyond politics or that reading literary texts is (or should be) no more than a sophisticated, politically neutral, and ultimately irresponsible parlour game for academic mandarins. Once appropriate questions are raised, whether explicitly or implicitly, it is up to the reader to decide whether and why and how to react to them or not in the world outside the text. That decision, however, belongs – at least for the kind of formalist reader envisioned and advocated here – more appropriately to the realm of practical politics than to that of the literary text.

1

Death in Venice: Narrative Situations in Thomas Mann's *Der Tod in Venedig*

One of the most fundamentally important implications of the gap between narrative discourse and the story it presents is that narrative is *always* implicitly both a producer and a product of irony.[1] Some writers naturally make considerably greater use of this latent discursive potential than do others – and few do so more than Thomas Mann, 'the ironic German,' as Erich Heller dubbed him in a classic study. Mann's early masterpiece *Der Tod in Venedig* (1912), translated into English as *Death in Venice*, allows us to examine one particularly interesting textual strategy employed by an exemplarily ironic narrator.

The story – as opposed to the discourse that presents it – is both uncomplicated and familiar. Gustav von Aschenbach, a middle-aged German writer at the height of his career, even recently raised to the nobility for his exemplary service in the cause of literature and moral enlightenment, decides on a sudden whim to indulge in a rare holiday, hoping that the change of scene will help to counter the first intimations of flagging creative energies. Encountering a strikingly beautiful fourteen-year-old Polish boy immediately after his arrival at a Lido hotel in Venice, he is delighted as an artist by the boy's beauty. Aesthetic appreciation, however, gives way for the lonely Aschenbach to a growing fascination and eventually the at once shocked and exhilarated realization that he is in love with the boy and can no longer live without him. Discovering shortly afterwards that Venice is in the grip of a cholera epidemic, he briefly considers warning Tadzio and his family to flee, then yields to a guilty desire to have the boy close to him at all costs. Cosmetically rejuvenated, he abandons all discretion, pursuing Tadzio openly through the reeking alleys of the diseased city. As the Polish family prepares of its own accord to leave after a few days, a delirious Aschenbach, watching the boy spending a few last minutes on the beach, succumbs to the cholera he has himself by now contracted. A respectful world is saddened to learn of the unexpected passing of a great artist.

I

Der Tod in Venedig is one of the fixed stars in the canon of modern German literature and has been the subject of extensive attention. Many critics have focused primarily on the development of Aschenbach as a character, and T.J. Reed speaks for many when he writes that Mann's *Novelle* 'is about psychological decay finding in the outside world pretext and occasion for its fulfilment. Aschenbach's creative discipline is essentially broken at the very outset. The long years of too deliberate application and self-control have begun to take their revenge' (1974: 171). Up to this point, indeed, Aschenbach, in spite of a frail constitution, has led a life of almost ascetic rigour and discipline. The first paragraphs of the text refer to his failing strength and the 'Müdigkeit' (10), the 'weariness' (198), that now increasingly threaten to overcome him.[2] The journey to Venice is also a journey into himself, initiating a midlife crisis that destroys him with stunning rapidity. Celebrated for an oeuvre marked by its Apollonian sobriety and serenity, Aschenbach experiences the violent eruption of his sudden love for Tadzio as a plunge into a realm of Dionysian abandon where the rigorous principles of artistic and personal restraint he has cultivated throughout his life prove entirely inadequate, leaving him finally 'kraftlos dem Dämon verfallen' (62) / 'powerlessly enslaved to the daemon-god' (257).

Other critics have focused instead primarily on Aschenbach's story as a tragic allegory of art itself, a symbolic confirmation that 'the disciplined forms of art require for their being the most intimate association with the dark ground of creativity' (Heller 1961: 104). The page and a half of 'erlesener Prosa' (44) / 'exquisite prose' (236) that Aschenbach will compose shortly before his death as a panegyric to Beauty in the shape of Tadzio, perfect pages written precisely out of an experience that is destroying his entire moral fibre, is a graphic illustration of the narrator's contention that 'es ist sicher gut, daß die Welt nur das schöne Werk, nicht auch seine Ursprünge, nicht seine Entstehungsbedingungen kennt' (44) / 'it is certainly as well that the world knows only the finished work of art and not also its origins, the conditions under which it came into being' (236). As Heller writes, Mann's text is in the end both parody and paradox: 'a work of art embodying so radical a critique of art that it amounts to its moral rejection' (1961: 113).

A very great deal has been written on Mann's almost obsessive preoccupation with the nature of art and the role of the artist, on his conception of the relationship of art, disease, and crime, and also, of course, on the autobiographical relevance of his story of Aschenbach.[3] Since our specific concern in this book, however, is with the relationship of story and discourse in narrative, I shall almost entirely ignore these important aspects of the text and limit myself instead to a consideration of one particular textual strategy (to my knowledge not yet discussed elsewhere in these terms) by means of which the world in which Aschenbach as character moves is constructed (rather than just reported) by the narrative discourse that presents it.

This process of construction begins with the very first sentence:

Gustav Aschenbach oder von Aschenbach, wie seit seinem fünfzigsten Geburtstag amtlich sein Name lautete, hatte an einem Frühlingsnachmittag des Jahres 19.., das unserem Kontinent monatelang eine so gefahrdrohende Miene zeigte, von seiner Wohnung in der Prinzregentenstraße zu München aus allein einen weiteren Spaziergang unternommen. (7)

On a spring afternoon in 19–, the year in which for months on end so grave a threat seemed to hang over the peace of Europe, Gustav Aschenbach, or von Aschenbach, as he had been officially known since his fiftieth birthday, had set out from his apartment on the Prinzregentenstrasse in Munich to take a walk of some length by himself. (195)

While thus ostensibly anchoring his story in a firmly realist setting, the narrator, as we may notice, simultaneously demonstrates his ability, even in his opening sentence, to influence the reader's understanding of that apparently so solid world. The details of Aschenbach's being raised to the nobility certainly contribute to the narrative verisimilitude of the account we are going to read – but we may also note that no sooner is Aschenbach introduced in the first two words than he is renamed in the next three. The pedantic refusal to name the exact year is likewise at once a comfortably old-fashioned convention for discreetly guaranteeing the realism of the story we are about to read and an indication of the narrator's ability to provide or withhold information as he chooses. Even the experienced reader is likely to miss the point that both the 'grave threat' of the political times and the lengthy 'walk' on which Aschenbach embarks are at once elements of a realistically portrayed story-world and ironic discursive commentaries on the story to come – ironic, that is to say, because the reader has simply no way of knowing at this point that he or she is indeed being offered this discursive 'assistance' in understanding the text.

For readers interested primarily in the semiotic relationship of story and discourse, as we are here, *Der Tod in Venedig* exhibits one particularly striking structural characteristic, namely, its domination by what modern linguistics would call the paradigmatic axis of narrative. Every narrative, in these terms, is characterized by the intersection of two axes, the syntagmatic and the paradigmatic.[4] Narrative, that is to say, always combines a syntagmatic or 'horizontal' thrust (namely, what *happens* in the *story*) and a paradigmatic or 'vertical' thrust (how what happens in the story is *presented* by a particular narrative *discourse*). In these terms, of course, the relationship of the syntagmatic and paradigmatic axes merely reflects that of story and discourse, and *Der Tod in Venedig* is hardly unique in being only one of very many narratives in which discourse dominates story. The interplay of the syntagmatic and paradigmatic axes takes place, however, not just *between* the narrative levels of story and discourse but also (though interdependently) *on* each of these levels, to the degree that the dominant characteristic in any particular case is either time or space. The syntagmatic axis is the axis of time and thus of actions, what happened and when it happened; these actions may be interrelated either in very simple or in very complex ways either on the level of story or on that of discourse or on both at once. The paradigmatic axis is the axis of space and thus merely of the *location* of those actions on the level of story, but of their *setting* (which is a very different matter) on the level of discourse. On the latter level, our primary concern here, the presentation of narrative actions thus operates on the syntagmatic axis and that of narrative setting on the paradigmatic axis, while that of character may be seen as a function of the intersection of both axes (cf. O'Neill 1994: 54–7).

As far as the story is concerned, our attention as readers of traditional realist narrative is usually firmly fixed either on particular characters or on the nature of the events in which they are involved or, of course, on a combination of the two. Most narratives indeed have a physical 'setting' of some sort, but very often the location in which characters engage in the particular events that define them is little more than a background, sometimes inconsequential, sometimes lending itself to the production of a greater or lesser degree of symbolic significance. There are relatively few narratives, however, in which the setting is more important than either the events portrayed or the characters who enact them – and *Der Tod in Venedig*, downplaying as it does either the development of a complex tapestry of narrative events or the development of intricately drawn characters in favour of an extremely rich narrative setting, is one of them.[5] One might even go so far as to say that the story of Aschenbach is predominantly the story of the setting, its development seen partly through Aschenbach's eyes, partly through those of the narrator and (eventually) the reader.

Our discussion of Mann's narrative is therefore almost entirely about description, about setting and its uses, and therefore about a very particular effect of narrative *discourse*, for while the physical locations in which the events of the story take place belong to the level of story, the description of those locations and the uses to which they are put in the narration of the story belong not to the realm of story but rather to that of discourse. Setting, moreover, includes not only physical locations but also characters of subsidiary importance whose real role in the narrative is not to be developed as characters in their own right but rather to serve as, precisely, a further element of the *setting* for the central story to be told.[6] *Der Tod in Venedig* is particularly rich not only in physical setting but also in characters used as elements of setting.

However, and this is the most interesting point in the context of our investigation, this markedly paradigmatic effect is achieved by textual strategies that are distinctly syntagmatic in their individual operation. That is to say, the overall setting in which Aschenbach's story takes place is presented in a markedly sequential and cumulative fashion, employing not just individual acts of description but a number of interactive descriptive *series*. These several series are by no means merely descriptive, however. They are also hermeneutic; for in their complex interaction they also variously and to varying degrees facilitate, impede, and complicate the reader's progression through the text.

This accounts to at least some extent for a peculiar obliquity of presentation in Mann's text, for one of its most important modes of narratorial irony is provided by this striking use of narrative setting – the central importance of which, of course, is already suggested by the title. Most obviously, Venice itself (surely the best imaginable setting for Aschenbach's story) clearly serves as a symbolic allegory of art and its duality: beauty and form arising miraculously out of – and continually threatening to sink back into – the formless sea. As Aschenbach's initially entirely dispassionate aesthetic pleasure in Tadzio's physical beauty develops into an overpowering and self-destructive passion, so too the beauty and serenity of Venice mask another city of the same name, an abode of corruption and dissolution, the mask of Apollo hiding the face of Dionysus.

Aschenbach's first dreamlike pursuit of Tadzio by gondola takes place in and through this labyrinth, this Dionysian netherworld:

Der Ruf des Gondoliers, halb Warnung, halb Gruß, ward fernher aus der Stille des Labyrinths nach sonderbarer Übereinkunft beantwortet ... Das war Venedig, die schmeichlerische und verdächtige Schöne, – diese Stadt, halb Märchen, halb Fremdenfalle, in deren faulige Luft die Kunst einst schwelgerisch aufwucherte ... (51)

The gondolier's call, half warning and half greeting, was answered from a distance out of the silent labyrinth, in accordance with some strange convention ... This was Venice, the flattering and suspect beauty – this city, half fairy tale and half tourist trap, in whose insalubrious air the arts once rankly and voluptuously blossomed ... (244–5)

All sense of moral and social dignity finally abandoned, Aschenbach, with dyed hair, rouged cheeks, and painted lips, 'am Narrenseil geleitet von der Passion' (65) / 'helpless in the leading strings of his mad desire' (259), eventually takes to pursuing Tadzio shamelessly through the 'krank[e] Stadt' (64), the 'sick city' (259), and it is here, exhausted by the heat, the humidity, and the turmoil of his own mind, disoriented and lost in a 'labyrinth' (64/259) of lanes and alleyways, that he eventually buys and eats the tainted strawberries that lead directly to his death.

The labyrinthine quality of Venice as a fatal and inescapable trap emerges not only from its physical description. Aschenbach does not set out to go there in the first place. His original plan is merely to spend a few weeks in the sun at some holiday spot or other, and he makes arrangements for a stay on a popular Adriatic island near Pola. Only after a few days, dissatisfied with his choice, does he suddenly realize that 'er war fehlgegangen. Dorthin hatte er reisen wollen' (17) / 'he had gone completely astray. *That* was where he had wanted to travel' (207) – to Venice, his real goal, though unadmitted even to himself. His journey to Venice is attended by ironically presented discursive portents of an uncertainly ominous nature. He obtains his ticket in Pola, signed with all the ceremony worthy of a diabolical pact, from an individual who behaves suspiciously like a stage Mephistopheles (18/208). Arrived in Venice, he is transported to his hotel under distinctly dubious circumstances by a surly individual whom the narrator is at pains to associate in the reader's mind with Charon, ferryman of souls (22/212). After only a day or two he is so affected by the sultry weather that he resolves to leave again, but he immediately regrets his decision and is secretly delighted when he is 'forced' to stay by the providential fact that a piece of luggage has been forwarded to a wrong destination (37/229).

The reader is permitted to assemble this complex picture of Venice only gradually and piecemeal, through a cumulative series of references. The Venice complex, indeed, can be read as the first of the several cumulative hermeneutic *series* that structure the discourse of *Der Tod in Venedig*, their common function the (paradigmatic) development of an editorial commentary, a discursive setting for the story told, rather than the (syntagmatic) development of a story-line. The labyrinth motif embodied in the Venice series, for example, is closely associated with a second series, constructed on the motif of the journey to the heart of darkness, and emerging most clearly in three clearly related episodes: an abrupt vision spurred by the sight of a vaguely exotic stranger glimpsed in Munich; the account of the spread of Asian cholera into Europe via Venice; and an orgiastic dream of Dionysian revels.

His imagination unaccountably stirred by the vision of the Munich stranger (to whom we shall return), Aschenbach is abruptly overcome by a momentary and completely uncharacteristic vision of disturbing intensity. For a fleeting instant he sees

eine Landschaft, ein tropisches Sumpfgebiet unter dickdunstigem Himmel, feucht, üppig und ungeheuer, eine Art Urweltwildnis ... sah zwischen den knotigen Rohrstämmen des Bambusdickichts die Lichter eines kauernden Tigers funkeln – und fühlte sein Herz pochen vor Entsetzen und rätselhaftem Verlangen. (9)

a landscape, a tropical swampland under a cloud-swollen sky, moist and lush and monstrous, a kind of primeval wilderness ... saw between the knotted stems of the bamboo thicket the glinting eyes of a crouching tiger – and his heart throbbed with terror and mysterious longing. (197)

Fading as abruptly as it appeared, this vision, which inspires Aschenbach's decision to take a holiday, finds its first correspondence shortly after he first admits to himself his love for Tadzio, at which point he also discovers the truth that Venice is indeed in the grip of plague, though this has been vigorously denied by the authorities, all too mindful of the tourist trade. A Thomas Cook clerk confidentially tells him the real story:

Seit meheren Jahren schon hatte die indische Cholera eine verstärkte Neigung zur Ausbreitung und Wanderung an den Tag gelegt. Erzeugt aus den warmen Morästen des Ganges-Deltas, aufgestiegen mit dem mephitischen Odem jener üppig-untauglichen, von Menschen gemiedenen Urwelt- und Inselwildnis, in deren Bambusdickichten der Tiger kauert, hatte die Seuche in ganz Hindustan andauernd und ungewöhnlich gewütet, (58)

For several years now, Asiatic cholera had been showing an increased tendency to spread and migrate. Originating in the sultry morasses of the Ganges delta, rising with the mephitic exhalations of that wilderness of rank useless luxuriance, that primitive island jungle shunned by man, where tigers crouch in the bamboo thickets, the pestilence had raged with unusual and prolonged virulence all over northern India, (252-3)

before spreading to the Mediterranean, including Venice, where 'geleugnet und vertuscht fraß das Sterben in der Enge der Gäßchen um sich' (59) / 'despite every denial and concealment, the mortal sickness went on eating its way through the narrow little streets' (253). The spread of the disease, the clerk further volunteers, is accompanied by a marked collapse in public morals, corruption in high places (60/254) mirrored in random acts of violence and even murder.

The third episode in the series is Aschenbach's dream of nameless Dionysian orgies immediately after receiving this information – and immediately after he has made the desperate and shameful decision not only to remain in Venice but also to remain silent rather than warning Tadzio and his family of the danger, as he had first immediately thought of doing.

In dieser Nacht hatte er einen furchtbaren Traum ... Angst war der Anfang, Angst und Lust und eine entsetzte Neugier nach dem, was kommen wollte ... Aber er wußte ein Wort, dunkel, doch das benennend, was kam: '*Der fremde Gott*' ... Und seine Seele kostete Unzucht und Raserei des Unterganges. (61-2)

That night he had a terrible dream ... It began with fear, fear and joy and a horrified curiosity about what was to come ... Yet he was aware of a word, an obscure word, but one that gave a name to what was coming: '*the stranger-god!*' ... And his very soul savored the lascivious delirium of annihilation. (255-7).

The first two episodes in this second series are a distorted reflection of Venice. The bacchantic howling of the devotees in the third, a long-drawn-out *u*-sound (61/256), links it unambiguously with Tadzio, whose unfamiliar name Aschenbach had first heard, called out by the boy's companions, only as two indistinct syllables ending in a long-drawn-out *u*-sound (31/223). Only in retrospect is the reader allowed to see that all three of the episodes in this second series anticipate the triumph of Dionysus, the god deemed a 'stranger' by the Greeks for having come (like the cholera) from India, his chariot drawn by the same tigers Aschenbach glimpses in his first vision, his milieu one of intoxication, sexual abandon, and final chaos.

Tadzio's metamorphosis by this point (paralleling that of Venice) from representative of Apollonian form to representative of Dionysian abandon has already been progressively adumbrated, however, in a third hermeneutic series, one in which characters are made to perform the role of setting, and to which we may now turn.

II

The central discursive armature upon which Aschenbach's world is constructed, indeed, is the series of 'messenger' characters he encounters, some of whom we have already met in passing. The degree to which the traditional iconography of Death, Dionysus, and Hermes is severally and collectively reflected in these 'messengers' has already been the subject of extensive discussion (cf. Vaget 1984: 171). What interests us here specifically is the *cumulative* manner in which the reader is allowed to become aware of what is happening in the text. The potential importance of these characters for the course of his own life is largely – if not entirely – lost on Aschenbach on the level of story, while the reader is permitted to realize only gradually what is taking place on the level of discourse.

The first of these characters to be described in detail[7] is the stranger Aschenbach sees on the steps of the mortuary chapel in Munich during the afternoon walk with which the story begins: 'Mäßig hochgewachsen, mager, bartlos und auffallend stumpfnäsig, gehörte der Mann zum rothaarigen Typ ... Offenbar war er durchaus nicht bajuwarischen Schlages' (8) / 'Moderately tall, thin, beardless and remarkably snub-nosed, the man belonged to the red-haired type ... He was quite evidently not of Bavarian origin' (196). The stranger, who wears a rucksack, a yellowish jacket, and a straw hat, also carries a rain-cape over his left arm, 'den er in die Weiche gestützt hielt, und in der Rechten einen mit eiserner Spitze versehenen Stock, welchen er schräg gegen den Boden stemmte und auf dessen Krücke er, bei gekreuzten Füßen, die Hüfte lehnte' (8) / 'which was propped against his waist, and in his right hand an iron-pointed walking stick which he had thrust slantwise into the ground, crossing his feet and leaning his hip against its handle' (196). Aschenbach (or is it just the narrator?) further notices a prominent Adam's apple, deep furrows between the eyebrows, and lips drawn back from the teeth in a grimace: 'So – und vielleicht trug sein erhöhter und erhöhender Standort zu diesem Eindruck bei – hatte seine Haltung etwas herrisch Überschauendes, Kühnes oder selbst Wildes' (8) / 'There was thus – and perhaps the raised point of vantage on which he stood contributed to this impression – an air of imperious survey, something bold or even wild about his posture' (196).

Aschenbach is both startled and embarrassed to find this somewhat odd apparition glaring angrily at him, possibly because he may inadvertently have been staring. Hastily continuing on his way, he promptly forgets the man – except to the extent that the unexpected apparition, as we have seen, suddenly inspires him with a powerful desire to undertake a trip abroad, an interruption the work-obsessed Aschenbach would normally be at pains to avoid. Unsuspecting readers may be equally likely to continue on their way without further thought at this point. Only much later will it become finally apparent that our stranger simultaneously combines the traditional attributes of Death (in his crossed feet and skull-like physiognomy), of Dionysus (in his strangeness, the wildness of his stare, and the unspecified air of danger he projects), and of Hermes (equipped as he is with the hat and staff of the god of travellers). The reader, in short, having reached no further than the fourth paragraph of the narrative, is already multiply and massively off balance, unknowingly already attempting to negotiate a labyrinth that mirrors on the level of discourse the wanderings of Aschenbach on the level of story.

Some two weeks later Aschenbach embarks on his journey via Trieste and Pola to an anonymous Adriatic island. 'Was er suchte, war das Fremdartige und Bezuglose' (17) / 'What he sought was something strange and random' (206). Bad weather, however, contributes to a sense of dissatisfaction with his choice, and after only a few days he departs again for a new destination, for 'auf einmal, zugleich überraschend und selbstverständlich, stand ihm sein Ziel vor Augen' (17) / 'suddenly his surprising yet at the same time self-evident destination stared him in the face' (207). The reader, of course, assisted by the title of the narrative, is not surprised at all, having the distinct advantage over Aschenbach of knowing that the latter has no choice but to go to Venice.

On boarding the steamer from Pola, Aschenbach is effusively greeted by

ein ziegenbärtiger Mann von der Physiognomie eines altmodischen Zirkusdirektors, der mit grimassenhaft leichtem Geschäftsgebaren die Personalien der Reisenden aufnahm und ihnen die Fahrscheine ausstellte ... Er schrieb große Krähenfüße, streute aus einer Büchse blauen Sand auf die Schrift, ließ ihn in eine tönerne Schale ablaufen, faltete das Papier mit gelben und knochigen Fingern und schrieb aufs neue. (18)

a goat-bearded man with the air of an old-fashioned circus director and a slick caricatured business manner, taking passengers' particulars and issuing their tickets ... He scribbled elaborately, shook some blue sand from a box over the writing and ran it off into an earthenware dish, then folded the paper with his bony yellow fingers and wrote on it again. (207)

As in the case of the stranger Aschenbach had encountered in Munich almost a month before, the ticket-seller may very well strike the reader at first sight as merely a colourfully overdrawn peripheral character, whose discursive role is little more than to demonstrate the narrator's eye for quirky detail. The reader probably begins to pay more serious attention when Aschenbach, idly glancing about the deck as the boat prepares for departure, also notices an odd and rather pathetic fellow passenger among a group of noisy young holiday-makers. 'Einer, in hellgelbem, übermodisch geschnittenem Sommeranzug, roter Krawatte und kühn aufgebogenem Panama, tat sich mit krähender Stimme an Aufgeräumtheit vor allen anderen hervor' (18) / 'One of the party, who wore a light yellow summer suit of extravagant cut, a scarlet necktie, and a rakishly tilted Panama hat, was the most conspicuous of them all in his shrill hilarity' (208). On closer inspection, however, Aschenbach is shocked to realize that the apparent youth is in fact a man of advanced years: 'Das matte Karmesin der Wangen war Schminke, das braune Haar unter dem farbig umwundenen Strohhut Perücke, ... sein gelbes und vollzähliges Gebiß, das er lachend zeigte, ein billiger Ersatz' (19) / 'His cheeks' faint carmine was rouge, the brown hair under his straw hat with its colored ribbon was a wig, ... his yellowish full complement of teeth, displayed when he laughed, were a cheap artificial set' (208).

The reader's attention is drawn to this particular apparition at least partly because of the narrator's account of Aschenbach's immediate and fastidious revulsion: 'Ihm war, als lasse nicht alles sich ganz gewöhnlich an, als beginne eine träumerische Entfremdung, eine Entstellung der Welt ins Sonderbare um sich zu greifen' (19) / 'He had a feeling that something not quite usual was beginning to happen, that the world was undergoing a dreamlike alienation, becoming increasingly deranged and bizarre' (209). Arrived in Venice and waiting to disembark, he is approached by the same pathetic old man, by now very drunk, who suggestively wishes him a pleasant stay, conveying lubricious compliments 'dem schönsten Liebchen' (22), to his 'beautiful sweetheart' (211), his effusion interrupted only when he almost loses his badly fitting false teeth. His departure is followed immediately, and without any apparent connection, by a reflectively rhetorical question on the part of the narrator:

Wer hätte nicht einen flüchtigen Schauder, eine geheime Scheu und Beklommenheit zu bekämpfen gehabt, wenn es zum ersten Male oder nach langer Entwöhnung galt, eine venezianische Gondel zu besteigen? Das seltsame Fahrzeug ... so eigentümlich schwarz, wie sonst unter allen Dingen nur Särge es sind, – es erinnert an lautlose und verbrecherische Abenteuer in plätschender Nacht, es erinnert noch mehr an den Tod selbst, an Bahre und düsteres Begräbnis und letzte, schweigsame Fahrt. (22)

Can there be anyone who has not had to overcome a fleeting sense of dread, a secret shudder of uneasiness, on stepping for the first time or after a long interval of years into a Venetian gondola? How strange a vehicle it is ... so characteristically black, the way no other thing is black except a coffin – a vehicle evoking lawless adventures in the plashing stillness of night, and still more strongly evoking death itself, the bier, the dark obsequies, the last silent journey! (211–12)

Though the voice is the narrator's, however, the sentiments are clearly now also Aschenbach's, tired from both his journey and his literary labours, and musing in such terms as he sinks gratefully into the comfortable seat of the gondola that is to take him ashore – only to realize after a few moments that the gondola is in fact heading towards the open sea instead. Assuming a misunderstanding, Aschenbach turns to the gondolier, towering over him on his raised deck,

ein Mann von ungefälliger, ja brutaler Physiognomie, seemännisch blau gekleidet, mit einer gelben Schärpe gegürtet und einer formlosen Strohhut ... verwegen schief auf dem Kopfe. Seine Gesichtsbildung, sein blonder, lockiger Schnurrbart unter der kurz aufgeworfenen Nase ließen ihn durchaus nicht italienischen Schlages erscheinen ... Ein paarmal zog er vor Anstrengung die Lippen zurück und entblößte seine weißen Zähne. (22–3)

a man of displeasing, indeed brutal appearance, wearing blue seaman's clothes, with a yellow scarf round his waist and a shapeless straw hat tilted rakishly on his head. To judge by the cast of his face and the blond curling moustache under his snub nose, he was quite evidently not of Italian origin ... Occasionally the effort made him retract his lips and bare his white teeth. (212–13)

Rather against his own principles, Aschenbach, after only a very cursory argument, gives in to the gondolier, who is clearly counting on a larger fare by taking him directly to the Lido rather than depositing him at the *vaporetto* station for a later crossing as he had requested. 'Ein Bann der Trägheit schien auszugehen von seinem Sitz, von diesem niedrigen, schwarzgepolsterten Armstuhl' (23) / 'A magic spell of indolence seemed to emanate from his seat, from this low, black-upholstered armchair' (213).

Attentive readers, by this time, will certainly have begun to recognize the signs of Aschenbach's gradual slide from a previously over-regimented way of life – already described in detail in the text – into a southern *dolce far niente*. They will very likely have noted the association of death and Venice in the evocation of a Venetian gondola. They will very likely also have already become aware that the several suspiciously similar descriptions of ostensibly peripheral characters so far quoted should evidently be read as constituting a series of some sort – but that is probably as far as they will have got. It is likely even at this point that all four of these characters – the stranger in Munich, the ticket-seller in Pola, the pathetic old man on the boat, the surly gondolier in Venice – are indeed peripheral in the sense that they all to some degree have only a walk-on role, that they are not vital elements in the *story*. The reader does not particularly expect to see them again, thus in effect already tacitly assuming that they are more importantly elements of the discursive *setting* for Aschenbach's story rather than elements of the story itself and reading them as contributing primarily to the development of a general sense of foreboding.

It is only with the appearance of a fifth member of the series that the reader finally feels authorized to indulge in a more definite interpretation of their combined discursive significance. While the first four are introduced in relatively quick succession, the fifth does not appear for another thirty pages, by which time Aschenbach's infatuation for Tadzio is already well advanced. Now in his fourth week in Venice, Aschenbach has admitted to himself his passion for the boy, has developed strong suspicions that the city is in the grip of plague, has confessed to himself that he would not be able to go on living (50/243) if Tadzio's family should leave Venice as a result. Sitting on the hotel terrace one evening sipping a drink and, as usual, surreptitiously observing Tadzio from a distance, Aschenbach is disturbed in his reflections by a group of street singers, and especially by their guitar-playing leader:

Er schien nicht venezianischen Schlages ... Sein Lied ... gewann in seinem Munde ... etwas Zweideutiges, unbestimmt Anstößiges. Dem weichen Kragen des Sporthemdes ... entwuchs ein hagerer Hals mit auffallend groß und nackt wirkendem Adamsapfel. Sein bleiches, stumpfnäsiges Gesicht ... schien durchpflügt von Grimassen und Laster, und sonderbar wollten zum Grinsen seines beweglichen Mundes die beiden Furchen passen, die trotzig, herrisch, fast wild zwischen seinen rötlichen Brauen standen. (55–6)

He was quite evidently not of Venetian origin ... His song ... had something inde-cent and vaguely offensive about it ... He wore a sports shirt, out of the soft collar of which his skinny neck projected, displaying a remarkably large and naked Adam's apple. His pallid, snub-nosed face ... seemed to be lined with contortions and vice, and the grinning of his mobile mouth was strangely ill-matched to the two deep furrows that stood defiantly, imperiously, almost savagely, between his reddish brows. (249)

What strikes Aschenbach most, however, is the strong smell of carbolic emanating from this somewhat dubious figure. The reader's questions as to the composite significance of the members of the series now seem to have found a satisfactory answer: the odour of carbolic ominously confirms Aschenbach's discovery that Venice is being disinfected, and already there have been enough hints of the possibility of plague that the reader, again remembering the foreboding title, is very likely in retrospect to see the snub noses and teeth-baring grimaces of the Munich stranger, the gondo-lier, and the street singer as a series of (distinctly ironic) evocations of the grinning death's head of medieval imagery. The ticket-seller who theatri-cally shakes the sand with which he had dried the ink of Aschenbach's con-tract for passage to Venice into an earthenware vessel before folding the paper 'mit gelben und knochigen Fingern' (18) / 'with his yellow bony fingers' (207) fits without difficulty into the same general mould – as does the painted old man, that false youth with his equally false complement of yellow teeth (19/208). The sense of general and undefined foreboding that accompanies each of these characters appears also to have found a satisfac-tory explanation.

Such a reading makes perfectly acceptable sense in the economy of a narrative account of Aschenbach's approaching death. In terms of literary history there is little that is new in the presentation of these metaleptic mes-sengers of death – other than the ironic tone in which most of them are introduced. The significance of the series is by no means exhausted by this reading, however. For one thing, it gradually becomes apparent that the beautiful boy Tadzio, though presented in a completely different key, must also be read as a member – the final member – of the series.

Only with Tadzio, indeed, is the reader for the first time fully in a position to make retrospective sense of the series of messenger figures. Aschenbach first notices Tadzio as ein langhaariger Knabe von vielleicht vierzehn Jahren. Mit Erstaunen bemerkte Aschenbach, daß der Knabe vollkommen schön war. Sein Antlitz, bleich und anmutig verschlossen, von honigfarbenem Haar umringelt, mit der gerade abfallenden Nase, dem lieblichen Munde, dem Ausdruck von holdem und göttlichem Ernst, erinnerte an griechische Bildwerke aus edelster Zeit. (26)

a long-haired boy of about fourteen. With astonishment Aschenbach noticed that the boy was entirely beautiful. His countenance, pale and gracefully reserved, was surrounded by ringlets of honey-colored hair, and with its straight nose, its enchanting mouth, its expression of sweet and divine gravity, it recalled Greek sculpture of the noblest period. (216)

Tadzio's beauty would seem initially to be worlds apart from the grimacing visages of the 'messengers.' The narrator, however, works with a suggestive blend of similarities and differences expressed in sometimes minute descriptive details: Tadzio's classically straight nose (26/216), for example, is strikingly different from the markedly snub noses of the stranger in Munich (8/196), the gondolier (23/212), and the street singer (55/249) alike. Tadzio's honey-coloured hair (26/216) likewise appears to have nothing in common with the red hair of both the stranger (8/196) and the street singer (55/249) or the reddish eyebrows shared by the gondolier (23/212) and the street singer (55/249), but is suggested by the curly blonde moustache (23/212) of the gondolier, while the colour red is repeated in the red necktie (18/208) of the drunken old man and Tadzio's beach costume, with its red breast-knot (29/220) or bow (67/263). The yellowish suit of the Munich stranger (8/196), the yellow fingers of the ticket-seller (18/207), the bright yellow suit and yellow teeth (18–19/208) of the old dandy, the yellow sash of the gondolier (23/212) recur ironically in the tone of Tadzio's skin, 'vom gelblichen Schmelze parischen Marmors' (29) / 'with the creamy luster of Parian marble' (220). Even the teeth-baring grimaces find an echo: Tadzio's physical perfection (26/216) is marred for Aschenbach only by the fact that his teeth do not look entirely healthy (34/224).

The most overtly marked similarity, however, is that between the physical stance of the Munich stranger and that of Tadzio on two separate and significant occasions. The stranger stands with his left hand 'in die Weiche gestützt ... und in der Rechten einen mit eiserner Spitze versehenen Stock, welchen er schräg gegen den Boden stemmte und auf dessen Krücke er, bei gekreuzten Füßen, die Hüfte lehnte' (8) / 'propped against his waist, and in his right hand an iron-pointed walking stick which he had thrust slantwise into the ground, crossing his feet and leaning his hip against its handle'

(196). Tadzio as he listens to the street singer likewise stands with 'die Füße gekreuzt, die rechte Hand in der tragenden Hüfte' (54) / 'his feet crossed, his right hand on the supporting hip' (248); and as Aschenbach sees him for the last time, the boy is turning towards him, 'eine Hand in der Hüfte' (68) / 'one hand on his hip' (263). Tadzio is thus unambiguously associated with the messenger-of-death imagery of this series, the skeleton imagery of medieval iconography transformed, however, into the beautiful boy who symbolized death for the Greeks.

Tadzio, however, is a highly complex figure, for he is also, as we have seen, associated in Aschenbach's dream with Dionysus, 'der fremde Gott' (61) / 'the stranger-god' (256). Tadzio himself is a 'stranger' in several senses. For a start, he is marked out – for Aschenbach at least – by his extraordinary beauty. Aschenbach further detects a striking contrast (26/216) between the way Tadzio and his sisters are being raised, Tadzio clearly, and quite unlike his siblings, being pampered by a doting mother. Most obviously, he is a foreigner, a Pole, and Aschenbach cannot understand a single word of his language (41/233). Finally, of course, the discourse associates him unambiguously with 'the stranger-god' by means of the long-drawn-out u-sound (31/223) with which his name ends, thus closing the series – and allowing the reader finally to perceive the significance of the recurring and teasingly parallel 'strangeness' in the description of the Munich stranger as being of non-Bavarian (8/196), the gondolier as of non-Italian (23/213), and the street singer as of non-Venetian stock (55/249). Retrospectively, through Tadzio, the harbingers of death become also, by way of their otherness, heralds of Dionysus, the stranger god.

The complexity of this series becomes even more evident when we reflect that the messengers can also be read as discursively prefiguring Aschenbach's fall from grace. As Tadzio is distortedly reflected in the series, so too is Aschenbach, though his exalted status and dignified character seem to have as little to do with their world as does Tadzio's beauty. Most obviously, the rejuvenated Aschenbach (64/259) physically becomes a mirror of the foolish old man who initially disgusts him, even down to the detail of the straw hat with its red ribbon. Less obviously, this same old man with painted face may be read as a travesty of an 'artist.' The street singer is likewise an artist, his vulgarity and crudity distortedly mirroring Aschenbach's devotion to formal purity. Both the street singer and the gondolier are described as physically frail, and both – again like the physically frail Aschenbach (12/201) – have to put enormous effort into plying their trade. The messengers, in short, are not only symbolic harbingers of dissolution and death, 'messengers' from the world of discourse in the world of story; they are also a composite distorting mirror of Aschenbach himself. They also, of course, mirror the fact that in an important sense the entire process of dissolution described in *Der Tod in Venedig* takes place most crucially inside the mind of its protagonist.

III

All three of the hermeneutic series so far discussed have their roots at least ostensibly in the realm of story reality, in the sense that all of them have a real existence for Aschenbach as an actor in that world: Venice and the various 'messenger' characters he encounters have a tangible existence in that world, while his visions of nature in the raw are clearly presented as the product of his own mind. There are also other such series at play in *Der Tod in Venedig* that have a similar overall function as far as the reader is concerned but give rise to a considerable degree of uncertainty as to whether they should be assigned primarily to the world of story or to that of discourse – which in effect means whether Aschenbach also has access to them or not. Indeed, the most interesting thing about these series is precisely the difficulty in assigning them unambiguously either to Aschenbach's consciousness or to that of the narrator.

The fourth of our series, for example, is made up of a complex web of allusions to classical mythology, some overt, some covert, and all occurring only after Aschenbach has reached Venice. The gondolier who ferries him across to the Lido, as we have seen, is overtly reminiscent of Charon, ferryman of souls, even before this is made explicit by Aschenbach's invocation of Aides/Hades (24/214). The labyrinthine quality of Venice is relevant in this context too, and Aschenbach's failure to 'escape' on his first attempt is reminiscent of various classical myths invoking an inability to escape from the Underworld. His return to Venice on this occasion takes place under the sign of 'der Gott mit den hitzigen Wangen' / 'the god with the burning cheeks,' Helios, who 'lenkte Tag für Tag ... nackend sein gluthauchendes Viergespann durch die Räume des Himmels' (39) / 'day after day ... soared naked, driving his four fire-breathing steeds through the spaces of heaven' (231), as Aschenbach yields ever more willingly to the effects of the sun, the sea, and his desire for Tadzio. His world is transformed into a vision of a world of myth, peopled by Achelous the river-god and his nymphs (42/235) and Eros the god of love (44/236), a world where Aschenbach the artist, invoking the story of Ganymede, sees himself transforming Tadzio's physical beauty 'ins Geistige ... wie der Adler einst den troischen Hirten zum Äther trug' (44) / 'into the spiritual world, as the eagle once carried the Trojan shepherd boy up into the ether' (236). The rising of the sun is 'eine beschwingte Kunde ... daß Eos sich von der Seite des Gatten erhebe' (45) / 'a winged message ... that Eos was rising from her husband's side' (238); in the waves of the sea 'die Rosse Poseidons liefen, sich bäumend, daher, Stiere auch wohl, dem Bläulichgelockten gehörig ... Eine heilig ent-stellte Welt voll panischen Lebens schloß den Berückten ein, und sein Herz träumte zarte Fabeln' (46) / 'the horses of Poseidon reared and ran; his bulls too, the bulls of the blue-haired sea god ... A sacred, deranged world, full of Panic life, enclosed the enchanted watcher, and his heart dreamed tender tales' (239).

Tadzio, the beautiful boy, is at one moment Ganymede (44/236), cup-bearer to the gods; at another Hyacinth (46/239), doomed to die because of the jealous love of two gods; at another Narcissus (48/241), intoxicated by his own godlike beauty – and whose fatally seductive smile eventually forces Aschenbach to admit his doomed love. From this moment of admission the mythological landscape darkens too. As Aschenbach listens to the street singer whose reeking clothes betray the presence of the plague, Tadzio's stance reminiscent of the 'stranger' in Munich evokes his role as Thanatos, while the pomegranate juice Aschenbach sips may remind us that the pomegranate was sacred not only to Dionysus, the god of passion, but also to Persephone, the goddess of the Underworld (54/248, 58/252). Very soon Aschenbach has his 'terrible dream' of Dionysus (61/254), a vision of dissolution and chaos, and as he sets off, painted and pomaded, to pursue Tadzio through the labyrinth of a diseased Venice, unclean spirits, malignant sea birds (64/259), seem to be abroad, vile har-pies who defile the food of the living and snatch away the souls of the dead. Within pages Aschenbach breathes his last, collapsing in the course of one final effort to follow Tadzio, whose designation as 'der bleiche und liebliche Psychagog' (68) / 'the pale and lovely soul-summoner' (263), standing at the edge of sea and land, lends him one final new identity, that of Hermes Psychopompos, another leader of souls to the land of the dead. Tadzio's final metamorphosis, of course, confirms that he is also the final link in the messenger series, the Grim Reaper transformed into the beauti-ful boy Thanatos, Death, twin brother of sleep. The combination of the mythological series and the messenger series also finally allows us to see that the strangers may be read as prefigurations not just of Death and Dionysus, but also of Hermes, master of metamorphosis and messenger of the gods – and, as one might say, metaleptic messenger also from the world of discourse to the world of story.

The messenger series, of course, is also an ironically angled series of *mises en abyme*. The fundamental difference between a character in a literary text and its reader, after all, is that the reader reads it *as* a literary text – and the character does not. 'If only' Aschenbach had been able to see these various ironically 'angelic' figures in the proper discursive light that the reader eventually learns to recognize, much could conceivably have been averted. The play with the Hermes characters, however, takes place entirely in the realm of discourse, to which Aschenbach has no access. It is indicative of the systemically ironic narratorial stance that while the mythological setting in which Aschenbach's fatal fall takes place is evidently at least largely the product of his own literary imagination, intoxicated with classical concepts of beauty, its simultaneous setting in the framework of the Hermes figures is certainly not. We may also observe that for all the mythological names actually mentioned in the text, that of Hermes himself, who is thus omnipresent, remains unspoken.

The fifth of our series, closely related to the mythological series, is equally ambiguous in this regard. This series is made up of a number of occurrences of a markedly hexametric diction throughout the text. The most obvious of these is the unattributed line of dactylic hexameter quoted by Aschenbach in amusement when he notices at breakfast on the day after he first sees Tadzio that the boy has apparently slept late: 'Nun, kleiner Phäake! dachte er ... Und plötzlich aufgeheitert, rezitierte er bei sich selbst den Vers: Oft veränderten Schmuck und warme Bäder und Ruhe' (29) / 'Well, my little Phaeacian! he thought ... And with his spirits suddenly rising, he recited to himself the line: "Varied garments to wear, warm baths and restful reposing"' (219). Alerted by the epithet 'Phäake'/'Phaeacian' the interested reader has little difficulty in locating the source of the quotation, namely, the eighth book of Homer's *Odyssey*.[8] Half a page later the narrator, describing Tadzio's appearance, mentions the collared blouse he is wearing: 'Auf diesem Kragen aber, der nicht einmal sonderlich elegant zum Charakter des Anzugs passen wollte, ruhte die Blüte des Hauptes in unvergleichlichem Liebreiz' (29) / 'But on this collar – which did not even match the rest of the suit very elegantly – there, like a flower in bloom, his head was gracefully resting' (220). The last words are again an exact – but this time completely unmarked – quotation from the same book of the *Odyssey* (8.19). The reader who notices may reasonably assume that these words, though ostensibly the narrator's, are actually 'thought' by Aschenbach, his mind still running on the *Odyssey* and the Greek world it evokes. A similar but considerably longer example occurs at the beginning of the fourth section of the text, after Aschenbach's attempt to flee Venice has (to his secret delight) been thwarted:

Nun lenkte Tag für Tag der Gott mit den hitzigen Wangen nackend sein gluthauchendes Viergespann durch die Räume des Himmels, und sein gelbes Gelock flatterte im zugleich ausstürmenden Ostwind. (39)

Now day after day the god with the burning cheeks soared naked, driving his four fire-breathing steeds through the spaces of heaven, and now too his yellow-gold locks fluttered wide in the outstorming east wind. (231)

Again the report is ostensibly the narrator's, and again the hexametric diction suggests that his description is focalized through the eyes of an Aschenbach who now sees himself as transported to a world of classical beauty and nearness to the gods.

Such discursive ruses might not be of any particular note if it were not for the ironic framework in which they too are employed. Again a page or so later, the narrator, describing Aschenbach's unexpected delight in being in Venice in these circumstances, observes that he occasionally

erinnerte sich seines Landsitzes in den Bergen, der Stätte seines sommerlichen Ringens, wo die Wolken tief durch den Garten zogen, fürchterliche Gewitter am Abend das Licht des Hauses löschten und die Raben, die er fütterte, sich in den Wipfeln der Fichten schwangen. Dann schien es ihm wohl, als sei er entrückt ins elysische Land, an die Grenzen der Erde, wo leichtestes Leben den Menschen beschert ist ... (40)

recalled his country house in the mountains, the scene of his summer labors, where the low cloud would drift through his garden, violent evening thunderstorms would put out all the lights, and the ravens he fed would take refuge in the tops of the pine trees. Then indeed he would feel he had been snatched away now to the Elysian land, to the ends of the earth, where lightest of living is granted to mortals ... (232)

and so on for several lines, which the reader may or may not again recognize as an unacknowledged quotation from the *Odyssey* (4.563–8). The reader may well also be struck, however, by the overtly clashing mythological worlds evoked here. We may have become used to the idea of the scholarly Aschenbach's mythologizing the world of Venice under the influence of his infatuation with Tadzio; the mythologization for good measure of his annual summer retreat to the Bavarian mountains in such ostentatiously Wagnerian terms as a primeval labour of creation worthy of a Wotan, complete with mythological ravens and meteorological special effects, is implicitly to ironize the whole mythological framework, whether we see it as the creation primarily of Aschenbach's consciousness or of the narrator's.

The hexameter series continues with a number of other examples at later points in the text, but we may conclude our consideration of this series by noting that while all the occurrences mentioned noted so far *could* be the (reported) work of Aschenbach's altered consciousness, there are in fact also examples that are unambiguously *not* the work of Aschenbach's mind. The first of these may be found as early as in the third paragraph of the narrative, where Aschenbach, still in Munich and just about to encounter the fateful stranger, gazes idly at the Byzantine styling of the mortuary chapel, decorated with Greek crosses and hieratic motifs, and which lay 'schweigend im Abglanz des scheidenden Tages' (7) / 'silent in the glow of the westering day' (196). The combination of the pointed references to art and death, the hints of exotic places and cultures, the gleam of a dying day, and finally the hexametric diction of the last words constitute an overall symbolic context in which the relationship of narrator, reader, and character is ironically skewed in a fashion typical of *Der Tod in Venedig*: the narrator is privy to all the implications involved, the reader only to some, and the character to none at all. To this extent the hexameter series allows the narrator to demonstrate at once his godlike power over Aschenbach's fate[9] and his almost equal capacity for ironic play with the reader – who again cannot possibly already understand at this early stage the particular implications of a dactylic rhythm rather than any other.

One further overtly ironic minor series is devoted in a similar vein entirely to highly stylized epithets for Aschenbach, constructed of an article and a nominalized adjective, parodically reminiscent of similar constructions in Homer, and forming in their sequence a minimal synopsis of the story: 'den Reiselustigen' (17) / 'him who was eager to travel' (206) in Munich, 'des Ruhenden' (20) / 'the resting one' (209) on the boat to Venice, 'der Reisende' (22) / 'he who traveled' (212) in his gondola, 'der Schauende' (26) / 'he who contemplated' (216), 'den Betrachtenden' (27) / 'him who observed' (217), 'der Reisende' (36) / 'the traveler' (226) who attempts to flee Venice, 'dem Alternden' (37) / 'the aging one' (228), 'der Reisende' (37) / 'the traveler' (229) who fails to flee Venice, 'den Wiederkehrenden' (38) / 'him who returned' (229), 'der Betrachtende' (41) / 'he who observed' (233), 'der Enthusiasmierte' (42) / 'he who was filled with the god' (234), 'den Berückten' (46) / 'the enchanted one' (239), 'der Heimgesuchte' (61) / 'the stricken one' (257).

The epithet series, indeed, can be read as just one component of an all-pervasive final series of textual leitmotifs and other devices that continually demonstrate the narrator's pervasively ironic attitude towards both Aschenbach and the reader. The use of the adjective 'verschwommen' (variously translatable as 'swimming, vague, cloudy, indistinct') and associated expressions, for example, continually hints discursively at the process of dissolution that is taking place in Aschenbach's world, whether the ostensible story context is the movement of a boat (19/209), the random impressions resulting from an idle glance (25/215), a hand hanging limply from the arm of a chair (39/230), the sound of Tadzio's uncomprehended foreign speech (29/219), or the final sight of the boy wading out to sea (68/263). The reader is continually and unavoidably forced to misread the significance of such details as the *u*-sound in Tadzio's name (31/223) or the ripe red strawberries that Aschenbach eats shortly after first seeing the boy (32/223). Missing a particular detail does not necessarily destroy the validity of an overall reading; seeing it certainly leads to a new appreciation both of the narrator's comprehensively ironic attitude and of the enormous richness of Mann's text.

IV

In *Der Tod in Venedig* the theoretical distinction between the syntagmatic and the paradigmatic axes of narration is systemically blurred. Venice is as much character as it is setting; the Hermes figures are more setting than they are characters; both are the product of a narrator whose primary interest is far less narration in any narrower sense than it is a highly ironic – and self-ironic – *presentation*. The narrator at once is at pains to present himself as a pompously moralizing commentator on the nature of art and continually reveals himself as a master of discursive ludicity, the style of his narrative becoming ever more formalized, ever more 'classical' – and the classical canon sedulously plundered for appropriate references, from Homer (29/219), Socrates (32/223, 43/235, 65/261), Plato (43/235, 65/261), and Xenophon (32/223) to Cicero (7/195), Louis XIV (16/205), and Hölderlin (40/231) – as Aschenbach increasingly forsakes Apollonian order for Dionysian abandon. This formalization is doubly (and thus ironically) focalized, as we have seen – and (again ironically) hypostatized in the Hermes characters as 'messengers' between story and discourse. The pervasive irony – sometimes amusing, sometimes poignant, sometimes painful – holds until the concluding sentences of the narrative, as Aschenbach, with his last breath, still attempts to follow Tadzio 'wie so oft' (68) / 'as so often' (263), a final ambiguity ironically equating the shame of the pedophile and the duty of the artist who spends his life in pursuit of beauty.

There is a final irony, of course, in the fact that the discourse of *Der Tod in Venedig*, as is well known, also toys with another (potential) story, the story of Mann's own homosexual leanings. The catalogue of Aschenbach's works (11/200) is also an ironically self-aggrandizing list of works that Mann himself had either written or contemplated writing over the past decade. And, indeed, Aschenbach evidently 'is' also Thomas Mann – at least as he might have been.[10] But it is at least equally evident that the narrator who systemically ironizes Aschenbach 'is' Thomas Mann too – and therein lies a fundamental difference between biography and literary fiction.

The appearance in the last page or so of Mann's *Novelle* of an unattended camera on its tripod, 'scheinbar herrenlos' (67) / 'apparently abandoned' (262), may serve as a graphic reminder to any reader who still needs it that there can, by definition, never be any unmediated access to the world of story, which is always necessarily filtered through the discourse that presents it. *Der Tod in Venedig*, in which Dionysian chaos is shown to triumph over Apollonian order in what is surely one of the most Apollonian texts imaginable, is a highly self-aware modernist text – and one that in the end is just as much about its own discourse as it is about the story it narrates. As such, it provides a classic and concrete realization of the irony that always latently characterizes the gap between story and discourse.

2

The Trial:
Paradigms of Indeterminacy
in Franz Kafka's *Der Prozeß*

There are several modern German writers whose work has been the subject of intense critical attention both in German and in English – Thomas Mann, for example, and Hermann Hesse, and Günter Grass. None, however, has been subjected to more intense scrutiny than has Franz Kafka, and none has produced a body of work that has been read in so great a variety of disparate and even openly conflicting ways.[1] Clearly, the most immediate reason for this multiplicity of readings is that Kafka's oeuvre is structurally characterized by a systemic indeterminacy that is unique in its range and pervasiveness. His uncompleted novel *Der Prozeß* (*The Trial*), written in 1914–15 and published posthumously (against Kafka's stated wishes) by his friend Max Brod in 1925, provides a key example both of this characteristic of Kafka's writing and of the concomitant interpretive challenges it presents to his readers.[2] In this chapter we shall therefore focus on the structural articulation of this indeterminacy in *Der Prozeß*, reading it as a function of the relationship of story and discourse. Specifically, we shall examine two particular (and related) ways of *seeing* the narrative events presented, whether 'seen' (or read) as by narrator, character, or reader, looking first at the use of narrative focalization and then (as in the case of *Der Tod in Venedig* but to very different effect) at the essentially paradigmatic structuration of the text.[3]

I

The presentation of the story is at once markedly straightforward, even schematic, as a whole and entirely enigmatic in its details. Josef K., a bank official in an unnamed city not unlike Prague, wakes up on the morning of his thirtieth birthday to find himself, for reasons unknown, under arrest at the hands of two likewise unknown men. He spends the whole of the following year attempting to establish his innocence, but all his efforts remain completely unavailing. On the evening before his thirty-first birthday, exactly one year after his arrest, he is led away, again by two unknown men, who, with impeccable formality, put him to death by plunging a dagger into his heart.

In spite of this ironically exaggerated overall symmetry in the presentation of K.'s story – neither the symmetry nor the irony of which its reader can fully discover until the very last chapter – its most immediately striking characteristics as far as its details are concerned are its continual 'dreamlike' distortions of reality and its pervasive and again dreamlike vagueness. Indeed, one immediately obvious (if in the end entirely disappointing) reading in realist terms is to see K.'s story, like Alice's adventures in Wonderland, as 'only' a dream: K. dreams that he wakes up at the beginning and dreams his own death at the end, just before he really wakes up from the nightmare in the blank space following the last sentence of the text. Such a readerly decision, of course, simply defuses the text's strangeness by means of a comfortingly realistic explanation imposed from without; as readers whose primary concern is the interactive relationship of stories and their discourse, we are still faced, dream or not, with the task of reading the text in its own terms – which is to say, precisely as literary narrative.

The nature of K.'s arrest, it quickly emerges, is to at least some degree dependent on how he chooses to see it, for he is both 'under arrest' and entirely free to carry on with his normal routine. And K. never does (never can) decide how to see his own situation. He is never informed what his offence has been or what sort of court or code of law he has come up against, but his guilt is evidently (or apparently) assumed by everyone except himself. Almost everyone, indeed, seems to be much more aware of the existence of this court than he is, but even its apparent officials, when he succeeds in questioning them, seem to be incapable of grasping the subtleties of its operation. But perhaps, as K. reasons, these officials, though in some cases clearly functionaries of considerable importance, are still simply too low down in the overall hierarchy to have any real information, for the high judges are so very remote that even their existence is not entirely certain.

Summoned at an early stage to a public interrogation in a squalid suburb, K., master of the situation, indignantly denounces the sham, hypocrisy, and illogicality of so iniquitous and even foolish a system – but at the same time, as we notice, implicitly accepts its authority in immediately setting out to prove himself innocent of whatever it is that he is being accused of.

Rather than attempting to discover what his alleged crime may have been, he elects instead to spend the entire year looking for people (most of them women) who may be able to help him, such as his fellow lodger, one Fräulein Bürstner (whom he almost absent-mindedly attempts to seduce while telling her of his arrest), his landlady, or a washerwoman whom he believes (for no immediately obvious reason) to be associated in some undefined capacity with the court. Initially full of self-confidence, K. becomes increasingly demoralized. With the help of an accommodating uncle, who even moves into town to help him, he succeeds in locating an ailing but reputedly powerful advocate named Huld – but while his uncle is discussing the complexities of K.'s case with the lawyer, K. himself slips out of the room to make love to the lawyer's nurse. A business associate points him towards a painter named Titorelli, who is allegedly the official portrait painter for the court. Titorelli, who seems (both to K. and to the reader) to be unusually well informed, explains at great length the three possible outcomes (according to himself) of K.'s trial: a definite acquittal, which, however, is unheard of; an ostensible acquittal, which does not prevent its recipient from possible re-arrest even before he leaves the courtroom; and an indefinite postponement, which simply leaves things exactly as they are. Not surprisingly, perhaps, all of Titorelli's paintings, as far as K. can see, also look exactly the same. (K., as character, can hardly be expected to see the discursive irony at play here; the reader is clearly challenged by Kafka's text to do so.)

K. duly abandons Titorelli, attempts to dismiss Huld, thinks about submitting a private plea on his own behalf even though there is no evidence that such a plea would ever be read by anybody (or have any effect if it were), and discusses his case at length with a ruined businessman named Block, who has also been arrested, who maintains a whole team of advocates all working away busily on his behalf, and whose case (according to himself) is none the less hopelessly bogged down, just as it has been for the last several years. In the cathedral of the unnamed city, where business affairs have taken K., he is addressed from the pulpit by an unnamed priest who claims to be a prison chaplain and officer of the court, and who informs K. not only that his trial is going very badly for him but that he has evidently completely misunderstood the entire nature of the proceedings (a 'misunderstanding' that is certainly shared by the reader).

The priest further recounts a parable about a 'Mann vom Lande' (182), a 'man from the country' (213) or country bumpkin, who comes to the door of the Law seeking admission, only to be informed by a doorkeeper that he cannot be admitted at the moment. For many years the man sits before the

Law, more and more feebly trying to persuade the doorkeeper to admit him. Finally his strength is exhausted, and as he lies dying he asks the doorkeeper why, since the door is always open, nobody else has sought admission to the Law in all these years. The doorkeeper replies that the door was always intended solely for the man from the country – and now he, as doorkeeper, is going to close it. Exactly one year after his initial arrest K. is visited by two further emissaries of the court, two plump and well-dressed men in top hats who lead him away unresisting. With great politeness they prepare his execution. At the last moment a window in a nearby house flies open, and a figure leans far out with arms outstretched, possibly to offer some help, possibly without any relevance whatsoever. At any rate it is too late. The knife is already embedded and twisted for good measure in K.'s heart, and his executioners are watching with polite interest as he dies, 'wie ein Hund' (194) / 'like a dog' (229).

'Jemand mußte Josef K. verleumdet haben, denn ohne daß er etwas Böses getan hätte, wurde er eines Morgens verhaftet' (7) / 'Someone must have been telling lies about Josef K., for without having done anything wrong he was arrested one fine morning' (1). Even the opening word of the narrator's account of K.'s story is characterized by the uncertainty and indeterminacy that pervade the entire narrative; even the opening sentence raises potential doubts as to the authority of the narrative voice. Who exactly is the 'someone' who 'must' have been telling lies? Who says he (or she) must have been lying? What sort of lies? What sort of 'wrong' has K. allegedly not done? Why does he not enjoy a full surname? Any such initial doubts on the reader's part will in fact turn out to be entirely justified, for the opening play with concealment and revelation is merely the first example of a technique massively employed throughout the narrative, namely, a deconstructive giving of information with one hand and taking it back with the other.

But whose is this narrative voice in the first place? Is it the voice of a narrator who is wholly external to the story narrated and merely records detachedly what he knows or has been told, without further involvement on his part? Or is it the voice of K. himself, the third-person form of the narration merely a very thin disguise for what is 'really' a first-person narrative? Or is it perhaps a voice whose ventriloquist owner cannot (or will not) quite decide whether it should be *projected* from the position of the detached observer or from that of the deeply involved protagonist? The answer, it will emerge, is yes to all three questions, for it is precisely the shifting narrative distance between narrator and character that is the primary source of the pervasive indeterminacy that characterizes Kafka's text.

Many readers have been seduced by the apparent closeness of the narrator and the main character into an incautious assumption that their perspectives are entirely identical – and throughout much of the text it is indeed quite impossible to distinguish them conclusively. There are also points in the text where the narrating voice does indeed step back and align itself, even if only fleetingly, with the position of an observer rather than of an observed – as when K., in the course of his arrest, 'machte eine Bewegung, als reiße er sich von den zwei Männern los' (8) / 'made as if to wrench himself away from the two men' (3), or remembers previous occasions on which he acted rashly and promises himself not to do so now, 'ohne daß es sonst seine Gewohnheit gewesen wäre, aus Erfahrungen zu lernen' (10) / 'though it was not usual with him to learn from experience' (4). For very much the most part, however, the narrative voice is characterized precisely by its indeterminacy – which is to say, of course, by its audience's inability to determine its location (mirroring K.'s inability to determine the nature of the charges – if any – against him).

'Shifting narrative distance,' however, is only a convenient misnomer. What we are really talking about is the strategic employment of a multiply shifting *focalization*, and it may be useful to examine that concept a little more closely at this point. Focalization, as Mieke Bal writes, is 'the most important, most penetrating, and most subtle means of manipulation' available to the narrative text, whether literary or otherwise (1985: 116). The term was introduced into critical discourse by Gérard Genette in the early 1970s, in order, as he says himself, to dispel 'a regrettable confusion' surrounding an 'apparently obvious but almost universally disregarded distinction,' namely, that 'between the question *Who is the character whose point of view orients the narrative perspective?* and the very different question *Who is the narrator?* – or, more simply, the question *Who sees?* and the question *Who speaks?*' (1980: 186). Focalization is thus most importantly a matter of presentational mediation: as Shlomith Rimmon-Kenan succinctly puts it, 'the story is presented in the text through the mediation of some "prism," "perspective," "angle of vision," verbalized by the narrator though not necessarily his' (1983: 71). Multiple varieties and operational subtleties of focalization may be distinguished (cf. O'Neill 1994: 83–106). The simplest and most radical distinction, however, is entirely adequate for discussing the fundamental opposition at play in *Der Prozeß*, namely, that between, on the one hand, a narrative focalized (in part or as a whole) through the eyes of a narrator who is detached from and external to the account he presents and, on the other, a narrative focalized through the eyes of a character *within* that account.

Der Prozeß achieves its pervasively enigmatic character largely from a sustained and masterly use of *indeterminate* focalization, that is to say, by a systemic blurring of the theoretically clear distinction between external narrator-focalization and internal character-focalization. The opening sentence, for example, already quoted, initially reads as if it were an uncomplicated narrator-focalization. Indeed, there is no technical reason why it should *not* be regarded as narrator-focalization pure and simple. 'Jemand mußte Josef K. verleumdet haben' / 'Someone must have been telling lies about Josef K.' could simply be an assumption made by a character-narrator realistically aware of his incomplete control of all the facts, as could the further statement that K. was arrested 'without having done anything wrong.' As sentence follows sentence, however, the cumulative effect is to cause the reader to wonder if the opening sentence too should not (or, at least, could not) retrospectively be read through the eyes of K. as character-focalization (CF) rather than narrator-focalization (NF) after all:

Die Köchin der Frau Grubach, seiner Zimmervermieterin [NF], die ihm jeden Tag gegen acht Uhr früh das Frühstück brachte [NF? CF?], kam diesmal nicht [NF?]. Das war noch niemals geschehen [CF?]. K. wartete noch ein Weilchen [NF], sah von seinem Kopfkissen aus [CF] die alte Frau, die ihm gegenüber wohnte [NF] und die ihn mit einer an ihr ganz ungewöhnlichen Neugierde beobachtete [CF], dann aber, gleichzeitig befremdet und hungrig [CF], läutete er [NF]. (7)

His landlady's cook [NF], who always brought him his breakfast at eight o'clock [NF? CF?], failed to appear on this occasion [NF?]. That had never happened before [CF?]. K. waited for a little while longer [NF], watching from his pillow [CF] the old lady opposite [NF], who seemed [CF] to be peering at him with a curiosity unusual even for her [CF], but then, feeling [CF] both put out and hungry, he rang the bell [NF]. (1)[4]

Even though the reader's initial assumption of narrator-focalization may be unsettled by this sequence, however, he or she is still not provided at any stage with *unambiguous* evidence that that first reading was either right or wrong. And that is precisely the point: the overall effect of the continually shifting, continually indeterminate focalization, which could equally easily be shown to obtain in almost any paragraph of the novel, is to create a pervasive sense of readerly uncertainty throughout the entire narrative.

This continual and unsettling movement between external narrator-focalization and internal character-focalization is reflected in (and emphasized by) a related and centrally important structural characteristic of the text, namely, the repeated thematization of *particular ways of seeing*, and the relationship between observers and observed, watchers and watched (cf. Allemann 1965: 261). The relationship of narrator and character in any narrative is always in principle that of observer and observed. It is also clear that, as readers, we always in principle have the choice of focusing our attention primarily on the story told or on the discourse that presents it. Concentrating on the story focuses our attention on the observed, in these terms, while concentrating on the discourse shifts our focus instead to the observer – and thus also to the relationship between the observing subject and the observed object. The narrator too, of course, is a special kind of reader, a reader who *reads* the possibilities of the situation described in the story precisely by *writing* the story in one way rather than another – or in a variety of ways. What is true of the narrator is evidently also true of the author (whether implied or real) who creates him.

From the very beginning, *Der Prozeß* is full of watchers observing Josef K. The old lady across the street watching him through the window as he lies in bed is soon joined by an old man and then by a young man, all of whom simply observe K. as he is arrested. This is their only function as characters. Once this function has been exercised, they simply disappear from the text and are never seen again. Their places are soon filled by a whole series of others, however: the 'Wächter' (literally, 'watchers') who arrest him, his fellow lodger Fräulein Bürstner, who acts as audience to K.'s re-enactment of that arrest, the spectators at K.'s interrogation, the girls who watch as he talks to Titorelli the painter, the priest who observes him as he explores the cathedral, the executioners who watch him as he dies. The central concept of a court that sits in judgment on K. is itself an institutionalization of the relationship of observer and observed, the watchers and the watched.

II

Sometimes, however (and such instances provide some of the most interesting passages in the text), it is K. himself who is allowed to be the focalizing observer (even if he remains largely unconscious of that fact). The most striking occurrence of this is in the fifth chapter, 'Der Prügler' / 'The Whipper,' where K. watches, in a room he had thought to be merely a 'Rumpelkammer' or lumber-room, as a man clad in black leather brutally whips the two warders involved in K.'s initial arrest – ostensibly in consequence of a complaint that K. has made concerning their behaviour on that occasion. As the alleged plaintiff, K. is thus in a transferred sense the whipper, but he simultaneously wonders uneasily if the whip really hurts as much as it seems to do, and is later made to reflect (or at least share in the reflection) that 'so wäre es ja fast einfacher gewesen, K. hätte sich selbst ausgezogen und dem Prügler als Ersatz für die Wächter angeboten' (78) / 'it would almost have been simpler to take off his own clothes and offer himself to the whipper as a substitute for the warders' (88).

In this crucial scene the narrative self-consciously refers to its own central structural principle, as K. is identified simultaneously as whipper, whipped, and observer. K. as observer, that is, projects himself (or rather, of course, is *made* to project himself) into two separate and complementary roles at once, focalizing himself as winner and loser, active and passive, subject and object. K., thus allowed to play with a possible decision between the two possibilities, eventually cuts the knot in this particular case by refusing to make the decision and simply slams the door. But the knot refuses to stay cut: next day he opens the door to the lumber-room again, 'wie aus Gewohnheit' (79) / 'as if out of habit' (89), and is faced with exactly the same scene, unchanged by any passage of time. Again, he responds by slamming the door, even attempts to erase it completely: 'Räumt doch endlich die Rumpelkammer aus!' he cries, almost in tears, to the bank attendants. 'Wir versinken ja im Schmutz!' (79) / 'Clear the lumber-room out, can't you? ... We're smothering in dirt' (90).

Josef K.'s momentary play (whether voluntary or involuntary) with the hypothetical choice of being *either* whipper or whipped is a reflection of the text's systemic structural play with the polar opposites of controlling and being controlled, as seen also in various other groupings, whether in the form of arrester and arrested, seducer and seduced, adviser and advised, doorkeeper and suppliant, or executioner and executed. This fundamental opposition, in turn – which is to say, this continued experiment in focalization and refocalization – operates self-reflexively at every structural level of the narrative transaction.[5] In the world of discourse the narrator continually balances K. the 'master' against K. the 'victim' – as, for example, during the first interrogation, in which K. is portrayed as pendulating between complete (apparent) domination of the situation and utter (apparent) defeat. 'Behind' the narrator, to go one step further, the implied author has the narrator now identify with K., whether victorious or defeated, now back off for impartial observation of the defeats or victories. Behind the implied author we may, of course, if we wish, catch glimpses of the real author, as he identifies now with this textual possibility, now with that, the perennial observer slamming and reopening an infinite series of lumber-room doors. In *Der Prozeß* as elsewhere, Kafka's pervasive use of indeterminate focalization coupled with a pervasive thematization of the embedded structuration of narrative provides him with a fundamentally refractive technique, a series of prisms continually rebreaking and restating, superimposed filters providing a play of contrastive colorations and effects.

Viewed in this light (and as readers we too always have the option of choosing or refusing this or any other angle of vision), *Der Prozeß* constitutes a narrative theatre of alternatives, an indefinitely extensible series of narrative paradigms that in the end, like Titorelli's landscapes, are in one sense all exactly the same. For all their surface difference, the reader is clearly invited to conclude that 'die Schrift ist unveränderlich und die Meinungen sind oft nur ein Ausdruck der Verzweiflung darüber' (185) / 'what is written is unalterable, and commentaries are often simply an expression of despair about that fact' (217), as the priest tells Josef K. in his explication of the parable of the man from the country. At the same time the text is unrelentingly lavish in its variations on the expression of this 'despair.' The discursive structure of *Der Prozeß*, in other words, is essentially paradigmatic rather than syntagmatic, implying the necessity of a reading that is primarily vertical or metaphoric, as one reads lyric poetry, rather than the horizontal or metonymic reading required by the cause-and-effect motivation of traditional realist narrative fiction. In other words, what *happens* to Josef K. is always less important than what can be *seen* to happen (or be capable of happening) to him.

From this perspective, of course, the attempts of Kafka scholars over the past half-century to establish a single correct chapter-order – for the traditional order has long been disputed[6] – are essentially irrelevant, as is also the fact that *Der Prozeß* is unfinished. From this perspective, nothing would be altered if it had been finished. The *story*, of course, like all stories, is linear, but the discursive series of hypothetical scenarios bracketed between Josef K.'s awakening and his execution is infinitely extendable, a latter-day demonstration of Zeno's proof of the impossibility of motion. Nor need K.'s final execution necessarily be regarded as in any way a definitive end, some Archimedean point of privileged knowledge. Chronologically it is indeed the final chapter of the narrative; structurally it is just one more tentative slamming of the lumber-room door. Josef K., as we know, will appear again, the same but different, as the protagonist of *Das Schloß* (*The Castle*).

Like Gregor Samsa in *Die Verwandlung* (*The Metamorphosis*), who wakes up one morning to find himself transformed into a 'monstrous vermin,' Josef K. wakes up one morning to find himself transformed into something that is no longer part of the familiar everyday world where it once belonged. Josef K. has been made strange, defamiliarized, 'arrested,' not only by the unseen Court, but also by the discourse itself, which will go on to submit him to an extensive array of experiments and monitor his reactions – and ours also, of course, since each of these 'experiments' influences our reaction to the text as a whole. We do not actually witness his arrest. Clayton Koelb even points out that K.'s alleged arrest in fact forms no part of the story, which deals only with its aftermath (1983: 38). The warder Willem, when K. attempts to leave the room, observes, 'Sie dürfen nicht weggehen, Sie sind ja verhaftet' (8), which, because of the force of the concessive particle *ja*, might be translated as something like 'You can't leave, you're under arrest *after all*' (3), to which K., accepting Willem's focalization, merely (and perhaps foolishly) replies, 'Es sieht so aus' (8) / 'So it seems' (3). In one sense, then, K. may be read as already 'under arrest' even before the story begins; in another, the whole thing is the result of his own originary misreading of the situation. K. indeed asks *why* – 'warum denn?' (8) / 'but what for?' (3) – but he never contests the situation, merely sets out immediately to find an explanation for it. As readers, we too are promptly manipulated into accepting (perhaps equally foolishly) K.'s reading (of the warder's reading) of the situation.

The first sentence seems indeed to suggest that the arrest has already taken place, but this suggestion is arguably retracted by the next three sentences, which show Josef K. first in relation to an unexpected absence – 'Die Köchin der Frau Grubach ... kam diesmal nicht' (7) / 'Frau Grubach's cook ... did not come this time' (1) – then as an object of observation for 'die alte Frau, die ihm gegenüber wohnte und die ihn mit einer an ihr ganz ungewöhnlichen Neugierde beobachtete' (7) / 'the old lady who lived opposite him and who was watching him with a curiosity quite unusual for her' (1); and finally as setting his own 'arrest' and 'trial' in motion by ringing the bell. 'Sofort klopfte es und ein Mann, den er in dieser Wohnung noch niemals gesehen hatte, trat ein' (7) / 'There was an immediate knock on the door, and a man whom he had never yet seen in that house entered' (1). The first words we witness Josef K. speaking are 'Wer sind Sie?' / 'Who are you?' directed to the man who turns out to be called Franz, Franz who is a 'Wächter,' a 'warder' who will 'watch' over K., and who is also a parodic representative in the world of story of that other Franz who operates vicariously in a different narrative world. Not only does K., of course, not know who Franz (or 'Franz') is; he even has momentary difficulty in proving who he is himself – beyond producing his bicycle licence. 'War es eine Komödie, so wollte er mitspielen' (10) / 'If it was a comedy, he was going to play along' (5).

It is a comedy, as we have seen, at least as far as its narrative structuration is concerned, but this fact is soon lost on Josef K. – and also, of course, on those readers who choose to emphasize the story rather than the discourse by means of which it is presented. Ostentatiously and symmetrically observed by three officials, three clerks from the bank, and the three watchers from across the street, K. is pointedly advised to collect himself: 'Denken Sie weniger an uns und an das, was mit Ihnen geschehen wird, denken Sie lieber mehr an sich' (16) / 'Think less of us and of what's going to happen to you, think more about yourself instead' (12). K., however, is too self-confident at this stage to be self-conscious and soon feels completely in control of the situation: 'Er spielte mit ihnen' (18) / 'He was playing with them' (14), as the text puts it, itself playing again, by means of indeterminate focalization, with both K. and the reader. K.'s self-esteem suffers only a very minor set-back when at the end of this episode he realizes that his conversation with the three bank clerks has prevented him from noticing the three officials leaving, just as earlier his dealings with the latter had prevented him from seeing the bank clerks in the first place. 'Viel Geistesgegenwart bewies das nicht' (19) / 'That did not show much presence of mind' (16), K. reflects, or the narrator observes, or both.

K.'s next 'trial' is the encounter with his fellow lodger, Fräulein Bürstner, which takes place in her bedroom. Once again the scenario is that of a contest, a game of victory or defeat this time in sexual terms, and at its conclusion K., having subdued Fräulein Bürstner with a long kiss, returns to his bed satisfied that the victory is his. The reader is perhaps less sure, since K.'s sexual 'victory' can also be read as having been carefully orchestrated by the presumed victim herself. The high point of K.'s 'seduction' is his narration, for Fräulein Bürstner's benefit, of the course of his first interview with the officials, a retelling ironically skewed by K.'s electing (or being made to elect) to play the role of the interrogating officer, while unaccountably 'forgetting' the role of the arrested K. 'Ja, ich vergesse mich. Die wichtigste Person' (28) / 'Why, I'm forgetting myself. The most important person' (27). The reader may also notice that as K.'s imitated (narrated) shout of 'Josef K.!' (29/27) shatters the silence, an irritated knocking from the room next door indicates that his cry has awakened a certain 'Hauptmann' Lanz – the title merely means 'captain,' of course, but it obviously can also be read as a verbal play on *Haupt-mann* as literally meaning 'the most important person.' K. himself, however, ignorant of all this, returns satisfied to his room and 'schlief sehr bald ein' (31) / 'fell asleep almost at once' (30).

The second, third, and fourth chapters are characterized by the same ironic dialectic of apparent victory and apparent defeat, perceived superiority versus perceived inferiority. K. completely cows his interrogators during the so-called first interrogation – which is really rather the third round in an ongoing interrogation. On his attempting to reprise the scene a week later, however, he is first thwarted by finding that no sitting has been scheduled. He is partially compensated for this set-back by another apparent sexual victory, this time over a casually encountered washerwoman, whom he perceives as being intimately connected with his tormentors, only to have her literally snatched from his grasp by the student Berthold. K. 'sah ein, daß das die erste zweifellose Niederlage war, die er von diesen Leuten erfahren hatte' (53) / 'recognized that this was the first unequivocal defeat that he had received from these people' (58). As readers, we are likely to see K.'s misinterpretation of the washerwoman's significance as merely foolish – but we are entirely likely (perhaps equally foolishly?) to accept at face value the interpretation offered here of the situation as a whole, even though the shifting focalization ensures our inability to determine unambiguously whether the view offered is the narrator's or K.'s.

Moving on immediately to the Law Court offices, K. high-handedly demonstrates his assumed superiority over a group of fellow defendants before being overcome himself by 'ein wenig Schwindel' (61) / 'a slight dizziness' (67): 'Wollte etwa sein Körper revolutionieren und ihm einen neuen Prozeß bereiten, da er den alten so mühelos ertrug?' (66) / 'Could his body possibly be meditating a revolution and preparing a new trial for him, since he was withstanding the old one with such ease?' (73), the text (again entirely indeterminately) asks, while K., having very quickly closed the door behind him and adjusted his rumpled appearance with the help of a pocket mirror, 'lief dann die Treppe hinunter, so frisch und in so langen Sprüngen, daß er vor diesem Umschwung fast Angst bekam' (66) / 'leapt down the stairs so buoyantly and with such long strides that he became almost afraid of his own reaction' (73). Chapter four finds him attempting to consolidate his earlier 'victory' over Fräulein Bürstner, but his efforts are decisively scotched by a discursive joke at his expense when he is confronted by a forbidding Fräulein 'Montag,' Fräulein Bürstner's Monday-morning friend.

We have already looked at the fifth chapter, 'Der Prügler' / 'The Whipper,' in some detail, and have seen that it too functions as a 'pocket mirror,' a 'Taschenspiegel' (66) in which Josef K. can adjust his appearance, demonstrating for K., had he but the eyes to see it, the indecisiveness of his accumulated gains and losses. 'Ich bin es!' / 'It's me!' he cries to the bank attendants who approach as he slams the lumber-room door, 'es schreit nur

ein Hund auf dem Hof' (77) / 'it was only a dog howling in the courtyard'
(87). As K. watches from his window the reflection of the moon in the windows across the street,

es quälte ihn, daß es ihm nicht gelungen war, das Prügeln zu verhindern, aber es war
nicht seine Schuld, daß es nicht gelungen war, hätte Franz nicht geschrien – gewiß,
es mußte sehr weh getan haben, aber in einem entscheidenden Augenblick muß
man sich beherrschen – hätte er nicht geschrien, so hätte K., wenigstens sehr wahrscheinlich, noch ein Mittel gefunden, den Prügler zu überreden. (77–8)

he was deeply disappointed that he had not succeeded in preventing the whipping,
but it was not his fault that he had not succeeded; if Franz had not shrieked – it
must certainly have been very painful, but in a decisive moment one must control
oneself – if he had not shrieked, then K., in all probability at least, would still have
found some means of persuading the whipper. (88)

This pivotal episode, the fifth of ten chapters in Brod's edition, foreshad-
ows Josef K.'s own execution down to the setting of moonlight, windows,
the executioners who watch the 'Entscheidung' (194) or 'decisive moment'
(229), and his dying words 'wie ein Hund' (194) / 'like a dog' (229). If the
implied author wanted to, he could certainly – or 'in all probability at least'
– find a way to avert or at least postpone K.'s execution. But would there
be any point? From the lumber-room scene on, K.'s mind is characteristically 'müde und gedankenlos' (79) / 'tired and blank' (90), and the remaining chapters – with the abrupt exception of the last – become
correspondingly and increasingly prolix, as the game scenarios of the earlier chapters give way to endless discussions in which an overwhelming
excess of information deconstructs into an entropic absence of certainty.

On the level of story, the level of Josef K.'s experience, the reader from
now on may well share K.'s growing hopelessness, while accompanying
him sympathetically in his futile attempts to achieve at least some degree of
clarity. On the level of discourse, however, K.'s doomed efforts are continually and ironically distanced by a variety of narrative stratagems related to
particular ways of seeing things. K.'s Uncle Karl, 'ein kleiner Grundbesitzer vom Lande' (80) / 'a small land owner from the country' (91), or, as
K. calls him, 'das Gespenst vom Lande' (80) / 'the ghost from the country'
(92), materializes in chapter 6, his epithet of 'Grundbesitzer' also ironically
suggesting one who 'possesses reasons' for his actions and the reference to
his country origins likewise ironically pointing forward to the 'man from
the country' in the priest's parable who comes to gain entry to the Law.

Uncle Karl, having heard of K.'s plight, is determined to expedite his affairs by resolute action and adroit use of professional connections, an attempt that is scuttled, however, by K.'s increasing irresolution and maladroit efforts to exert an oblique influence himself through Leni, the advocate's nurse. 'Je ruhiger ich bin, desto besser ist es für den Ausgang' (82) / 'The quieter I am, the better it will be in the end' (94) is now K.'s motto; his uncle, by contrast, continues the energetic line of attack that had been Josef K.'s in the earlier chapters. 'Deine Gleichgültigkeit bringt mich um den Verstand' (85) / 'Your indifference is driving me insane' (97), he upbraids the now increasingly passive K.

This 'Onkel Karl,' in fact – who later metamorphoses without explanation into 'Albert K.' (91/100) – clearly functions as a discursive synecdoche for that side of K.'s nature which still believes that there is some point in continuing the obviously uneven contest. The reverse synecdoche is presented in chapter 8, where K., during a momentary revival of confidence, is contrasted with the completely defeated Block, who treats even his own defence lawyer with all the dread of one facing his executioner. 'Dieses Kapitel wurde nicht vollendet' (168) / 'This chapter was never completed' (196), an editorial note at the end of the chapter observes, implicitly if unconsciously revealing the endlessly extensible nature of the text.

The two ostensible information givers of these chapters, the advocate Huld and the painter Titorelli, whose 'explanations' occupy the long chapter 7, describe endless circles around the very absence of any explanation, never making a statement without simultaneously retracting it or qualifying it into meaninglessness. 'War es Trost oder Verzweiflung, was der Advokat erreichen wollte? K. wußte es nicht' (107) / 'Was it reassurance or despair that the lawyer was aiming at? K. did not know' (125). In similar vein, at the conclusion – or interim conclusion – of Titorelli's lengthy explanations, when he finds that the artist's studio is itself actually part of the law courts, 'K. erschrak nicht so sehr darüber, daß er auch hier Gerichtskanzleien gefunden hatte, er erschrak hauptsächlich über sich, über seine Unwissenheit in Gerichtssachen' (141) / 'K. was startled not so much because there were Law Court offices here too; he was chiefly startled by himself, by his own ignorance of the affairs of the Court' (164). K.'s bafflement is again ironized by the discourse when he is made to buy several of Titorelli's heathscapes, each quite indistinguishable from all the others.

If the early chapters dealing with the possibility of achieving some sort of privileged Archimedean point of external vantage are summarized and deconstructed in the relativity of chapter 5, 'Der Prügler' / 'The Whipper,' the later chapters, more overtly thematizing indeterminacy, are summarized and deconstructed in the relativity of chapter 9, 'Im Dom' / 'In the Cathedral.' As the whipper chapter provides a *mise en abyme* of the text's discursive method or narrative expression, so the cathedral chapter provides a *mise en abyme* of the story or narrative content in the parable of the 'man from the country' or country bumpkin who attempts with enormous perseverance (but complete lack of success) to gain entry to 'das Gesetz' / 'the Law.'

'Das Gesetz,' however, literally that which is 'set down' (*setzen*), that which is fixed, is as much subject to infinite regression as 'das Gericht' / 'the Court,' that which enunciates a final decision (*richten*), for Josef K. and the man from the country share the same crime, ignorance of the law, just as they are condemned to the same unappealable sentence, which is to remain ignorant of the law. The final chapter, 'Ende' / 'The End,' portraying K. awaiting his executioners in a scene that parodically draws attention to its own theatricality (190/223), may be read as an ironic reflection of this central and irresolvable paradox of Kafka's thinking. As he walks to his death, K. is grateful – and the narrator, uncharacteristically, reports that fact in tagged direct monologue – 'daß man es mir überlassen hat, mir selbst das Notwendige zu sagen' (192) / 'that it has been left up to me to say all that is needed to myself' (226). 'Alle drei zogen nun in vollem Einverständnis über eine Brücke im Mondschein' (192) / 'All three now made their way in complete harmony across a bridge in the moonlight' (226) – a perfect scene of harmonious reconciliation, as it might appear. K.'s moment of insight, long postponed, is apparently now at last at hand:

K. wußte jetzt genau, daß es seine Pflicht gewesen wäre, das Messer, als es von Hand zu Hand über ihm schwebte, selbst zu fassen und sich einzubohren. Aber er tat es nicht ... Vollständig konnte er sich nicht bewähren, alle Arbeit den Behörden nicht abnehmen, die Verantwortung für diesen letzten Fehler trug der, der ihm den Rest der dazu nötigen Kraft versagt hatte. (194)

K. now realized quite clearly that his duty was supposed to be to seize the knife as it passed from hand to hand over him and stab himself. But he did not do so ... He could not completely rise to the occasion, could not relieve the authorities of all their tasks; the responsibility for this last failure lay with him who had refused him the remnant of necessary strength. (228)

As K.'s ironically vouchsafed glimpse of his own narrator exposes the parodic theatricality of the hypothetical happy ending, all his doubts revive, and he dies, as he must, 'wie ein Hund' / 'like a dog,' watching his executioners watching him and his 'Entscheidung' (194) – the word ironically suggesting not only a 'decision' or 'decisive moment,' but also an 'unsheathing.' The final decision, this 'unsheathing' of the butcher's knife, is not one determined by Josef K., but one that terminates his futile search by abruptly cutting it short; an arbitrary end, at an arbitrary point, imposed from without. 'Es war, als sollte die Scham ihn überleben' (194) / 'it was as if the shame must outlive him' (229), reflects the text with its usual indeterminacy of focalization as K. dies – and there is certainly no reason why it should not in the text's own terms, for K. (whatever about the reader) has made no headway at all.

III

Throughout the earlier chapters of *Der Prozeß* the narrative voice parodically balances victory and defeat in a dazzling display of narrative relativity. The later chapters explore the possibilities of indeterminacy as both an epistemological and a narrative problem. The element of discursive play, at least potentially alerting the reader to the dual world of the narrative, is present from the first sentence. The ludic dialectic of concealment and revelation (and relativization) is carried even by such minute qualifications as that involved in the assertion that Frau Grubach's room after the arrest looks *'fast* genau' (8) / '*almost* exactly' (2) the same as it did the day before, or the observation that Franz 'sah K. mit einem langen, wahrscheinlich bedeutungsvollen, aber unverständlichen Blick an' (11) / 'gave K. a long, probably significant, but incomprehensible look' (6). There is continual parodic play with psychiatry's predilection for the unconscious mind, not only in the lumber-room episode but also in the 'unnützen Kram' (55) / 'useless rubbish' (60) of the attics where the court offices are housed.

The central structural principle of *mise en abyme* is continually referred to and foregrounded. Other than the whipper scene and the parable recounted by the priest in the cathedral, there are K.'s own account of his arrest, ostensibly for Fräulein Bürstner's benefit; K.'s encounter with the caretaker's son at the door of the building he himself lives in; the filthy pictures in the law books at the first interrogation, lacking in all sense of perspective (48/52); and Titorelli's unvarying heathscapes. There is also K.'s piecemeal examination of the picture in the cathedral, where his fascination with the figure of a knight in armour distracts him from realizing that the knight is only a very peripheral figure in the overall context of the painting as a whole (175/205). As well, we have both the continual observers throughout and the continually recurring framing device of doors and windows, each one suggesting a hitherto unsuspected entrance into a possible new reality, a possible new way of seeing things, or of reading things. Finally, there is the constant play on various levels of identity: Josef K.'s 'Wer sind Sie?' (7) / 'Who are you?' (1) addressed to Franz; the thrice-repeated cry 'Josef K.' (first from the supervisor of the warders, then from K. himself for Fräulein Bürstner's benefit, then from the priest in the cathedral); K.'s Uncle Karl, who metamorphoses inexplicably into an Albert K.; K.'s 'Ich bin es' / 'It's me!' after the lumber-room scene; K.'s unprovoked inquiry of the merchant Block 'Ist das Ihr wirklicher Name?' (144) / 'Is that your real name?' (168), paralleling the earlier information that Titorelli's name is only a pseudonym (117/136).

Throughout, there is unrelenting play with the reader, who is repeatedly invited to resolve the narrative dilemmas in terms of Kafka's own biography, to which the text provides numerous references. Josef K.'s name is an entirely transparent play on Kafka's own name, as is that of the warder Franz who arrests him. The three bank clerks who witness his interview with the 'inspector' are called Kullich, Kaminer, and Rabensteiner, the first two sharing the initial already shared by K. and Kafka, the third containing the German translation of Czech *kavka*, namely 'raven, jackdaw.' Fräulein Bürstner's initials, F.B., are of course also those of Felice Bauer, with whom Kafka had broken off a very brief engagement immediately before he began to write *Der Prozeß*. There is further parodic authorial self-reference of various kinds in the narrative side-glances at K.'s 'Verurteilung' (49) or 'judgement' (53), his 'Verwandlung' (61) or 'metamorphosis' (67), his recurring 'Schwindel' (61, 133) – the term connoting a 'swindle' or 'fraud' as well as 'dizziness' (67, 155) – and the fact that 'Franz hier wollte heiraten' (74) / 'Franz here wanted to get married' (84).

Structurally, as we have seen, K.'s story is constituted as a highly indeterminate series of events taking place between two very definite ones, his arrest and his death. In the course of this 'process,' K. is continually faced with situations that are essentially *mises en abyme*, each chapter, as Allemann observes (1965: 264), presenting the same basic situation anew, paradigmatic variations on a single fundamental theme, namely, how to 'see things' – in other words, how to read a text.[7] K.'s interpretive endeavours are mirrored in those of the reader, for while the Court, as Sussman puts it, 'serve[s] as a medium for an endless exchange of interpretations,' the novel itself likewise 'admits of no authoritative reader' (1977: 48, 53). *Der Prozeß*, in Heller's phrase, 'confronts the reader and interpreter not so much with difficulties as with inescapable defeat' (1974: 94). There is an evident sense, however, in which the discourse of *Der Prozeß* encourages us to read not for any narrative product – the story presented – but rather for its own process of production. As readers primarily of a story, we instinctively read greedily for closure, for a narrative product; as readers primarily of discourse rather than story, we learn to read the text less as product than as process. K. suffers from a number of pronounced weaknesses of character: his arrogance, his inflexibility, his objectivization of other people, and so on – but most important of all, he never succeeds in distinguishing between what is important and what is not. He is a failure as a reader, incapable as he is of understanding his own 'guilt,' of *reading* the hermeneutic situation in which he finds himself (cf. Allemann 1965: 257). The reader is implicitly challenged to do better, for K.'s 'trial' is the reader's also, inviting and repelling interpretation, provoking readerly decisions on both Josef K.'s and the reader's part that immediately deconstruct into the necessity for further interpretive decisions.

Der Prozeß thematizes a central focus of contemporary critical thought, namely, the role of undecidability and indeterminacy as fundamental constraints of hermeneutic performance (cf. Culler 1981: 39). Like many of Kafka's protagonists, Josef K. is before anything else an interpreter of undecipherable 'texts.' As Naomi Schor writes, the prevailing rule in the world of *Der Prozeß* is that 'the absolute necessity to interpret goes hand in hand with the total impossibility to validate interpretation' (1980: 177; cf. Elm 1979: 423–6). K.'s readings are in turn embedded in further readings, for the acts of interpretation he is made to undertake are simultaneously acts of interpretation on the part of the narrator, of the implied author, and, of course, of the implied reader, the reader demanded by the text. As the discourse projects a series of K.s in shifting contexts and shifting possible worlds, so the reader is required to project a series of texts, of possible interpretations, hypothetical scenarios, possibilities of meaning – or rather of a plurality of meanings. For, as readers, we too are cast like K. in the dual role of observer and observed, offered the opportunity not just to witness the hapless K.'s efforts but also to reflect on our own (perhaps not much less hapless) efforts to emulate them, to read ourselves reading.

3

Harry Haller's Records:
The Ludic Imagination in
Hermann Hesse's *Steppenwolf*

Hermann Hesse's novel *Der Steppenwolf* (1927) has been the object of a great deal of critical attention over the years. By and large, however, critics have concentrated on its proper place in the overall development of Hesse's thinking and its relevance to his troubled biography. Thomas Mann's praise of the novel as being just as bold a formal experiment as Joyce's *Ulysses* or Gide's *Faux-monnayeurs* is indeed regularly rehearsed, but remarkably few critics have taken him at his word with any degree of rigour.[1] In an attempt to do so, we shall limit ourselves here to a resolutely formalist consideration, specifically of the narratological implications of the way(s) in which Harry Haller's story is presented, for there are very few narratives, German or otherwise, in which narrative discourse itself is so flamboyantly – and so playfully – foregrounded.

I

The concept of humour plays an overtly central thematic role in Harry Haller's story, but little attention has to date been paid to its overall structural role in the novel, which finds discursive expression through the play of an ironic, metanarrative reflexivity. The story of Hesse's novel is straightforward: a once-popular but now bitterly disaffected German writer approaching his fiftieth birthday in the unsettled years between the two world wars suffers a protracted midlife crisis that leads him close to suicide before he recovers his equilibrium. This essentially very thin story, however, is presented in so complex a form that the result is one of the most intriguing examples of narrative discourse among twentieth-century novels. Early critics reacted with bewildered indignation to what they perceived as the entire formlessness of the account of Harry Haller's troubles;

and more than one subsequent reader has deplored the gratuitous self-indulgence and self-dramatization of Haller's first-person account.[2] In both cases, however, the reaction stems from a debilitating underreading of the textual play that, far from being some mere ornamental flourish, is the central discursive characteristic of *Steppenwolf* as a literary text.

Haller's autobiographical 'Aufzeichnungen' (29) or 'Records' (27) take up more than four-fifths of Hesse's novel.[3] It is preceded by a twenty-page 'Vorwort des Herausgebers' (7–28) or editorial 'Preface' (3–25), for once having completed his account Haller dismissively hands it over to his land-lady's decidedly strait-laced nephew to do with as he pleases. Haller's account is thus relativized first of all – and in advance – by its anonymous editor's consciously 'bourgeois' perspective (a mixture of scandalized rejection and hero-worship) on Haller's 'bohemian' travails. It is further relativized both by an ironic essay it contains of almost thirty pages (46–74/46–75) on the implications of Haller's psychological state, ostensibly written by yet a third hand, and by its own climactic conclusion, an almost fifty-page account (189–237/198–248) of Haller's overtly drug-induced experiences shortly before he abruptly disappears from view. *Der Steppenwolf* as a literary text is centrally about the way in which these several presentations of his situation intersect and mutually reflect one another.

Haller suffers from an acute disgust with bourgeois society, against which he perceives himself to be in revolt. Only on rare occasions is he able to rise above his habitual *ennui*, as when, listening to a favourite piece of old music,

war zwischen zwei Takten ... wieder die Tür zum Jenseits aufgegangen, ich hatte Himmel durchflogen und Gott an der Arbeit gesehen, hatte selige Schmerzen gelitten und mich gegen nichts mehr in der Welt gefürchtet, hatte alles bejaht, hatte an alles mein Herz hingegeben. (34)

between two beats ... the door to the other world had once again opened. I had traversed the heavens and seen God at his work, had suffered holy pains, feared nothing in the world, had accepted all things and to all things had given up my heart. (34)

As he colourfully paints his own situation, Haller swings between such all too infrequent euphoric states, typically engendered by music, poetry, or philosophy – or even occasionally 'wenn ich bei meiner Geliebten war' (34–5) / 'in the presence of my beloved' (35) – and an avowed desire to end it all as quickly as possible, or, as Haller puts it, 'dem Beispiele Adalbert

Stifters zu folgen und beim Rasieren zu verunglücken' (29) / 'to follow the example of Adalbert Stifter and have an accident while shaving' (30). The latter states heavily predominate, for 'Ach, es ist schwer, diese Gottesspur zu finden inmitten dieses Lebens, das wir führen, inmitten dieser so sehr zufriedenen, so sehr bürgerlichen, so sehr geistlosen Zeit' (35) / 'it is hard to find this track of the divine in the midst of this life we lead, in this besotted, humdrum age of spiritual blindness' (35). Haller's ultimate (and, for him, tragic) dilemma, however, is that he feels himself, as an artist and a 'Steppenwolf,' excluded from *both* these realms of experience simultaneously, 'longing for a bourgeois life that he cannot hope to rejoin and doubting the ideal that he cannot hope to attain' (Ziolkowski 1965: 226). His 'Aufzeichnungen' or 'Records' essentially concern the relationship and results of a number of disparate manifestations of the world of the ideal in the desert of his everyday life.

The first of these to be actually described by Haller occurs as he walks along a rainy street late one evening engrossed as usual in 'diesen gewohnten Gedanken' (35) / 'these familiar thoughts' (36). Over a gateway in a wall – perhaps already seen a hundred times but never really noticed, as Haller says (36/36) – he suddenly notices a shield, 'auf dem stand, so schien mir, irgend etwas geschrieben' (36) / 'on which, it seemed to me, there was something written' (36), and deciphers the words 'Magisches Theater / Eintritt nicht für jedermann' (37) / 'Magic Theater / Entrance Not For Everybody' (37). The gate, however, refuses to open, and the letters quickly disappear, only momentarily replaced by a second flickering inscription on the wet pavement: 'Nur – für – Ver – rückte!' (37) / 'For Madmen Only!' (37). As he admires the play of the dancing letters, 'fiel mir plötzlich wieder ein Bruchstück aus meinen vorigen Gedanken ein: das Gleichnis von der golden aufleuchtenden Spur, die so plötzlich wieder fern und unauffindbar ist' (38) / 'a fragment of my former thoughts came suddenly to my mind; the parable of the golden track that shines forth and then is so suddenly gone and no longer to be found' (38).

Betraying remarkably little surprise at this apparition, Haller continues morosely on his nocturnal way, 'jener Spur nachträumend, voll Sehnsucht nach der Pforte zu einem Zaubertheater, nur für Verrückte' (38) / 'still following that track in my dreams, full of longing for the door to a magic theater, for madmen only' (38). Making his way home later in an even blacker mood, he glimpses a lonely figure with a placard that again seems to promise a 'Magisches Theater' (45/45). The figure responds to Haller's excited advances, however, only by mechanically thrusting a booklet into his hands and quickly disappearing. Haller's reaction is again oddly (or alcoholically) inconsequent: 'Ich nahm es schnell und steckte es ein' (45) / 'I took it quickly and put it in my pocket' (45); and he finds it again only when taking his coat off at home. Poorly printed on cheap paper, the booklet, as Haller reports with surprising insouciance, is entitled 'Traktat vom Steppenwolf. Nicht für jedermann' (46) / 'Treatise on the Steppenwolf. Not for Everybody' (46).

The complete text of this magical booklet is then faithfully (as we must assume) reported by Haller, some thirty pages set in italic type (46–74/46–75). Contrary to Haller's report, we notice, the actual German title of the booklet as thus reprinted is in fact 'Tractat vom Steppenwolf,' and it lacks any subtitle, beginning instead with the epigraph 'Nur für Verrückte' (46) / 'For Madmen Only' (46) – the magic inscription from the wet pavement – as do Haller's own 'Records' (29/29). The 'Tractat' or 'Treatise,' as the title suggests, is indeed a retelling, or a restaging, of the story of Haller's existential malaise, but the tone is entirely different from both the mixture of awe and disapproval with which the landlady's nephew introduces it and the mixture of occasional euphoria and otherwise uninterrupted despair presented as Haller's natural state of mind. The 'treatise' adopts a quizzically ironic tone from the beginning:

Es war einmal einer namens Harry, genannt der Steppenwolf. Er ging auf zwei Beinen, trug Kleider und war ein Mensch, aber eigentlich war er doch eben ein Steppenwolf. Er hatte vieles von dem gelernt, was Menschen mit gutem Verstande lernen können, und war ein ziemlich kluger Mann. Was er aber nicht gelernt hatte, war dies: mit sich und seinem Leben zufrieden zu sein. (46)

There was once a fellow by the name of Harry, called the Steppenwolf. He walked on two legs, wore clothes and was a human being, but nevertheless he was in reality a wolf of the steppes. He had learned a good deal of all that people of good intelligence can, and was a fairly clever fellow. What he had not learned, however, was this: to find contentment in himself and his own life. (46–7)

The treatise maintains its almost euphorically ironic tone throughout, based essentially on the premise that while Haller's sufferings may well be very real as far as he is concerned, they are neither at all unique nor at all necessary when seen in a broader perspective.[4] What *is* necessary, indeed, is precisely to find this Archimedean point of vantage from which one's day-to-day struggles may be viewed at least theoretically *sub specie aeternitatis*. Various philosophical systems have devised ways and means of attaining this perspective, but, as the treatise suggests, there is a simpler and equally effective (if regrettably only temporary) method freely available to every-body, namely the cultivation of a sense of humour, 'vielleicht die eigenste und genialste Leistung des Menschentums' (62) / 'perhaps the most charac-teristic and most brilliant achievement of the human spirit' (63).

In der Welt zu leben, als sei es nicht die Welt, das Gesetz zu achten und doch über ihm zu stehen, zu besitzen, 'als besäße man nicht', zu verzichten, als sei es kein Verzicht – alle diese beliebten und oft formulierten Forderungen einer hohen Le-bensweisheit ist einzig der Humor zu verwirklichen fähig. (62)

To live in the world as though it were not the world, to respect the law and yet to stand above it, to have possessions as though 'one possessed nothing,' to renounce as though it were no renunciation, all these favorite and often formulated proposi-tions of an exalted worldly wisdom – it is in the power of humor alone to realize. (63)

If Haller were to discover this 'Zaubertrank' or 'magic draught,' the trea-tise suggests, 'dann wäre er gerettet. Noch fehlt ihm dazu vieles' (62) / 'his rescue would be assured. But much is yet lacking' (63).

In narratological terms, we may note, what the treatise is suggesting is that Haller needs to be able to see himself, if only purely provisionally, from the external and detached vantage point of *discourse* rather than the internal and very much involved experience of being a character in a *story*: to exist as a character is to inhabit a world over which one has absolutely no control; to exist as a narrator is to invent worlds over which one has total control. A central theme of *Der Steppenwolf* is the metaleptic inter-changeability of the two worlds, for to narrate a story in the first place is to choose just one of the innumerable ways in which this is possible. Most of us, the treatise observes, spend our entire lives trapped (as 'characters') in one paralysing version or another of some particular psychological 'narra-tive,' some 'vereinfachende Mythologie' (64) / 'simplifying mythology' (65), when what we really need is (as 'narrators') to *see* ourselves as less some closed final *product* than 'ein Bündel aus vielen Ichs' (66) / 'a bundle of many selves' (67), an ongoing, alterable, open *process*. To have reached one's fullest possible extension in these terms, to have 'narrated' *all* one's possible stories, is 'seine Seele so erweitert haben, daß sie das All wieder zu umfassen vermag' (72) / 'to have expanded the soul to such an extent that it is once more able to encompass the All' (73), and only a very few of the greatest saints, geniuses, and artists can be said to have joined the ranks of these 'Unsterbliche' (73) or 'immortals' (74) – who are contrasted by the treatise to both the stolidly unproblematic 'Bürger' or 'bourgeois' who are blissfully unaware of their status as 'characters' and the 'Selbstmörder' or 'suicides' like Haller who experience that status as a tragic and unsolvable dilemma.

When Haller has duly read the lengthy and anonymous 'Tractat,' written precisely from the serenely detached perspective of these hypothetical 'immortals,' his first reaction is again peculiarly oblique: 'Als ich zu Ende gelesen hatte, *fiel mir ein*, daß ich vor einigen Wochen einmal in der Nacht ein etwas sonderbares Gedicht aufgeschrieben hatte, das ebenfalls vom Steppenwolf handelte. Ich suchte danach im Papiergestöber meines vollgestopften Schreibtisches, *fand es* und las' (74; emphasis added) / 'When I had read it to the end it came to my mind that some weeks before I had one night written a rather peculiar poem, likewise about the Steppen-wolf. I looked for it in the pile of papers on my cluttered writing table, *found it*, and read (75–6; emphasis added). What follows is an extremely bad piece of doggerel, whose hopelessly lachrymose and self-pitying tone is struck in the very first lines: 'Ich Steppenwolf trabe und trabe, / Die Welt liegt voller Schnee ... ' (74) / 'A Steppenwolf, I trot and trot, / The world lies deep in snow ...' (76). 'Da hatte ich nun zwei Bildnisse von mir in Händen,' reflects Haller with his usual gloomy relish, 'So now I had two portraits of myself before me,' the one his own 'schwermütig stammelndes Gedicht' / 'sad and sorry doggerel,' the other 'die kluge Studie von unbe-kannter Hand' / 'the clever study by an unknown hand.' Each of them, for Haller, sufficed to show 'die Unerträglichkeit und Unhaltbarkeit meines Zustandes' / 'how unbearable and untenable my situation was' (75/76–7), to show clearly that there were only two options left to him now as always: on the one hand, suicide; on the other, 'er mußte, geschmolzen im Todesfeuer einer erneuten Selbstschau, sich wandeln, seine Maske abreißen und eine neue Ichwerdung begehen' (75) / 'molten in the fire of a renewed self-knowledge, he would have to undergo a change, tear off his mask and become a new self' (77). And this he has often done already, the reader is now informed, for Haller at this point, for the first time, provides some details of the multiple crises that have cumulatively turned a once-successful young poet into such a terminally soured misanthrope, whose life is a 'Dreckhölle der Herzensleere und Verzweiflung' (83), a 'filthy hell of emptiness and despair' (85).

In spite of the theoretical insights of the treatise, however, Haller quite inexplicably sees it as irrelevant to his personal situation, and although he subsequently rereads it several times (80/81), he completely ignores any help it might provide and sinks into a state of even deeper depression,

'meistens betrunken' (92) / 'usually drunk' (94) , consoling himself only
with the bleak promise that he will definitely put an end to his own life the
next time it becomes completely unbearable.

Haller's 'Aufzeichnungen' or 'Records' are largely concerned with the
development of his brief relationship (over a period of some four or five
weeks) with two inhabitants of a world that is entirely foreign (and initially
abhorrent) to the reclusive intellectual, namely Hermine, a proverbially
gold-hearted prostitute, and her friend Pablo, a saxophone player in a jazz
band. Hermine is initially the more important of the two for Haller, whom
she treats with scant ceremony as a recalcitrant child, scolding him repeatedly for his self-importance and his absurd obsessions. For his part,
Haller's portrayal of Hermine throughout is an oddly double one, sometimes overtly and sometimes less overtly so. On the one hand he is well
aware of her real occupation, of which she makes no secret, on the other he
completely idealizes her from the beginning as a shifting combination of
mother, lover, and mirror of his own better, younger, still-idealistic self.
Between teaching a protesting Haller to dance the foxtrot and slipping off
to assignations with other men, Hermine is thus, at least by Haller's
account, able to indulge easily in high philosophical debate with him, sees
deep into his soul, knows his innermost fears and desires, and comforts him
as a kindred soul.

Their relationship is initially a non-sexual one, though Hermine
thoughtfully provides a very agreeable substitute in the form of her friend
and colleague Maria, who helps the only initially reluctant Haller to redis-
cover neglected pleasures. His newly acquired prowess as a ballroom
dancer is to be put to the test at a grand masked ball that is soon to be held,
and it becomes clear that this will also be the occasion when Hermine is to
replace Maria as Haller's lover. The voluptuary Pablo, meanwhile, whose
importance now begins to increase, has introduced him to the joys of drug-
induced hallucination and invites him to join in a particularly interesting
experiment to take place immediately after the masked ball.

The evening of the masked ball provides Haller's narrative with two parallel climaxes, first the ball itself and then Pablo's 'Magisches Theater' or
'Magic Theater.' Searching through the masked throng for Hermine and
eventually finding her costumed as none other than his own long-lost
'Jugendfreund' Hermann (181), 'the friend of my youth' (189), Haller
dances himself into a state of frenzied euphoria, his personality 'aufgelöst
im Festrausch wie Salz im Wasser' (184) / 'dissolved in the intoxication of
the festivity like salt in water' (193), rediscovers Hermine dressed as a
woman, rapturously feels as if all the different women he has danced with

throughout the long evening were now 'zusammengeschmolzen und eine einzige geworden, die in meinen Armen blühte. Lange dauerte dieser Hochzeitstanz' (187) / 'melted together and become one, the one who blossomed in my arms. This nuptial dance went on and on' (196). The dance eventually coming to an end just before dawn, Haller and Hermine are led upstairs by Pablo for the second act of the evening's entertainment, the 'magic theatre' made possible by courtesy of Pablo's expert knowledge of pills and potions.

If the masked ball provides Haller with a euphoric experience of a totality of one sort, the experience of all become one in the 'Unio mystica der Freude' (183–4), the 'mystic union of joy' (192), Pablo's magic theatre graphically provides him with the reverse of this coin, namely, the chemically induced insight that if all may become one, then so may one contain all, each individual be potentially capable of all the heights and depths alike of human behaviour. In a mirror held by Pablo, Haller sees reflected not just his present divided self but all the selves he ever was, ever might have been, or ever will be; from a chess player (208/218) who may possibly also be Pablo he hears that one's life is an endlessly renewable and replayable game, in which the various complementary or conflicting faces of one's real and possible personalities are mere counters that may be repositioned at will (209–10/219). In Pablo's theatre of alternatives Haller accordingly experiences the savage thrill of random destruction and indiscriminate killing, experiences the joy of reliving and rewriting every amorous encounter he has ever had or almost had, watches horrified a trained wolf eating chocolate while a man very like himself savagely tears a live rabbit apart with bloody fangs. Long a convinced pacifist, Haller is now in a position to reflect that no madman crazed with power was capable of dreaming up atrocities any worse than he could devise all on his own (214/224) – an insight graphically underlined when, discovering Pablo and Hermine naked and asleep in each other's arms, he unhesitatingly plunges a dagger into Hermine's heart (228/238). His final vision is of his own trial, with Mozart as judge, for the murder of Hermine – or rather on the charge that he 'ein gespiegeltes Mädchen mit einem gespiegelten Messer totgestochen hat' (234) / 'stabbed a reflected girl to death with a reflected knife' (245), for which imaginary crime he is sentenced both to 'eternal life' (234/245) and to be soundly laughed at for his lack of perspective and good humour. As the hallucinated Mozart metamorphoses into the smiling Pablo offering him one more of his helpful cigarettes, a completely exhausted Haller is suddenly and euphorically aware that at long last he understands everything, wußte alle hunderttausend Figuren des Lebensspiels in meiner Tasche, ahnte erschüttert den Sinn, war gewillt, das Spiel nochmals zu beginnen, seine Qualen nochmals zu kosten, vor seinem Unsinn nochmals zu schaudern, die Hölle meines Innern nochmals und noch oft zu durchwandern. (237)

knew that all the hundred thousand pieces of life's game were in my own pocket, glimpsed its meaning, was ready to begin the game all over again, to taste its torments, to shudder at its senselessness, to traverse the hell of my inner being once more and again and again. (248)

'Einmal würde ich das Figurenspiel besser spielen,' Haller's account concludes. 'Einmal würde ich das Lachen lernen' (237) / 'One day I would be a better player of the game. One day I would learn how to laugh' (248).

II

All this the reader discovers only through the first-person account of Harry Haller, who is both the narrator and the protagonist of his own narrative. How we judge that relationship will materially affect how we react to the story we read. And critical reactions differ significantly, even on so basic an issue as whether the novel ends on a positive or a negative note. Hesse himself, for example, saw the ending as portraying a process of healing rather than failure (Michels 1972: 160). Most critics share this view: the novel 'recounts the development of Harry Haller from the brink of despair to the heights of humor that make life tolerable' (Ziolkowski 1965: 180); for others, however, 'the underlying pessimism of the novel is not effectively offset by the optimistic look to the future in the final lines, which have a tacked-on effect' (Dhority 1974: 64).[5] The significance of Hermine's death is likewise much debated, taken as evidence of Haller's failure by some (e.g., Boulby 1967), as evidence of spiritual or psychological growth by others (e.g., Mileck 1978). There are certainly readers who will reject Haller's entire account out of hand because of the degree to which it seems self-indulgently to romanticize and dramatize his own allegedly tragic lot and heroic sufferings. Such readers might also be tempted to extend their censure to Hesse's writerly abilities as well. That would certainly be a mistake – but it is a mistake that is not just made possible but positively encouraged by the particular strategy of Haller's (and Hesse's) narrative.

In any narrative, as already observed, readers 'see' events as focalized, whether consistently or with varying degrees of alternation, through the eyes either of the narrator or of one of the characters the narrator presents.

In the case of a first-person narrator the distinction between the vision of the narrating and that of the experiencing self becomes considerably more difficult to identify – and in the case of *Steppenwolf* the distinction is even further blurred because of the particular narrative means Haller as narrator chooses to employ to present his consciousness as a narrated character. Dorrit Cohn has demonstrated that while the most usual mode chosen by a narrating self in presenting the narrated self is traditional omniscient discourse, in Haller's account the overwhelmingly predominant mode is self-narrated monologue (or first-person *erlebte Rede*), which has the systemic effect of radically blurring the distinction between the experiencing and narrating selves, between Haller 'then' and 'now.'[6]

Cohn notes several instances where Haller's account alternates between past-tense and present-tense verbs (1969: 130–1) and reads this alternation as demonstrating that there has essentially been no change in Haller's way of seeing the world, but it is in fact evident that while Haller has indeed not reached any ultimate state of unshakeable stability, and in all likelihood will never do so, he certainly *has* become able to play better the game learned from the chess player of the magic theatre. Cohn likewise sees the unparalleled predominance of self-narrated monologue in Haller's account as indicating that the narrator 'abandons his present vantage point and surrenders to his past self' (129) – in fact, however, the doubled reading that characterizes all *irony* is also ideally enabled by the constantly ambiguous focalization that is guaranteed by this particularly elusive discursive mode.

Hesse criticism has focused almost unanimously on Haller the experiencing character, whether seeing him with Field (1970: 104) as existing essentially in a Romantic fairy-tale world[7] or with Ziolkowski as possessing an eidetic imagination, abetted by alcohol and drugs, that reshapes everyday reality into the rarefied world of his philosophical obsessions (1965: 197, 213). Very little attention has been devoted to the fact that Haller is a once-successful writer who seems to have spent very little of his time writing during the time portrayed in his narrative – but who now has produced a major work of art in the form of the very narrative we are reading.[8] The crucial difference between Haller then and now, in other words, is quite simply that the latter has written a much more complexly structured account of his perceived predicament than any he had ever managed before, his earlier productions amounting only to a few stray poems (74/76, 170/177). The difference is indeed one of degree rather than kind, but the degree is decisive: for while the narrated Haller experiences life as an almost unremitting tragedy, Haller's account as narrator is a highly stylized, highly *ludic* presentation of his former woes, to a degree that makes it clear his formerly tragic sense of life has matured with his development as a writer into a pervasively ironic vision.

Irony, however, is always significantly in the eye of the beholder, always a matter of agreeing to read information in one way rather than another. A phrase like 'You're looking very cheerful today!' can mean either exactly what it says or its complete opposite, depending on whether the semantic information (what the words appear to say) and the signal information (how we are invited to react to what the words appear to say) are, either implicitly or by inference, consonant or dissonant. The relationship of the *what* and the *how* of irony, in short, corresponds exactly to that of story and discourse in narrative – and indeed all narrative *is* ultimately an ironic structure as far as theory goes. Some narratives, however – and *Steppenwolf* is one of them – exploit this inherent structural possibility to a much greater degree than others.

Clearly both the treatise and the magic theatre are playfully ironic by any yardstick, and both (unless we accept a 'magic' origin for the treatise) are evidently the work of Haller. So too, however, are passages that may certainly seem very far from any saving irony. 'Ich weiß nicht, wie das zugeht, aber ich, der heimatlose Steppenwolf und einsame Hasser der kleinbürgerlichen Welt, ich wohne immerzu in richtigen Bürgerhäusern, das ist eine alte Sentimentalität von mir' (32) / 'I don't know how it comes about, but I, the homeless Steppenwolf and lonely hater of life's petty conventions, always take up my quarters in just such properly bourgeois houses, an old weakness of mine' (32). Readers who see Haller as intolerably maudlin understandably point to such all too melodramatic self-characterizations as this in making their case. However, the alternative interpretive possibilities offered by Haller's three narrated encounters with Goethe offer a significantly different model for reading the overall discursive strategy of *Der Steppenwolf*.

The first of these involves Haller's description of a disastrous dinner party to which he is invited by a young professor of his acquaintance. The climax of the evening occurs when Haller mortally insults his hosts by ridiculing a sentimental picture of Goethe they possess, on the grounds that it completely misrepresents a great poet. Shortly afterwards, trying to explain his outrage to Hermine, he is scoldingly told that his reaction was childishly intolerant and that in spite of all his book-learning he is little more than an 'absolute baby' (101/104). Later, falling into an exhausted sleep, he has a dream in which he meets the pompously self-important elder statesman Goethe and accuses him in turn of having cynically betrayed in his later work his own tragic awareness as a young man of the utter hopelessness of human existence (105/108) – and is soundly laughed at for his pains by a maliciously gleeful Goethe who mockingly urges him to try to acquire a sense of humour too.

Haller as narrator thus provides three separate presentations: the first, from the unrelentingly tragic perspective of the distempered 'Steppenwolf,' presents just one more example of the way in which truth and beauty are inevitably destroyed in a barbarous world; the second, from that of a robustly commonsensical Hermine, momentarily deflates Haller's rampant self-dramatization without causing him to alter his behaviour in any significant way; and the third, from the narrator's own newly achieved ironic perspective, pokes fun at an earlier Haller incapable of ever learning anything – typically for this earlier Haller, when he wakes up he has forgotten the dream: 'erst später fiel er mir wieder ein' (109) / 'only later did it occur to me again' (112).

The most significant argument for seeing Haller's account as self-ironic is the flaunted centrality of play in his narrative as a whole – a structural feature which would otherwise lack any determinable textual function. Many critics have already noted the highly important role of mirrors in his account, for example: the word *scheinen* ('to seem') is employed with notable frequency (Ziolkowski 1965: 207); mirrors and mirroring devices abound; Hermine and Pablo are both overtly treated by Haller as mirrors of his own soul on several occasions; the magic theatre is a hall of mirrors where every reflection becomes a possible reality; indeed, 'the whole world in which Harry Haller moves may be interpreted as merely the reflection of his own mind' (Boulby 1967: 186).[9] The importance of the mirror imagery has been seen primarily in psychological terms: Haller comes to self-knowledge by being exposed, through a form of quasi-magical therapy (however explained), to previously underdeveloped facets of his own personality. This mirroring goes well beyond what might reasonably be considered *necessary* to make such a point, however. Even a minor character like the idealistic (and nameless) young professor of philosophy (85/87) can clearly be read as a projection of one aspect of Haller's personality – Hermine calls Haller clever in a silly sort of way, just like a professor, as she adds (99/102). Hermine, who 'magically' metamorphoses into Haller's 'boyhood friend' Hermann (181), teases Haller that Harry is not a grown-up's name; the professor takes issue with the political opinions of a 'different' Haller – who turns out to be the same one; Haller's attempts to regain psychological equilibrium take place in the all too aptly named Hotel Balances; and so on. Ultimately, indeed, there is only one character in Haller's memoirs, who goes through a 'school of humour' based on the premise that 'aller höhere Humor fängt damit an, daß man die eigene Person nicht mehr ernst nimmt' (193) / 'all true humour begins with one's ceasing to take oneself seriously' (202).

In such instances we seem to be in a realm of play that is purely for its own sake – a realm that may remind us, indeed, of the sovereign humour of the 'immortals' of the treatise and the magic theatre. This playfulness for its own sake is also apparent in the very structure of Haller's narrative, with its spendthrift threefold telling (by Haller, by the treatise, and through the magic theatre) of the 'same' story. The treatise, for its part, concludes by ironically undermining its own theoretical explanations in drawing attention to the provisionality of *all* theory (63). The parallel climaxes of the masked ball (Haller finally wins Hermine) and the magic theatre (Haller finally loses Hermine) likewise parodically (and 'unnecessarily') reflect each other. We can even speak of a *doubled* mirroring in the text, again an 'unnecessary' doubling that points to a primarily ludic motivation on the part of the narrator. The hall of mirrors of the magic theatre is the episode that is most obviously so doubled, presented first as the vividly experienced fantasy of the narrated Haller and subsequently as the ironizing account of Haller the narrator. Ultimately, however, the same is true of all the 'magic realism' we encounter: the narrated Haller, who lives essentially in a world of books and ideas, a latter-day Don Quixote, always to some extent sees himself as a literary character, dramatizes and exaggerates his own tragic sense of life, and half-consciously puts the words he wants to hear into the mouths of Hermine and Pablo, while his perceptions are in turn ironically – theatrically –presented by Haller the narrator.

Irony is never so much a matter of what is said as of how it is seen to be said. Once we have *decided* that Haller's narration is driven by self-irony rather than self-pity – once we have made the same leap from tragic to ludic vision that Haller himself makes, in short – then the entire narrative takes on new contours, and scenes and details that were previously embarrassingly lugubrious, sentimental, or exaggeratedly mannered take on an entirely new significance. The fact that Haller's dilemma is in the best tradition of Faust's 'two souls in one breast' and of countless German artist novels for example, now emerges as parodic rather than derivative. His repeated 'forgetting' of desperately needed insights, his inexplicable refusal to see the obvious relevance of the treatise, his insistence on misery at all costs – all now become key elements in the comedy of an entirely one-dimensional Haller's wilful and ridiculous blindness – as presented by a Haller who is now (however temporarily) *magister ludi*.

III

The process of ludic reflexivity in *Steppenwolf* goes beyond the boundaries of Haller's autobiographical reminiscences, however. The editorial preface is generally regarded as an unimaginatively traditional introduction to the 'real' story, somewhat weakly corroborating the alleged realism of Haller's account. Such readings are no doubt encouraged by the knowledge that the preface was a hesitant afterthought on Hesse's part, his original concept apparently having been to begin with a first-person introduction by Haller himself (Voit 1992: 65–7). Whatever Hesse's authorial intentions may or may not have been, however, the preface deserves to be read as a crucial component in the highly self-reflexive structure not only of Hesse's but also of Haller's text.

Boswell to Haller's Johnson, the editor, though initially claiming to know very little about Haller, gradually reveals a considerable knowledge of his comings and goings and is eventually – though on his own admission no psychologist – even willing to venture a comprehensive psychological explanation of Haller's condition. Very quickly at pains to characterize himself as a non-smoking, non-drinking *bon bourgeois*, punctilious, conscientious, and unproblematically content with his lot, he at first is irritated by Haller's nonconformism, then gradually becomes fascinated by him. Secure in his own way of life, 'ein kleines und bürgerliches, aber gesichertes und von Pflichten erfülltes' (26) / 'a narrow, middle-class life, but a solid one, filled with duties' (23), the editor develops an almost comically exaggerated reverence for Haller's ostensibly deeper insights into the workings of the world.[10] Reacting to a pompous public lecture they attend together, for example, Haller, by the editor's account, shoots him a glance, 'einen unvergeßlichen und furchtbaren Blick' (13) / 'an unforgettable and frightful look' (10). Not only does Haller's quite remarkably expressive look completely demolish the inflated pretensions of the lecturer, moreover, the editor goes on,

nein, der Blick des Steppenwolfes durchdrang unsre ganze Zeit, das ganze betriebsame Getue, ... das ganze oberflächliche Spiel einer eingebildeten, seichten Geistigkeit – ach, und leider ging der Blick noch tiefer, ging noch viel weiter als bloß auf Mängel und Hoffnungslosigkeiten unsrer Zeit, unsrer Geistigkeit, unsrer Kultur. Er ging bis ins Herz alles Menschentums, er sprach beredt in einer einzigen Sekunde den ganzen Zweifel eines Denkers, eines vielleicht Wissenden aus an der Würde, am Sinn des Menschenlebens überhaupt. (13–14)

no, the Steppenwolf's look pierced our whole epoch, its whole overwrought activity, ... the whole superficial play of a shallow, opinionated intellectuality. And, alas, the look went still deeper, went far below the faults, defects, and hopelessness of our time, our intellect, our culture alone. It went right to the heart of all humanity, it spoke eloquently in a single second the profound doubt of a thinker, of one who perhaps was fully aware of the worth and meaning of human life but none the less doubted their value. (10)

One is immediately struck by the self-confessedly bourgeois editor's equally remarkable ability to read quite so much out of (or into) a single glance. Can this be the same man who later pompously records his own indignation when he discovers Haller seated on the stairs one day admiring a potted plant instead of going about his proper business like a normal person (18/15)? Or who (Wagner to Haller's Faust) is so naïvely impressed by Haller's piles of books that he feels sure he must be a great scholar – especially as the room is full of cigar smoke, as one would also expect of a great scholar (17/13)?

The relationship of simultaneous distance and affinity between the two is striking. On the one hand the editor is allegedly a completely down-to-earth type who has little patience with the pretensions of self-glamourizing intellectuals; on the other, as his baroque overreading of a sideways glance shows, he is entirely capable on occasion of out-Hallering Haller. For all his alleged lack of knowledge about Haller's past, he also claims to have 'every reason to suppose' (15/12) that Haller was brought up by over-protective parents, who by trying to break his will for his own good succeeded only in teaching him to hate himself (16/12). He is likewise able to characterize Haller as a potential suicide who has too much respect for the value of suffering for its own sake ever to commit suicide (26/23). Finally, somewhat portentously, the editor volunteers that he would never have allowed Haller's memoirs to be published if they were not also

ein Dokument der Zeit, denn Hallers Seelenkrankheit ist – daß weiß ich heute – nicht die Schrulle eines einzelnen, sondern die Krankheit der Zeit selbst, die Neurose jener Generation, welcher Haller angehört, und von welcher keineswegs nur die schwachen und minderwertigen Individuen befallen scheinen, sondern gerade die starken, geistigsten, begabtesten. (27)

a document of the times, for Haller's sickness of the soul, as I now know, is not the eccentricity of a single individual, but the sickness of the times themselves, the neurosis of that generation to which Haller belongs, a sickness, it seems, that by no means attacks the weak and worthless only, but rather precisely those who are strongest in spirit and richest in gifts. (23–4)

Haller's memoirs – 'einerlei, wie viel oder wenig realen Erlebens ihnen zugrunde liegen mag' (27) / 'however much or however little of real life may lie behind them' (24) – are an attempt to portray this sickness of the times. 'Sie bedeuten, ganz wörtlich, einen Gang durch die Hölle, einen bald angstvollen, bald mutigen Gang durch das Chaos einer verfinsterten Seelenwelt' (27) / 'They mean, literally, a journey through hell, a some-times fearful, sometimes courageous journey through the chaos of a spir-itual world of darkness' (24). This particular reading, the editor dutifully notes, he owes to a remark of Haller himself.

Most interestingly of all, the editor proffers the advance information (a good two hundred pages ahead of the event) that Haller, even after all the unprecedentedly mind-expanding experiences he himself describes, carries on exactly as before, all hard-won insight once again completely aban-doned. For the magic theatre, the editor tells us, was followed immediately by a new and even deeper depression, a violent quarrel with his lady friend, who puts in another appearance, and Haller's subsequent disappearance, to carry on, the editor has no doubt, exactly as he has always done, 'und das dies Leiden es sei, woran er sterben müsse' (26) / 'and that it is of this suf-fering that he must die' (23).

Certainly our reading of the apparently euphoric conclusion of Haller's account is significantly relativized by these proleptic observations as to Haller's presumed future conduct. They can, indeed, evidently be read as suggesting three quite different possibilities: first, that our thesis as advanced so far of a sovereignly ironic narrating Haller is just plain wrong; second, that while our thesis may indeed be defensible in the internal context of the 'Aufzeichnungen,' Haller's ironizing proves entirely self-deluding in the external context of the editor's superior knowledge and is itself subjected to the editor's irony; and third, that our thesis holds for both the memoirs and the preface, for the editor too is merely an ironic figment of the newly invigorated imagination of the creative artist Haller.

Most Hesse critics tacitly agree that the author of the treatise is Haller's 'higher self' (Mileck 1978: 190); that the editor is also Haller's creation, has, to my knowledge, never been suggested – though Pfeifer notes (1980: 185) that the editor's character too is reminiscent of Hesse. The third of the options just given is clearly the most attractive in the overall economy both of Haller's and of Hesse's text, however. Esselborn-Krummbiegel observes that the numerous correspondences between the treatise and the magic the-atre suggest their common origin in a single consciousness (1988: 36); the weight of the evidence as so far adduced strongly suggests that the same argument holds for the preface as the product of a Haller who has become an adept in the chess game of life. If Hermine and Pablo are discursively constructed fragments of Haller's own self within the confines of his memoirs, so too, by the same criteria, is their ostensible editor, strategically equipped with conveniently appropriate bourgeois stuffiness, neatly bal-ancing 'from below' the perspective of the treatist and the magic theatre 'from above' – and nephew to the very same 'aunt' (7/7) Haller playfully sees as his own. We might do well to recall at this point the pointed refer-ence in the treatise to literary works such as *Faust*, which constructs out of Faust, Mephisto, Wagner, and all the other characters 'eine Einheit, eine Überperson, und erst in dieser höhern Einheit, nicht in den Einzelfiguren, ist etwas vom wahren Wesen der Seele angedeutet' (67) / 'a unity, a composite person, and it is in this higher unity alone, not in the individual characters, that something of the true nature of the soul is suggested' (69).

The playfully ironic reflexivity that pervades Haller's memoirs, in short, can clearly (and productively) be read as extending to the preface as well. The editor's ironic ambivalence with regard to Haller's way of life is made very clear, as we have seen. He ironically both supports and undermines the memoirs: at once professing to authenticate them as an eyewitness and classifying them as 'zum größten Teil Dichtung' (25) / 'for the most part fictitious' (22). He plays an ambiguous role in being at once their first reader (27/23) and the primary determiner of how they will be read by others. The preface itself is likewise ambiguously both 'inside' and 'out-side' simultaneously, ironically confusing Haller's text and Hesse's text: even Ziolkowski, who sees it as an essential constitutive element in what he calls the sonata-form opening of 'the novel,' also opposes the preface to 'the book itself' (1965: 182; likewise Mileck 1978: 194).

Suggestive structural links between the treatise and the preface are like-wise supportive of such a reading. The anonymous editor is a homodiegetic narrator (an *I* who talks of a *he*), the anonymous treatist is heterodiegetic (a *he* who talks of a *he*), Haller himself is autodiegetic (an *I* who talks of an *I*). The treatist's text is embedded in Haller's, which in turn, at least by impli-cation, is embedded in the editor's. The treatise functions multiply as a for-eign body: by virtue of its ostensibly non-fictional role, its status as an alleged *objet trouvé*, and its particular location in Haller's memoirs, whereby its role is essentially proleptic since Haller is not yet ready to take advantage of the insights it offers.[11] The preface is likewise marked as a foreign body by virtue of an ostensibly non-fictional role; an ostensible status as *objet trouvé*, the editor's rather than Haller's idea; and its situation (ostensibly) outside Haller's text, where it also has a significantly proleptic function in 'revealing' what happened after the events with which the novel concludes. Accepting the editor as one more of Haller's invented *personae* finally allows at least one more ironically relativizing turn of the screw, for an editor is playfully both less and more than an author, 'inferior' in his role-specific lack of creativity and imagination, 'superior' in that he always potentially has the last word, the power, whether exercised or not, to shape the author's shaping, to authorize (and relativize) the author.

IV

What is the advantage of such a reading? Quite simply that it produces a better text – and that is always the essential role of the reader, for literary texts are always negotiated settlements, constructed *between* the shaping author and the shaping reader. It produces a better text not least because it makes a more complexly textured and more interesting whole of *both* texts bearing the title *Der Steppenwolf*: the one written by Harry Haller, the other, in exactly the same words, by Hermann Hesse. For the final turn of the textual screw, of course, is that Harry Haller both 'is' and 'is not' Hermann Hesse. Critics are unanimous in finding *Steppenwolf* the most overtly autobiographical of Hesse's many works. Haller's marital and political problems were closely modelled on Hesse's own experiences. Haller's two poems (one dreadful, one competent) were even originally published as Hesse's own work some six months before the novel appeared. Letters and other writings during the period when he was working on the novel include several gloomy references to himself as a 'Steppenwolf'; a claim to be able to keep going only because he has promised himself the luxury of suicide on his fiftieth birthday if necessary; references to his childish pleasure at eventually learning to dance the foxtrot; and a description of his delight on attending a masked ball for the first time – in the company of a Swiss sculptor named Hermann Haller.[12] Masks and mirrors continue to be the order of the day as the ludic reflexivity that structures the narrative extends its reach to include its author.

What is finally most central to *Steppenwolf*, both thematically and structurally, is the sovereignty of play, the narrative hypostatization of that laughter of the immortals that so persistently eludes the narrated Haller – but *not* Haller the narrator.[13] Haller's narrative is the story of his continuing quest for a theoretically available Archimedean point enabling him 'in der Welt zu leben, als sei es nicht die Welt' (62) / 'to live in the world as though it were not the world' (63), and the comedy of his own account of his efforts resides in his continual failure to reach it, or, having once glimpsed it, his immediate and entirely predictable backsliding. The gap between tragedy and comedy is the gap between story and discourse.

It has been wittily suggested that Proust's *Recherche* can be more briefly restated as 'Marcel becomes a writer' (Genette 1980: 30); Hesse's novel can with equal validity be minimally paraphrased as 'Harry becomes a writer.' But Haller has been a writer all along: it is necessary for him not just to *become* a writer but to *remember* that he has become a writer, one who shapes, moulds, creates fictional realities – including the fictional reality in which he himself resides. Haller's accomplishment is essentially to learn to abandon a highly oversimplified psychological fiction in favour of a much more complex one, to abandon a closed text for an open one. *Steppenwolf* systemically reflects that openness. Thus even the fact that Haller has finally reached a point of vantage where he can see (and shape) his own progress with such lucid irony need certainly not be read as implying that he will never again abandon it. The (invented) editor's assumption as to his future conduct is an ironic acknowledgment of this by Haller himself – as is, of course, the radically blurred focalization throughout that virtually ensures confusion of his narrating and narrated selves. Haller's uninterrupted pendulation between reality and vision – a process, however, that is crucially recontextualized in his narration as comedy rather than tragedy – is structurally reflected in the text's own refusal to accept closure, for the ultimate textual point of *Der Steppenwolf* is precisely the play of alternatives, not the necessity of any final choice between them. Few texts so consistently exploit the primacy of narrative discourse to this end; and few so consequently remind us that the literary text is essentially silent until the reader makes it work – and play.

4

Auto da fé:
Reading Misreading in
Elias Canetti's *Die Blendung*

To read is also, always and necessarily, to misread. Few novels demonstrate the consequences of this interpretive maxim so graphically as Elias Canetti's remarkable novel *Die Blendung* (1935) – translated into English as *Auto da fé* – whose central character is the professional (and obsessional) reader Peter Kien, forty years old, 'Gelehrter, Sinologe von Hauptfach' (8) / 'man of learning and specialist in sinology' (12), perhaps even the greatest living scholar of ancient Chinese philosophy.[1] 'Unzählige Texte verdankten ihre Herstellung ihm' (14) / 'Countless texts owed their restoration to him' (20). Revered and envied by his peers as the unchallengeable authority in his field, the reclusive Kien 'drückte sich lieber schriftlich als mündlich aus. Er beherrschte über ein Dutzend östliche Sprachen ... Keine menschliche Literatur war ihm fremd' (14) / 'preferred to express himself in the written rather than the spoken word. He knew more than a dozen oriental languages ... No branch of human literature was unfamiliar to him' (20).

Kien's readerly skills fail him entirely, however, when it comes to the world beyond the walls of his private library. Completely misreading almost everyone with whom he comes in contact, he is successively deceived and defrauded by a shrewish wife, a conniving dwarf, and a brutish ex-policeman. Only the intervention of his psychiatrist brother – a professional reader of misreadings – seems capable of saving the day. Safely restored to his precious library, Kien promptly barricades it against intruders – and burns it to the ground. 'Als ihn die Flammen endlich erreichen, lacht er so laut, wie er in seinem ganzen Leben nie gelacht hat' (414) / 'When the flames reach him at last, he laughs out loud, louder than he has ever laughed in all his life' (522).

I

Kien regards the world beyond the library as at best a regrettably necessary evil, to be kept in its place by a rigidly unchanging routine that assigns only a minimum of time to such daily irritations as sleeping and eating. Even his scrupulously timed daily walk is preceded by a lengthy selection of the books he will carry with him in his briefcase in order to mitigate even such a momentary absence from his only proper milieu. *Die Blendung*, entirely predictably, is the story of the inevitable destruction of this all too fragilely protected intellectual idyll at the hands of that everyday world it affects to ignore, a theme that might, of course, lend itself just as easily to a tragic as to a comic treatment. Canetti unambiguously chooses the latter option, and *Die Blendung*, from beginning to end, displays its credentials as a remarkable comic performance. A latter-day Don Quixote, Kien is presented by Canetti's narrator as far less a character than a caricature.[2] The world that destroys him, however, is also peopled almost entirely by caricatures, and of these the most notable examples are certainly provided by the redoubtable trio of Therese Krumbholz, Siegfried Fischerle, and Benedikt Pfaff.

Therese Krumbholz has been in Kien's employ as a housekeeper for eight years without his ever having paid the slightest attention to her. In a momentary fit of weakness Kien one day very grudgingly lends her one of his least treasured books to read, only to discover her strategically adopted regard for learning to be so high that she reverently reads every page at least a dozen times before continuing, 'sonst hat man nichts davon' (38) / 'otherwise you can't get the best out of it' (51). Suddenly recognizing the perfect potential guardian of his library should such an emergency as a fire ever occur, Kien, seizing the moment, immediately proposes marriage. Therese, however, whose most striking personality trait is a highly starched and perennially worn bright blue skirt, turns out in fact to be a formidable adversary, largely because of her indomitable stupidity. With a vocabulary of only about fifty words, as Kien once scathingly estimates, she is rarely silent once she becomes the lady of the house. 'Wenn sie fertig war, fing sie von vorne an' (95) / 'When she had reached the end, she began at the beginning' (122). Disappointed by Kien's total rejection of the physical joys of matrimony, Therese soon gives way to delicious fantasies mostly involving Kien's immediate death and her inheriting vast sums of money. Having badgered a demoralized and exhausted Kien into making out a will in her favour, she is highly indignant that the sum involved falls so far short of her expectations and promptly improves the situation considerably by adding several zeros to the unsatisfactory figure (115/147). When this solution proves to be less permanent than she had hoped, she resorts to starving Kien for several days, beats him black and blue for good measure, and eventually ejects him bodily from house and home.

Kien escapes Therese's clutches only to fall immediately into those of Siegfried Fischerle, a misshapen, hunchbacked Jewish dwarf who lives by his wits and the avails of prostitution. Fischerle is characterized by a rapaciousness at least the equal of Therese's and by an overwhelming passion for chess. In Fischerle's view, all that stands between him and the world championship is the lack of adequate funds, and Kien is exactly the kind of involuntary patron he has long been looking for. He swiftly worms his way into Kien's confidence, ruthlessly exploits his accelerating dementia, plays on his multiple fears and weaknesses, and helps himself with great liberality to his money whenever possible. Fischerle's long-cherished dream is to escape to America, trounce the reigning chess champion, have his hump removed, and live in a mansion with a millionaire's daughter. Thanks to Kien's involuntary largesse, he eventually sees himself in a position to begin this odyssey, buys himself a suit of appropriate quality and pattern – 'schwarz-weiß kariert' (312) / 'black and white checks' (393) – for a man of his anticipated standing, spends an afternoon learning American (317/399), and indulges in a first-class ticket to Paris. At the last moment, Fischerle – or Doctor Fischer, as his newly forged passport now more appropriately has it – decides to return to his room for a forgotten address book containing the names of all possible competitors for the world title that is now rightly his. There he unfortunately encounters one of his wife's customers, a 'blind' beggar whom he has grievously insulted just a few days before and who promptly throttles the would-be world champion and savagely hacks off his hump with a blunt bread-knife – considerately shoving the corpse under the bed before resuming his interrupted love-making with the wife of the deceased.

The third member of the trio through whom Kien traumatically experiences the outside world is the caretaker Benedikt Pfaff. Kien originally sees Pfaff (like Fischerle) as an ally, for Pfaff has no time for the jumped-up Therese, whom he classifies with elegant simplicity, as he does all the other undesirables he encounters in the course of his duties, as a 'Scheißgefrieß' (73), a 'shithead' (95). Pfaff's favoured method of reasoning with such 'Subjekte' (73) or 'suspects' (95) of this kind as are incautious enough to attempt to venture past his porter's lodge is to fling himself on them from his lair and beat them senseless. A now-retired policeman, 'Oberbeamter in Pension' (345/437), Pfaff is wholly devoted to Kien, since before his eviction the latter has paid him a handsome monthly tip to ensure his undisturbed privacy. In happier days, Pfaff, 'der gute Vater' (326) / 'the kind father' (413), had conscientiously terrorized, beaten, and sexually exploited both his wife and his daughter, partly for their own good, partly to remind them of the respect due to himself as husband, father, and breadwinner. His wife 'starb unter seinen Händen. Doch wäre sie in den nächsten Tagen bestimmt und von selbst eingegangen. Ein Mörder war er nicht' (327) / 'died under his hands. But she would certainly have pegged out of her own accord in the next few days anyway. A murderer he was not' (414). When his daughter dies too some years later, he walls up the bedroom in which they were all three once so happy together and sadly devotes his fists to the re-education of uninvited visitors. Pfaff's success as guardian of the gate is largely due to his patented method of observation: all day long and much of the night he squats at a knee-high peephole in the wall of the entrance hall and watches the trousers and skirts that pass by. An instant evaluation of any previously unseen garment guarantees either safe passage or instant demolition for its wearer. When Kien, dazed from his experiences in the outside world, instinctively returns to his former address, he is first greeted with joy by Pfaff on account of the expected continuation of the monthly tip, then press-ganged into service at the peephole, and finally held to ransom in Pfaff's boarded-up lair for the price of his meals.

Like Kien himself, Therese, Fischerle, and Pfaff are far less characters in any realistic sense, capable of change and development, than they are caricatures, identified by just two or three static characteristics. Therese is characterized mentally by her stupidity, cupidity, and entirely groundless vanity, physically by her stiff blue skirt, in which she seems less to walk than to glide ominously as if on castors, her unusually large ears, and her pronounced body odour. Fischerle is characterized mentally by his cunning, his venality, and his contempt for anyone he can outsmart – which means most people, 'weil alle Menschen dumm sind' (297) / 'for they're all fools' (374); physically by his dwarfish stature, his hump, and a gigantic nose. Pfaff is characterized mentally by his stupidity, his obsequiousness in the face of authority, and his belief in force as the answer to all problems; physically by his gigantic fists, his red hair, and his great roaring voice. All three are united not only by their consuming greed for money but also by their total disregard of the rights of other people: Therese happily leaves her husband for dead, Fischerle ruthlessly exploits his wife and routinely cheats anyone who can't stop him, Pfaff beats his wife to death and sexually abuses his daughter for years. Therese and Pfaff, for all that, both see themselves as pillars of society: Therese is proud to be an 'anständige Person' (24), a 'respectable person' (33), as opposed to the 'Gesindel' (22) or 'riffraff' (30) that are everywhere rampant; Pfaff, as one-time policeman and servant of the state, swears by law and order and the sanctity of family values. Fischerle, for his part, lives only for the day when, rich and famous, he will be in a position to occupy his rightful place in the scheme of things.

Therese, Fischerle, and Pfaff are the three most closely described inhabitants of the unnamed Vienna represented in Canetti's novel.[3] There are numerous others who make briefer but still memorable appearances: the smooth Herr Grob (whose name means 'rough'); tiny Herr Groß ('great') and his domineering mother; Fischerle's wife, known as 'die Pensionistin' or 'the Capitalist' because of her steady income from a particular long-term customer; his friend 'die Fischerin' ('the Fishwife,' as C.V. Wedgwood felicitously translates it), so called because, a misshapen, hunchbacked dwarf herself, she is hopelessly in love with Fischerle; his murderer, Johann Schwer, alias 'der Knopfhans' / 'Johnny Button,' obsessed by the fact that his professional blindness prevents an appropriately violent reaction (except eventually in Fischerle's case) when he plainly sees buttons rather than coins being thrown into his beggar's hat; and the police Kommandant, perpetually devastated by the size of his hopelessly underdeveloped nose.

It is among this collection of Dickensian grotesques populating the world beyond the library – 'Here be monsters' – that Kien, the scholar and thinker, is obliged to move, at his peril, once he is ejected from his own book-lined world. To take Kien at face value as the representative of intellect in a hostile world, however, is to oversimplify drastically the complexity of the discursive situation presented in *Die Blendung*. Kien has completely rejected the outside world, the world of the 'Masse' (12), the 'mob' (18), devoted as he is to his

Dienst an der Wahrheit. Wissenschaft und Wahrheit waren für ihn identische Begriffe. Man näherte sich der Wahrheit, indem man sich von den Menschen abschloß. Der Alltag war ein oberflächliches Gewirr von Lügen ... Das wußte er zum Vorhinein, Erfahrung war hier überflüssig. (12)

service in the cause of truth. Knowledge and truth were for him identical terms. You drew closer to truth by shutting yourself off from people. Daily life was a superficial clatter of lies ... He had always known this, experience was superfluous. (18)

Before Therese finally outflanks him, he adamantly rejects the thought of ever taking a wife: 'Im Hauptfach ist eine jede *Frau* und stellt Ansprüche, die ein ehrlicher Gelehrter nicht im Traum zu erfüllen gedenkt' (10) / 'Each is a specialist first and foremost as a woman, and would make demands which an honest man of learning would not even dream of fulfilling' (15). As far as Kien is concerned, he is a scholar first, last, and always, and his entirely indiscriminate contempt for other people in general is founded on their unprincipled failure to emulate him in likewise adopting a rigidly unswerving course towards the truth and then adhering to it at all costs: '*Er legte seinen Ehrgeiz in eine Hartnäckigkeit des Wesens. Nicht bloß einen Monat, nicht ein Jahr, sein ganzes Leben blieb er sich gleich*' (12–13) / '*His* ambition was to persist stubbornly in the same manner of existence. Not for a mere month, not for a year, but for the whole of his life, he would be unchangingly true to himself' (18).

Kien's preferred method of dealing with this rejected world is to ignore it. 'Soviel Passanten, soviel Lügner. Drum sah er sie gar nicht an' (12) / 'Every passer-by was a liar. For that reason he never looked at them' (18). He achieves similar success with this method when he learns to ignore Therese's newly acquired furniture (an inconvenience he had previously avoided) by training himself to walk around the apartment with his eyes firmly closed except when he is sure he is standing in front of a bookcase (59/78). 'Die Möbel existieren für ihn so wenig, wie das Heer von Atomen in ihm und um ihn. "Esse percipi", Sein ist Wahrgenommenwerden, was ich nicht wahrnehme, existiert nicht' (61) / 'The furniture exists as little for him as the army of atoms within and around him. *Esse percipi*, to be is to be perceived. What I do not perceive does not exist' (79). Therese herself, unfortunately, is not quite so easy to rationalize out of existence. As an alternative strategy, Kien heroically attempts to mobilize his library in its own defence, addressing his army of books in martial terms before turning their twenty-five thousand backs to the wall – since that is exactly where the world of learning now finds itself in the face of a creeping 'Schlamm des Analphabetensumpfes' (79), an advancing tide of 'slime from the bog of illiteracy' (102). A victim of his own eloquence, he succeeds only in falling from the library ladder and spending six bedridden weeks a helpless victim of Therese's unending tirades (93/120). Once she turns to actual blows, Kien has to resort to yet more rigorous methods of defence and turns himself to stone: 'Seine Augen blickten ins Weite. Er versuchte sie zu schließen. An ihrer Weigerung erkannte er sich als ägyptischen Priester von Granit. Er war zur Statue geworden' (141) / 'His eyes were fixed on the distance. He sought to close them. From their refusal to do so he recognized that he was the granite image of an Egyptian priest. He had turned into a statue' (179). Only Therese's incurable ignorance, which extends also to matters Egyptian, causes this excellent plan to fail also.

Kien is likewise no match at all for the wily Fischerle. Kien cannot, of course, afford to be without his research library, so when Therese expels him from it he goes to enormous pains to reassemble the entire library by visiting bookshops – and carrying the volumes thus 'acquired' in his head. In order to sleep, of course, he then has to unload the entire library every night, requiring ever-larger hotel rooms as the collection grows. Fischerle busily assists him in this endeavour, even suggesting various refinements to ensure as orderly a procedure as possible (171/217). He also informs Kien in confidence that the state pawn office, the ominously (and fictitiously) named Theresianum (181/231), houses a particular official whose sole duty and pleasure it is to devour on the spot all books pawned by their unsuspecting owners. Appalled by this barbarous plot – 'Wieviel sieht man von all dem furchtbaren Elend, das einen umgibt?' (189) / 'How little do we see of the fearful misery which lies about us?' (241) – Kien immediately decides to devote his entire remaining fortune to saving the books, takes up sentry duty at the door of the establishment, and hands out ever larger sums of money to erring individuals wishing to pawn their books – and who are, of course, all in Fischerle's temporary employ.

Or rather, not quite all, for one day Therese and Pfaff, having in the meantime joined forces, also turn up with large parcels of Kien's own books to pawn. This apparition considerably disturbs Kien, for in the meantime he has been reliably informed, by one of Fischerle's henchmen, of Therese's unhappy death: '"Sie ist leider gestorben", erklärt der Blinde mit aufrichtiger Trauer, "und läßt schön grüßen"' (228) / '"I'm sorry to say she's dead," said the blind man with genuine regret, "and sends you her kind regards"' (288). Faced with such solid evidence, Kien has concluded that he himself was undoubtedly responsible for her death, for after he so narrowly escaped her clutches by locking her into the apartment, he reasons, she must no doubt have died a slow and very likely excruciating death of starvation. Her sudden appearance at this point is therefore obviously a hallucination of some kind, he further concludes, presumably due to overwork – certainly not to remorse, for Kien accepts his guilt with great equanimity: 'Sie hat diesen Tod verdient. Ich weiß noch heute nicht bestimmt, ob sie geläufig lesen und schreiben konnte' (233) / 'She deserved such a death. Even today I don't know for certain if she could read and write with any ease' (294). Some days later Kien strangles Pfaff's four singing canaries because their 'blue' plumage reminds him of the fatal blue of Therese's skirt, which comes to symbolize all that is evil in the world for him. Throwing their corpses out the window, he also tosses out the little finger of his left hand, which he has just cut off to test the sharpness of his dinner knife. 'Kaum hat er alles Blau aus dem Zimmer entfernt, da tanzen die Wände los. Die heftige Bewegung löst sie in blaue Flecken auf. Es sind Röcke, flüstert er und kriecht unters Bett. Er beginnt an seinem Verstand zu zweifeln' (350) / 'Scarcely has he thus expelled everything from the room when the walls begin to dance. Their violent movement dissolves in blue spots. They are skirts, he whispers, and creeps under the bed. He is beginning to doubt his reason' (442–3).

The reader has no doubt entertained similar reservations for some time already. And at just this point in the proceedings a second Professor Kien is introduced, namely, Kien's brother Georg (or Georges), the brilliantly successful director of a large psychiatric hospital in Paris. In striking contrast to Kien's determined misanthropy, Georg's success rests above all on his ability to empathize completely with his disturbed patients, to enter completely into their individual fantasy worlds on their own terms, and to treat them with all the respect due as appropriate to a Napoleon or a Goethe or a Jupiter. 'So lebte er in einer Unzahl von Welten zugleich' (353) / 'Thus he lived simultaneously in numberless different worlds' (446), a master of metamorphosis (360/455). Perhaps the most interesting of the many hermeneutic enigmas faced by Canetti's reader is why Georg, who has been so successful at entering into the fantasy worlds – the *Blendungen* or 'delusions' – of his other patients, fails so spectacularly when it comes to his own brother.

II

Die Blendung was originally intended as one of a cycle of eight novels that would constitute a 'Comédie Humaine an Irren' (Canetti 1975: 127), a '*Comédie humaine* of lunatics.' In the entropically degenerate world it portrays, rapacity, stupidity, brutality, and cunning fight constantly for supremacy. Critics are virtually unanimous in their reading of Canetti's narrative on this level. This is a novel about the emergence of the monstrous out of the everyday (Moser 1983: 54), a diagnostic portrayal of the sickness of the times (Busch 1975: 31), a revelation of all that is inhuman in society (Piel 1984: 16), a pandemonium of latent aggression (Barnouw 1979: 21–2). The degree to which social order has disintegrated is perhaps best illustrated by the fact that both Therese, the incarnation of stupidity and greed, and Pfaff, the incarnation of brutality and violence, appeal entirely confidently to the concept of law and order. The direct consequences of this social anomie are portrayed in various vicious (and historically prophetic) mob scenes – as when 'die Fischerin,' for example, is savagely beaten up and left for dead because of her hump (294/371).

The title *Die Blendung* has various possible connotations: the action or result of literal blinding, figurative blinding (as by bright lights), or metaphorical blinding (as by the deceit of others or by self-delusion). The term can also denote a 'blind' in the hunting sense, a shelter (or fiction) behind which to conceal one's true intentions – whether from others or from oneself. The novel plays with these various conceptions of blindness throughout.[4] One of Kien's greatest fears as a scholar, for example, is that of blindness, though the blindness he eventually falls victim to is metaphorical rather than physical; he deliberately 'blinds' himself on several occasions, quite literally closing his eyes to a reality he does not wish to see; and he is involuntarily 'blinded,' has the wool pulled over his eyes, in almost all his encounters with other characters. With the possible exception of Georg, all the inhabitants of this narrative world are represented as cripplingly limited by their assorted obsessions, each of them living in an almost entirely isolated fictional world of his or her own creation. Their grotesquely curtailed characterization corresponds to the grotesque limitations they impose upon their own development by the single-minded rigidity of their assorted *idées fixes* – graphically emblematized by Pfaff's knee-high peephole.

The narrative abounds in instances of voluntary or involuntary self-delusion as a means of controlling a rejected reality, typified by Kien's apologia: 'Ich weiß, diese Wahrheit lügt' (271) / 'I know this truth is a lie' (342). The most significant implication of this ubiquitous *Blendung* is that any form of real communication is practically impossible: nobody in this monoglot world talks *to* anyone else, rather everyone talks *past* his or her interlocutor, talks in the end only to him- or herself. The world becomes a lunatic asylum, with each individual hermetically sealed inside his or her own fantasy, reading everything that happens completely unreflectingly in accordance with the dictates of this system. One of the most graphic illustrations is provided by the farcical police interrogation of Kien, who is fully prepared to defend his 'murder' of Therese before any court, and is duly given that opportunity (though he is the only one who knows this) in the course of an interrogation (convened for quite different reasons) during which total confusion reigns, volubly enhanced by frequent interventions on the part of the murder victim.

Canetti's novel achieved recognition in the German-speaking countries only extremely belatedly, almost thirty years after its first appearance.[5] It has been variously noted that a central reason for this may be found in the wholly unflattering picture it paints of the role of the intellectual in society, in the egregious failure of its intellectual protagonist to come to any sort of terms with the barbarous world in which he lives.

Kien, in fact, quickly becomes tainted by the reality he so sedulously endeavours to ignore. He is immediately infected by Therese's greed for money, for example – not for any base reason, of course, but because he can buy more books with it. He quite happily accepts that he is, as he thinks, a murderer – though likewise in a good cause, of course. His delirious solution for the ills of the civilized world is a simple one: 'Ein Dekret betreffs Abschaffung des weiblichen Geschlechts wird vorbereitet' (340) / 'A decree for the abolition of the female sex is in preparation' (430) – a view interestingly paralleling Fischerle's contention that 'Die Weiber richten einen Mann zugrund" (175) / 'Women destroy men' (223) or Pfaff's that 'Die Weiber gehören totgeschlagen' (96) / 'Women ought to be beaten to death' (124). Pfaff's respect for law and order parodically reflects Kien's own fanatic devotion to order (13/19) in his daily routine. Forced by Pfaff to take his place at the peephole, Kien very soon becomes fascinated by the exercise and even considers the possibility of a brief monograph on his observations in the field (344/433). And in the end, of course, Kien becomes his own worst nightmare, a destroyer of books.

'Kein Mensch ist soviel wert wie seine Bücher, glauben Sie mir!' (191) / 'Believe me, no mortal man is worth his weight in books!' (242–3), Kien, a crazed Don Quixote in a fantasy world of book-devouring 'cannibals' (216/273), preaches in what he sees as his role as a more intellectually responsible Christ, saviour of books rather than of men (213/269). As long as he stays in his library, Kien's eccentric vision of the world is essentially unchallenged. With his expulsion from this paradise, his vision becomes entangled with numerous other and equally eccentric visions of the world. The three divisions of the narrative show Kien sliding increasingly rapidly from an ostensibly sovereign idealism ('Ein Kopf ohne Welt'/ 'A Head Without a World') through a hopelessly ineffective encounter with the real world ('Kopflose Welt' / 'Headless World') into outright madness ('Welt im Kopf' / 'The World in the Head').

Thematically, the reader's attention is thus drawn in turn to *Kopf*, *Welt*, and the reading of the latter by the former. Semiotically, a central strand – almost entirely ignored by Canetti criticism so far – is the parodic juxtaposition of three radically different portrayals of the intellectual in society. *Die Blendung* employs two main (and continually interlinked) strategies of narrative discourse: first, the systemic problematization of reading; second, as one aspect of this, the parodic evocation of the 'intellectual' by a process

of synecdochic, stereographic characterization. The character thus obliquely evoked is not so much that of Kien, who remains a caricature throughout; rather it is that of the intellectual per se, implied rather than portrayed
by virtue of the interaction of Kien and those about him. The resultant and
highly satirical portrayal of the intellectual in society emerges from a double procedure of contrast: Kien is contrasted on the one hand to Therese
and Pfaff as representatives of the forces that militate against intellect, and
on the other to Fischerle and Georg as representatives of intellect.

Therese and Pfaff are purely one-dimensional caricatures; Fischerle and
Georg are both more complicated figures. Having fought and lost his epic
battle with Therese in Part One of the narrative, Kien – whose apartment
does not contain a mirror (13/18) – is doubly reflected discursively in what
follows: first, more grotesquely, in the comico-pathetic figure of Fischerle
in Part Two, and then, more essayistically, in the figure of his long-lost
brother Georg in Part Three. The result is a composite picture of the intellectual as deliberate outsider, as trickster (with physical deformities to
match the intellectual ones), and as would-be saviour of a world that ener-
getically resists any such salvation.

Fischerle, in whom Kien immediately believes he detects a fellow spirit –
'Das Schachspiel ist seine Bibliothek' (164) / 'Chess is his library' (209) –
functions as a distorted image of Kien, a grotesque (and criminally minded)
Sancho Panza to Kien's equally grotesque Quixote. Like Kien, he is totally
obsessed, specifically by his ambition to become world chess champion.
Where Kien's intellectual interests are entirely disinterested, however, Fischerle's, indicatively, are purely a means to an end. His real ambition is to
become as rich as possible as soon as possible, and any means he may have
to employ are secondary to this end. He is easily able to outwit Kien, as we
have seen, but his own delusion eventually takes him over completely, just
as Kien's does him. Where Kien arrogantly ignores other people, Fischerle
contemptuously exploits them. Kien's arrogance leads ultimately to his
own death, since his total exclusion of other people from his world leads,
so to speak, to a complete loss of immunity, a complete defencelessness in
the face of others. Likewise, it is his contempt for others that finally leads
to Fischerle's death, as the result of a gratuitous taunt. It is indicative also
that while very few readers are likely to feel any sympathy with either
Therese or Pfaff, some readers may well feel that, for all his ruthlessness
and depravity, Fischerle is at least to some extent as much sinned against as
sinning. Branded a natural victim in the dog-eat-dog world in which he
lives by both his physical deformities and his Jewishness, Fischerle, as
'cripple' (290/365), needs all the considerable intelligence at his disposal to

survive. We may note a number of occasions when the discourse parodically connects Kien and Fischerle in the choice of words: Therese, for example, also calls Kien a 'Krüppel' (134/171); Fischerle himself sees Kien as a fish and himself as a fisherman (155/199); 'Bin i a Hund?' (154) / 'I'm not a dog, am I?' (198) are the first words we hear Fischerle utter, addressed to a Kien whom Therese also thinks of on occasion as a dog to be whipped; he even masquerades as Kien in his faked (but entirely accurate) telegram to Georg: 'Bin total meschugge' (300) / 'Am completely nuts' (377); and so on.[6]

Indicatively, perhaps, Georg never actually meets Fischerle, but becomes involved in his brother's affairs precisely as a result of that telegram, sent by Fischerle in Kien's name as a malicious joke just before his own unforeseen death. Since Georg is an outsider – and a psychoanalyst – his arrival on the scene seems to promise an imminent solution to the proliferating hermeneutic confusion (Dissinger 1971: 55). His failure provides the reader with the interpretive crux of the novel. For some readers, Georg fails quite simply because he never realizes that his brother, a 'listenreicher Odysseus' (379), a 'warywise Odysseus' (479), who refuses to reveal his madness, *needs* curing in the first place: Georg, that is to say, expects to find a world of lunatics only inside the walls of his asylum (Dissinger 1971: 98). Other readers are struck more forcefully by the fact that Georg, the master healer, prefers not to heal some of his favourite patients at all, judging their fantasized private worlds to be infinitely richer than the shared world of normality.

Georg's (putative) blindness to his brother's (metaphorical) blindness is ironically anticipated when he encounters a blind fellow passenger on the train from Paris to Vienna, remembers his brother's terror as a small boy with measles that he was going blind, and anticipates that Peter's present problems may well arise from a renewed fear of (actual rather than metaphorical) blindness as a result of too much reading. Dissinger notes that Georg, like Peter, also initially misreads both Therese and Pfaff (1971: 98). Georg, however, quickly corrects his reading in both cases and has little difficulty in saving his brother from this combined threat from without. The threat from within apparently escapes his diagnosis, however, and during the long and (grotesquely) learned debate with his brother he even inadvertently hastens Kien's self-destruction by citing as an example of a ludicrous and completely unlikely eventuality that Peter should voluntarily burn down his own library – an idea that in fact has long been present to Kien as a nightmare and now seizes the upper hand in his rapidly failing mind.

Kien, who had broken off all communication with his brother eight years previously (43/57), none the less thinks of him as his potential protector: he wishes Georg were there (43/57) as soon as he realizes his mistake in marrying Therese; a silent cry for help to Georg (413/520) is one of his last thoughts before the final flames reach him. Yet he also instinctively mistrusts Georg, the one person who might be capable of saving him. The brothers, unacknowledged patient and would-be doctor, are presented as being in many ways two sides of the same coin. Georg at one point observes that together they would constitute one real human being, 'ein geistig vollkommenes Wesen' (388) / 'a spiritually complete man' (490). Rigidity and abstraction are Peter's milieu, flexibility and human sympathy are Georg's: determined isolation as opposed to equally determined openness, abstraction versus empathy, misanthropy versus philanthropy, Peter's vain attempts at petrifaction versus Georg's constant metamorphosis in entering into the fantasies of his patients. Indicatively, where Peter wishes to be stone, Georg(es), whose name metamorphoses easily with his surroundings, is 'eine spazierende Wachstafel' (367) / 'a walking wax tablet' (464). But how sane is a psychoanalyst who at least selectively prefers insanity to sanity? While earlier critics understandably tended to see Georg as a wholly positive counterpart to Peter, Dagmar Barnouw, for example, argues that both of them behave with a completely irresponsible combination of political ignorance and arrogance (1979: 23). Georg, she argues, is an undisciplined dilettante delighted more by his own ingenuity as a healer than by any real interest in his patients, and consequently both irresponsible and potentially dangerous – as his behaviour with Peter shows.[7]

Kien, Fischerle, and Georg are all presented as master readers, master interpreters in their several specialized fields, whether oriental philology, chess, or the human psyche. Kien, the reclusive scholar, sees his field as a place of refuge from the real world; Fischerle, the crook, sees his field as a way to improve the real world in the most immediately practical way by making him rich and famous; Georg, the idealist, sees his field as a way to help people who need help, to make the world a better place for all. By the same token, however, all three are failed readers in one way or another.

Kien the celebrated scholar would certainly not have neglected to examine conflicting versions of a text before deciding on the correct reading – but he subscribes blindly, and eventually fatally, to a single and highly limited reading of the world he lives in. Fischerle, like Kien, becomes so completely enmeshed in his private vision of how the world works (or how it *should* work) that he forgets equally completely to apply even the elementary rules of his own area of specialized knowledge. As a chess player he would certainly not have carried out a single move with anything approaching the degree of reckless overconfidence that leads, off the board, to the immediate checkmate of his plans – in the form of his own savage murder. Georg, whose *métier* is the reconciliation of conflicting visions of reality, a brilliantly successful listener in his dealings with the mentally disturbed inmates of his asylum, likewise apparently fails to observe his own basic diagnostic rule as a psychiatrist in failing to enter into Kien's fantasy world – because he fails to recognize a patient when he sees one.

One of the major challenges presented to the reader of *Die Blendung* is to decide just how seriously this composite picture of the intellectual should be taken. One basic question to consider is to what degree Kien, Fischerle, and Georg really are the authorities in their respective fields they are presented – and accepted by most critics – as being. The role of narrative focalization in Canetti's text – the fact, that is to say, that so much of the text we read is presented by the 'voice' of the narrator but seen through the 'eyes' of particular characters – is crucial in this respect. The question of Fischerle's credentials as a chess player is a good example of the implications.

The reader may not be surprised that, true to his criminal instincts, Fischerle cheats even at chess. Indeed, Fischerle's credentials as a potential chess champion are openly undermined by the narrator when the dwarf is shown dazzling his drinking companions by demonstrating the mistakes allegedly made by reigning champions – but 'von seiner Bedeutung war er selbst durchaus nicht überzeugt. Die wirklichen Züge, die er unterschlug, gaben seinem gescheiten Kopf bitter zu denken' (159) / 'He was by no means convinced of his own importance. He racked his brains furiously over the actual moves he concealed' (204). The reader tends to assign less importance to this information, however, than to the information that 'während des Spiels fürchteten ihn seine Partner viel zu sehr, um ihn durch Einwürfe zu stören. Denn er rächte sich furchtbar und gab die Unbedachtheit ihrer Züge dem allgemeinen Gelächter preis' (156) / 'during games his partners were far too much afraid of him to interrupt him with objections. For he took a terrible vengeance and would hold up the foolishness of their moves to general derision' (200). So strong and so persistent is Fischerle's conviction of his own skill, in other words, that the reader tends to ignore the possibility that the account of his victories, though presented by the narrator, may be envisioned solely through Fischerle's eyes – tends, in fact, to accept Fischerle's vision of how things should be rather than the narrator's statement of how they in fact are.

Doubts as to Kien's being a professor are likewise raised (and apparently rejected) at a very early stage, when the boy Franz Metzger observes in the dialogue with which the narrative commences that 'Die Mutter sagt, Sie sind kein Professor. Ich glaube schon, weil Sie eine Bibliothek haben' (8) / 'My mother says you aren't a real Professor. But I think you are – you've got a library' (12).[8] The nine-year-old schoolboy's apparent correction of his mother's erroneous opinion is immediately reinforced by the fact that the narrator's initial reference to Kien is to 'Professor Peter Kien' (8/12). Since the reader has no reason to assume at this point that the narrator is presenting anything other than verifiably authentic facts, this reference and many others like it will naturally be read as entirely valid. A systematic analysis of focalization in the text, however, has convincingly shown that the narrator's various references to the extent and quality of Kien's scholarship all occur in narrative contexts where Kien's focalization can be read as predominating (Darby 1992: 23).

That Kien owns a large library seems to be beyond dispute, if only because we see Therese and Pfaff attempting to pawn large numbers of his books. That Kien is a world-renowned scholar, however, may be no less a private fantasy than are Fischerle's dreams of glory – we note, for example, that Kien eschews all contact with professional colleagues, whom he ostensibly despises. That Georg is a psychiatrist also seems beyond dispute, if only because the telegram Fischerle sends to his clinic in Paris actually reaches Georg there. But what of the reports of his astonishing success? Is the reported fact that his eight hundred patients regard him as a 'Heiland' (359), a 'saviour' (454), to be taken as a statement of narrative fact on the part of a reliable narrator – or as evidence that Georg, like his crazed brother Peter, also sees himself as a new and improved version of Christ the Saviour?[9] Can readers trust their own reading? Can readers trust the narrative presentation on which they have no option but to base that reading? In the absurd world of *Die Blendung* – in which its readers too must dwell for the duration of their reading – the yardstick that divides reading from misreading, the normal from the abnormal, the sane from the insane remains systemically uncertain, systemically subject to *Blendung* in its application.

III

Kien, the absent-minded professor, falls successively into the hands of a shrew, a crook, a murderer, the police, and a psychiatrist, all of them likewise portrayed as comic figures – including even Georg, the famous psychiatrist who cannot tell sane from insane. In the case of Georg, however, the comedy is in quite a different key, the grotesque slapstick of the earlier episodes giving way to a more ironically tinged picture of a world entirely out of joint, a world in which disorder reigns supreme – and a world that is also, of course, the creation of the narrator. Canetti's narrator is a master of grotesque invention, one who lives, like Georg, in a multitude of worlds at once – and allows the reader to do so too, though naturally at the latter's own risk. It is entirely in line with the thematic thrust of *Die Blendung* that instead of character development we are given character confrontation, conflicting visions of the intellectual juxtaposed rather than harmonized; it is entirely in line with the semiotic thrust that Georg's therapeutic practice, as reported, functions as a *mise en abyme* of the narrator's presentational strategy. Georg's belief that he can probe the relationship of the individual and society from the behaviour of the patients he leaves happily insane – 'In seinem eigenen Bewußtsein näherte er die getrennten Teile des Kranken, wie er sie verkörperte, und fügte sie langsam aneinander' (353) / 'In his own consciousness he would gradually draw the separate halves of the patient, as he embodied them, closer to each other, and thus gradually would rejoin them' (446) – is clearly paralleled by the narrator's practice, metamorphosing easily as he does, like Georg, between one exclusive fantasy world and another.

One can agree with Annemarie Auer when she sees *Die Blendung* as constructed essentially along entirely conventional lines, but hardly when she calls it a novel innocent of all experimentation (1983: 33). Canetti's narrator is one of the most devious in literature. The novel's elusiveness is in large part due to what one might describe as an ostentatiously backgrounded narrator. Indeed, the narrator is almost entirely 'absent' from his own account, as Dissinger observes (1971: 23), leaving his characters to speak for themselves, whether in the form of interior monologue (on a relatively few occasions) or, much more frequently, that of narrated monologue (*erlebte Rede*). The central significance of the latter device in Canetti's novel is that it almost always employs the third person and past tense of (apparently) omniscient (and thus completely authoritative) narration but is focalized through a character rather than by the narrator – and thus effectively leads to systemic ambiguity as far as the reader is concerned. For the options of unambiguous identification of the focalization with *either* the narrator or the character are rare; what are stressed are precisely the grey and frequently entirely indeterminable areas in between. The crucial difficulty is in determining just when the particular focalization involved should be read as the narrator's presumably authoritative and reliable report and just when as the deluded fantasy of one of his characters.

As we have seen, even a reference like 'Professor Peter Kien' demands two entirely different readings, depending upon whether we see it as focalized by an authoritative narrator or by a deluded character. In a narrative which centres on the fundamental ambivalence of narrative focalization, indeed, every single sentence is in principle ambivalent. Constant ironic change of perspective is thus a central feature of this narrative, obliging the reader constantly both to identify with *and* immediately to question the readings of the characters (Dissinger 1971: 33). The novel ironically comments on its own technique in Kien's dismissive statement that 'Romane sind Keile, die ein schreibender Schauspieler in die geschlossene Person seiner Leser treibt' (35) / 'Novels are so many wedges which the novelist, an actor with his pen, inserts into the closed personality of the reader' (47).

It is hardly surprising that before the appearance in 1960 of Canetti's major anthropological study *Masse und Macht* (*Crowds and Power*), criticism of *Die Blendung*, whether at home or abroad, was characterized by and large by bewilderment – and quickly moved towards an exclusive reliance on the theoretical categories developed in Canetti's apparently 'explanatory' later work concerning the relationship of the individual and the collective. Such readings, while of considerable value in non-literary terms, tend to underplay drastically the primarily literary status of the narrative. Avoiding this explanatory paradigm, David Darby persuasively analyses the text as primarily an open system of meaning, concentrating especially on the degree to which a continually shifting and radically ambiguous focalization systemically undermines the reliability of the narrative account and produces an informational disorder that overtly challenges the reader's powers of structuration throughout (1992: 24–38). The point in such instances – which are legion – is precisely their uncertainty, precisely their challenge to the reader.

'The narrator of *Die Blendung* provides no commentaries, offers no opinions, makes no attempt to provide the kind of insight into motivation and behaviour that calms and consoles,' as Stevens aptly observes (1991: 114–15). Instead, without comment, he presents a monstrous world, peopled by monstrous characters – and leaves the reader to decide where to locate its edges. It is also, however, a comic world, based on disorientation and disproportion, bearing comparison with those of Céline, Beckett, or Heller. Several (at least) of the chapters are frankly comic set pieces, especially, for example, 'Der Dieb' (251–64) / 'The Thief' (316–32) or 'Privateigentum' (264–89) / 'Private Property' (333–64). Canetti's narrative is also a comedy on another level, however, in that there is a second 'story' in progress of which the characters, by definition, can never know anything.

Lacking almost entirely any character development, and with only a minimal plot, the narrative is held together on the level of discourse by a network of parodic linking devices. These are of two main kinds: first, a variety of discursive leitmotifs, such as the occurrence of the colours blue and red; and second, a variety of teasing discursive parallels between characters.

Dissinger, for example (1971: 135–38), meticulously traces the occurrence of the colours blue and red, associated initially with Therese's skirt and Pfaff's hair respectively – and by extension with the threat to the intellectual life constituted by Therese and Pfaff as representatives of the unthinking mob, an elemental force of destruction like (blue) water or (red) fire. Kien's implication in his own downfall is minimally hinted at by references to his 'wasserblaue Augen' (152) / 'watery blue eyes' (195) and Georg's dream of him as a fighting cock, 'der rote Hahn' (372), literally 'the red rooster' (470), but in German also a traditional literary expression for a destructive fire. And so on. Other ostensibly symbolic series involve recurring numbers, mythological references, and repeated references to the relationship of individuals and collectives, parts and wholes. The point of all of this quasi-helpful information, however, is not that it leads the reader closer to some grand unitary meaning but rather that it teasingly offers the possibility of generating further meanings that may or may not be significant.

The narrator's parodic attitude is perhaps most evident in onomastic terms. Canetti, as we know, originally intended calling the novel, as a satire on the Cartesian *cogito*, 'Kant fängt Feuer' / 'Kant catches fire,' then changed the protagonist's name first to Brand, then to Kien, in each case retaining the ominous connection with fire: Kien's very name contains his own destruction from the beginning (Canetti 1975: 124, 127, 135). The term *Kien*, derived from a root meaning 'to hew, to split off,' denotes a long, flat shingle of resinous wood split off from a larger log and originally used especially as a torch. Onomastically Kien (whose unusual height and striking emaciatedness are also frequently mentioned) is thus ironically marked from the beginning not only as both a potential fireraiser and a potential victim of fire, but also as one 'split off.' The phrase *auf dem Kien sein*, we may also note, means 'to be alert,' a quality scarcely attributable to Kien, who allows himself to be swindled by almost everybody with whom he comes in contact. To add insult to injury, Kien, stamped by his surname as wood, is even ironically linked to Therese, the embodiment of all that is inimical to his way of life – and whose surname is Krumbholz, literally 'wood bender' (a term originally associated with the wheelwright's trade).

The reader may even wish to see a trilingual pun on Kien's first name, Peter: parodically connecting the Greek *petros* 'stone' (recalling Kien's unavailing efforts to become a statue) via English *rock* to German *Rock* 'skirt,' the most striking external manifestation of Therese's personality.

We find the same parodic play in the entirely inappropriate odour of onomastic sanctity doubly informing the reprobate 'Benedikt Pfaff' (the two names literally meaning 'blessed' and 'cleric' respectively) as well as in the obsequiously smooth Herr 'Grob' ('rough') or the tiny Herr 'Groß' ('great'). We note the parodic inappropriateness of Fischerle's given name, Siegfried; note the fact that Georg (like Siegfried) is onomastically stamped as a dragon-slayer; notice that Georges from Paris loses his -*es* in Vienna, just as Fischerle, en route to Paris, loses his -*le* when he promotes himself to Doctor Fischer, an orthographic correlative of the hump he wishes to lose – and will soon lose to a kitchen knife, just as Kien cuts off his own finger. How seriously readers choose to take all this all too generously provided information is left entirely up to them.

The presence of such caricatures as carriers of the narrative action might likewise suggest that the central thematic thrust of the narrative should most appropriately be read as bluntly satirical. Such a reading is certainly possible – as when Dissinger observes that one of the novel's central themes is to show the folly of greed (1971: 63; 1982: 35) – but though this is demonstrably the case, recognizing it also constitutes only the very beginnings of an adequate reading. What is far more striking, at least for an approach that privileges the semiotics of narrative discourse, is the number of loose ends that teasingly escape any such tidily attempted hermeneutic closure and demand a more differentiated and a more open reading. Darby thus responds far more adequately to the semiotic demands of the text in his discussion of the various (quasi-)symbolic strategies that are employed by the narrator – the use of colours, the opposition of the individual and the social mass, the use of 'significant' numbers, the play with proper names and mythological references –in concluding that their explanatory value is highly limited and their function essentially parodic, gesturing only vaguely towards possible systems of meaning but remaining fragmentary, hermeneutic red (or blue?) herrings for the benefit of readers hungry for closure (1992: 149–58).

IV

'Lesen kann jeder' (104) / 'Anyone can read' (134), as Therese sagely observes. Not just Kien, Fischerle, and Georg but also Therese (who rereads and rewrites her future by adding an appropriate number of extra zeros to her anticipated legacy), Pfaff (who rereads and rewrites the past by walling it up) and almost all the minor characters are *all* readers of texts deemed in need of emendatory rereading. *Die Blendung* overtly thematizes the problematics of reading and writing, overtly challenges its reader to demonstrate those powers of interpretive discrimination so signally lacking among its characters. Any text presents its readers to some degree with a similar challenge, of course; *Die Blendung* offers more than fair warning of the likelihood of hermeneutic failure through a discourse characterized by unreliability and indeterminacy.

The central enigma of the narrative, Georg's apparent failure as a reader, needs to be read in this context. The account of his career makes it clear that his psychiatric practice differs radically from an 'offizielle Psychiatrie' (351) / 'official psychiatry' (443) whose aim is to replace a deviant reading of reality with a socially authorized one. Georg rejects this aim in favour of a radically different understanding of his role as psychiatrist, refusing to subject his patients' reading of reality, albeit deviant, to a unitary master-reading: 'Der Verstand, wie wir ihn verstehen, ist ein Mißverständnis' (360) / 'Understanding as we understand it is a misunderstanding' (455–6). In refusing to heal his favourite patients, in short, Georg shows himself to be the open reader Canetti's text demands.

At the same time, of course, Georg, revered by his (mad) patients as a 'saviour,' characterized by his (translingually unstable) name as both a dragon-slayer and a mover between worlds, completely unsuccessful in his attempt to cure his own brother, and possibly a brilliant success only in his own imagination, is heavily ironized by the narrator. Readers, for their part, are left in the end with several possible interpretations of Georg's reading, none of which, however, can be considered definitive. First, we may conclude that Georg, outwitted by his brother's lunatic cunning, simply does not realize that Kien is mad: in this case Georg is either completely incompetent or insane himself – or, like all the other characters in the novel, he lives in a world where the distinction has become unrecognizable. Second, we may conclude that Georg does realize that Kien is mad – and unsuccessfully attempts to treat him as he does his other patients, by all too successfully entering into his fantasy world, 'including its intensely reductive, rational, hermeneutic reading' (Darby 1992: 138) of the external world. Third, we may conclude that Georg's failure is really a success, for, realizing that Kien is indeed mad, he none the less allows him not only to persevere in his rejection of the outside world but to take it to its logical conclusion: Kien's final *auto da fé*, after all, parodically conflates his total failure (as the destroyer of his own world) and his success in finally achieving complete (physical) unity with the world of his books in the flames that devour them both. Kien's final – and uninterpretable – laughter marks this conflation.

Darby aptly observes that while *Die Blendung* draws on the sensibility of literary modernism in its thematization of disintegration, it already displays facets of a postmodern consciousness in its parodic play with hermeneutic indeterminacy and the structuration of meaning (1992: 175–89). Reading and misreading, blindness and insight, are relative and mutually defining concepts, for all reading, however authorized or authoritative it may also be, by the nature of things necessarily also involves a concomitant degree of misreading, a degree of what Canetti's novel, ironically challenging its reader even in its title, memorializes as the perpetual possibility of *Blendung*.

5

The Tin Drum:
Implications of Unreliability
in Günter Grass's *Die Blechtrommel*

Günter Grass's extraordinary novel *Die Blechtrommel* (1959) – translated into English as *The Tin Drum* – is without any doubt one of the most impressive German literary texts of this or any other century, and has gradually assembled around itself an entire army of analysts, interpreters, and exegetes who have variously illuminated and occluded the object of their scrutiny according to their particular critical lights. In the present chapter I will limit myself to the central role played in the reading experience of this narrative by the flaunted unreliability of its narrator.[1] Few narrators, as almost all critics of Grass's novel observe, advertise their own unreliability as immediately and as blatantly as Oskar Matzerath, the narrator and central character, who begins his lengthy and complex autobiographical narrative with the provocative concession: 'Zugegeben: ich bin Insasse einer Heil- und Pflegeanstalt' (9) / 'Granted: I am an inmate of a mental hospital' (15).[2] Evidently, this initial 'zugegeben'/ 'granted' potentially undermines every subsequent statement over the next five hundred pages, invites the reader to weigh every single subsequent statement against that crucial – and flaunted – opening admission that the entire account must be considered suspect. While it may of course be true that not every inmate of a psychiatric hospital is necessarily insane or unbalanced or even unreliable, Oskar more than bears out the implication of unreliability suggested by his opening statement by flamboyantly and repeatedly demonstrating throughout his lengthy narrative just how little he is to be trusted. Neither, however, can we assume him to be *consistently* unreliable. For one thing, as John Reddick puts it, 'the question as to whether Oskar is truly mad, or only pretending to be mad, remains one of the ultimate ambiguities of the fiction' (1974: 50). It is certainly not the only one insofar as Oskar's narration is concerned.

I

By his own account not only is Oskar (at least by implication) the child of
two fathers, one Polish and one German, he is also born with a fully developed adult ability to make reasoned decisions: 'Ich gehörte zu den hellhöri-
gen Säuglingen, deren geistige Entwicklung schon bei der Geburt
abgeschlossen ist und sich fortan nur bestätigen muß' (35) / 'I was one of
those clairaudient infants whose mental development is completed at birth
and after that merely needs a certain amount of filling in' (47). Weighing his
(German) father's ambition that Oskar should grow up to be a shopkeeper
like himself against his mother's ambition to buy him a tin drum as soon as
he is three years old, Oskar decides that only the latter prospect justifies
anything but an immediate return to the womb. 'Zudem hatte die
Hebamme mich schon abgenabelt; es war nichts mehr zu machen' (37) /
'Besides, the midwife had already cut my umbilical cord. There was nothing more to be done' (49). Having duly reached the age of three, and finally
in possession of his first drum, Oskar further decides that, based on his
experience of life so far, he has no desire to join the world of adults but prefers to retain the permanent stature of a three-year-old instead, a compact
ninety-four centimetres. In order to provide a 'plausiblen Grund fürs aus-
bleibende Wachstum' (48), a 'plausible ground for my failure to grow' (61),
since grown-ups notoriously need explanations for things, as he relates, he
carefully flings himself head first down the cellar stairs: 'schon anläßlich
meines ersten Trommeltages war es mir gelungen, der Welt ein Zeichen zu
geben' (49) / 'on my very first day as a drummer I had succeeded in giving
the world a sign' (63). After the fall and four weeks of convalescence Oskar
develops not only a lifelong passion for prolonged bouts of drumming but
also a glass-shattering scream that is both very useful for protecting his
drum and turns out eventually to have various other practical and even
artistic applications as well.

But does 'after' the fall mean 'because' of it or not? That, indeed, is
exactly the sort of interpretive decision *Die Blechtrommel* continually and
consistently demands of its reader. In this particular case, for example,
there are several possible conclusions we may reach as to what 'really' happened. First, we may take Oskar completely at his word, and according to
Oskar's account it wasn't a fall at all but a carefully orchestrated jump,
designed to provide an apparent explanation for a previous and calculated
decision on his part. Second, however, even if that was indeed Oskar's
original plan, there is the obvious possibility that the plan went wrong and
he sustained at least some degree of mental as well as physical injury: to

take Oskar's account at its word again, his original plan was simply to stage a fall that would explain why he wasn't growing any taller; there is no mention of the glass-shattering voice as part of any plan. A third possibility is that there never was a plan in the first place; Oskar simply fell down the stairs as a three-year-old, sustaining permanent mental and physical injury, including the extraordinary vocal side-effects. Fourth, Oskar's mental and physical growth were both affected by his fall as a three-year-old, but there never was any glass-shattering voice in the first place: Oskar himself admits that at the time of writing his memoirs he has no such voice (57/72). Fifth, there was never any plan, there was never any fall, there was never any glass-shattering voice, and Oskar, possibly as the result of horrors experienced during the war years and suppressed or disguised in the account we read, simply lost his mind at some point and invents everything as a lunatic rationalization of how things 'must' (or might) have been – with the one exception of his diminutive stature, which is independently reported by Oskar's keeper, Bruno (356/428). Sixth, even his midget stature is simply an invention, for Oskar invents Bruno's narrative too, just as he invents everything else we read; in which case Oskar is either indeed completely insane, as his unbelievable narrative makes abundantly clear – or he is quite simply an author, whose job it is to invent things, including unbelievable things, just like his creator, Günter Grass, who after all *does* invent everything we read, including Oskar himself. One could, indeed, make a plausible case for any one of these options – and no doubt for other possibilities as well. The crucial question is evidently how the reader is to decide which reading is more appropriate than any other, and this in turn boils down to just how reliable or unreliable the reader believes – or wants – Oskar to be both at any given point and as a whole.

Traditionally, the status of the narrator in a work of narrative fiction was regarded as entirely above any suspicion of unreliability. From Homer right down to the late 1700s, whether the narrator was a so-called 'third-person' narrator endowed with narrative omniscience and total recall or a 'first-person' narrator who related his own story or someone else's, the reader was essentially in a position to take whatever he (or occasionally she) said completely at face value. The odd rogue elephant like *Tristram Shandy*, in which the ostensible reliability of the narrator was shown to be purely a literary convention, was very much the tolerated and well sign-posted exception that proved the 'natural' rule that the narrator, by definition, spoke the truth. Only during the last two centuries has the narrator been displaced from his position of God-like objectivity and infallibility and repositioned as an often all too human, all too subjective, and frequently highly fallible individual. Indeed, it would not be going too far to say that the history of modern narrative has essentially been the history of what one might call the fallibilization of narrative discourse, based essentially on the wholly 'obvious' but entirely crucial insight, central to our present endeavour, that the story presented is always completely inextricable from the discourse that presents it. But while a central discursive function of most narratives, fictional or otherwise, is to assist us in our readerly endeavours to reconstruct the story, *Die Blechtrommel* gains much of its distinctive fascination precisely from the way in which the discourse pervasively *hinders* us in determining what exactly the story told really is. Grass's text, once again, is by no means unique in this respect among modern and postmodern narratives, but it is a particularly brilliant example of the genre.

Clearly, however, it is not especially productive to regard the notion of 'discourse' as meaning a single, undivided narrative voice that is either reliable or unreliable. The question immediately arises as to how we know (or think we know) that a narrator is being unreliable. One of the most impressive features of *Die Blechtrommel* is that although almost all of Oskar's very tall stories are individually unbelievable if not downright impossible, taken as a whole they paradoxically generate their own reality, their own credibility. Most readers will none the less instinctively feel that certain episodes (the death of the Jewish shopkeeper Markus, for example) should be taken more seriously than others (some of Oskar's glass-shattering exploits, for example). We react in this way precisely because we consider ourselves *authorized* to do so by our overall perception of how the book we are reading *should* be read – or, as the narrative theorists tell us, we derive the sense of authorization from our reading of the particular role in that text of its 'implied author.'[3] The implied author of any text is thus essentially the hypostatization of the reader's perception as to how that text requires him or her to behave as a reader – and might thus, indeed, more usefully be thought of as an *inferred* or *textually reconstructed* author. The implied author, moreover, is (at least theoretically) wholly independent of the real author, for we can, as readers, evidently develop a very clear picture of how a particular text should be read even if we have no idea of the real author's identity. The narrator's reliability is gauged by the degree to which his or her account accords or conflicts with this overall interpretive vision. Narrative discourse, in other words, is thus not single but double, not monologic but dialogic, to employ Bakhtin's terminology: narratorial discourse, the narrative voice we 'hear,' is judged against the standard of the implied authorial discourse we 'read' from the text as a whole; what Oskar says, in other words, is judged against what *Die Blechtrommel* says. One may thus qualify Volker Neuhaus's contention when he writes that in a first-person narration like this the narrating *I* is our *only* guarantor of the truth about the narrated world (1979: 32). The concept of the implied author essentially involves seeing the narrator's discourse as always *positioned* against the implied authorial discourse, and thus allows for the possibility of at least an *implied* corrective. The degree to which we can practically apply that possibility as readers, of course, depends on our overall reading of the text as a whole – depends, that is to say, on our particular reconstruction of the implied author the text demands.

In the case of a narrator deemed reliable, the theoretical distinction between the two levels of discourse can for all practical purposes be simply ignored, and that is exactly what we usually do. In the case of a narrator deemed unreliable, it is precisely this distinction that allows us to sense that unreliability in the first place – though it will not, of course, necessarily help us to measure the precise degree of unreliability involved. Moreover, paradoxically, so strong is our ingrained desire as readers of narrative to believe in the imaginary world presented to us, to believe at all costs in the world-creating narrator's truthfulness and reliability, that even when a narrator like Oskar quite conclusively demonstrates his own unreliability we stubbornly tend in spite of everything to believe his various accounts, however extravagantly unbelievable they may turn out to be or even openly advertise themselves as being.

. One of the reasons why *Die Blechtrommel* has emerged so decisively as 'one of the monumental reference points of post-war writing' in Germany (Reddick 1974: 3) is very clearly the relationship of Oskar's eccentric narrative style and the half-century of modern German history over which his highly unlikely story is made to unfold. The ambiguity of the German term *Geschichte*, encompassing both 'story' and 'history,' permeates Oskar's account of his life and times, for his personal story (to the extent that it is possible to speak of one in any realistic sense in the first place) is told against and intimately implicated in the constant backdrop of the course of German history in the twentieth century. Oskar begins his autobiography, like Tristram Shandy, long before his own birth, for 'niemand sollte sein Leben beschreiben, der nicht die Geduld aufbringt, vor dem Datieren der eigenen Existenz wenigstens der Hälfte seiner Großeltern zu gedenken' (11) / 'no one ought to tell the story of his life who hasn't the patience to say a word or two about at least half of his grandparents before providing information about his own existence' (17–18). Chronologically the story thus begins with the (alleged) impregnation of Oskar's grandmother Anna Bronski in

1899 in a rainy potato-field near Danzig by his grandfather, Joseph Koljai-czek, a fugitive from the law because of his political activities on behalf of Polish independence. The result of their union, whether then or later, is Oskar's mother, Agnes, born 'Ende Juli des Jahres nullnull – man entschloß sich gerade, das kaiserliche Schlachtflottenbauprogramm zu verdoppeln' (18) / 'at the end of July of the year zero-zero – they were just deciding to double the imperial naval building program' (26). Eighteen years later Agnes, now a nurse in Danzig, meets Alfred Matzerath, a wounded German soldier. 'Der Krieg hatte sich verausgabt. Man bastelte, Anlaß zu ferneren Kriegen gebend, Friedensverträge' (32) / 'The war had spent itself. Peace treaties that would give ground for further wars were being boggled into shape' (43). By 1920, 'da Marszalek Pilsudski die Rote Armee bei Warschau schlug' (33) / 'when Marszalek Pilsudski defeated the Red Army at Warsaw' (44), they are engaged, and Agnes's former lover, Jan Bronski, possibly in pique, as Oskar suggests, takes out Polish citizenship, though without entirely abandoning his interest in Agnes. Three years later, 'da man für den Gegenwert einer Streichholzschachtel ein Schlafzimmer tapezieren, also mit Nullen mustern konnte' (33) / 'when you could paper a bedroom with zeros for the price of a matchbox' (44–5), Agnes and Matzerath get married and open a grocery store, where in September 1924 Oskar is duly born, to the great pride of Matzerath, 'der in sich meinen Vater vermutete' (35) / 'who presumed himself to be my father' (47).

Oskar's autobiography – written from his hospital bed over the two-year period from September 1952 to September 1954 – maintains this con-stant but entirely oblique relationship with the course of modern German history as the events of the next thirty years are presented, events of world-shattering importance serving merely as an offhandedly reported temporal grid against which the daily life of Oskar and his family is carefully (if entirely idiosyncratically) plotted. Oskar's boyhood years, chronicled *in extenso* and with great imagination, coincide with the rise of Nazism in the Reich and in Danzig and conclude with the death first of his mother and then of Jan Bronski, 'mein mutmaßlicher Vater' (187) / 'my presumptive father' (230), whose death coincides with the fall of the Polish Post Office in Danzig in September 1939. The rapid triumph and eventual fall of Nazism form the background to Oskar's narrative of his adolescent years, during which, according to his own account, he vies with Matzerath, 'den ich der Einfachheit halber wieder meinen Vater nenne' (213) / 'whom for the sake of simplicity I shall once more call my father' (261), for the affections of 'Oskars erste Liebe' (216) / 'Oskar's first love' (264), Maria Truczinski, who duly, again according to his own account, bears him a son,

Kurt – though Kurt is regarded by everybody else, including Maria, as Matzerath's son and Oskar's brother.

During these years Oskar also becomes a member of a touring troupe of midgets that performs for the German occupying forces in France, where he duly sees the Western Front at first hand and witnesses the death of another love, his exotic fellow midget Roswitha Raguna, who, 'durch die beginnende Invasion geweckt' / 'wakened by the beginnings of the invasion,' leaves Oskar's bed to fetch his coffee on the morning of 6 June 1944, and 'erreichte den heißen Morgenkaffee gleichzeitig mit einer dort einschlagenden Schiffsgranate' (285) / 'reached the steaming hot morning coffee exactly at the same time as a shell from a naval gun' (345). Returning home a sadder and a wiser man, Oskar briefly throws in his lot with a street gang of juvenile delinquents in the dying months of the war. As Russian forces in turn invade a ruined Danzig in June 1945, he witnesses the death of Matzerath, shot by a jumpy young recruit as he attempts to dispose of the incriminating evidence of his Nazi party pin.

Oskar's adult years begin at Matzerath's funeral, where either a second blow to the head or a fall or another conscious decision – for this is one of the points where Oskar generously provides us with several possible but conflicting explanations – causes him to resume his interrupted growth, though only at the expense of developing a twisted back and a pronounced hump, whereupon Oskar, now twenty-one years old and four feet tall rather than three, decides to flee Danzig and travel west with Maria and Kurt in search of fame and fortune. As the Economic Miracle of the West German postwar years slowly begins to create a new prosperity for all, Oskar becomes in succession a stone mason specializing in grave markers, an artists' model, and, eventually, a highly celebrated drummer in a jazz band. His efforts to assert himself as Kurt's father, however, fail, his marriage proposal to Maria is likewise rejected, and he becomes involved in a series of abortive sexual liaisons, always with nurses, one of whom he is eventually suspected of having murdered. Oskar flees the country, but gets only as far as Paris before he is arrested, eventually convicted of murder, and found to be criminally insane. As he finishes his five-hundred-page account, it is two years later, it is his thirtieth birthday, and he is still, as he volunteered in his first sentence, the inmate of a mental hospital.

II

Thus, at any rate, the general outline of Oskar's story – and that, of course, is the problem, for the whole thing *is* precisely Oskar's story, not only the story *of* Oskar but also and very emphatically the story *by* Oskar. Oskar himself obligingly draws our attention at an early stage to the most essential characteristic of any story: its arrangeability. 'Wie fange ich an?' / 'How shall I begin?' Oskar, as narrator, asks himself and the reader with ostensible ingenuousness and proceeds to develop one or two of the options available:

Man kann eine Geschichte in der Mitte beginnen und vorwärts wie rückwärts kühn ausschreitend Verwirrung anstiften. Man kann sich modern geben, alle Zeiten, Entfernungen wegstreichen und hinterher verkünden oder verkünden lassen, man habe endlich und in letzter Stunde das Raum-Zeit-Problem gelöst. Man kann auch ganz zu Anfang behaupten, es sei heutzutage unmöglich, einen Roman zu schreiben, dann aber, sozusagen hinter dem eigenen Rücken, einen kräftigen Knüller hinlegen, um schließlich als letztmöglicher Romanschreiber dazustehen. (11)

You can begin a story in the middle and create confusion by striking out boldly, backward and forward. You can be modern, put aside all mention of time and distance and, when the whole thing is done, proclaim, or have someone else proclaim, that you have finally, at the last moment, solved the space-time problem. Or you can declare at the very start that it's impossible to write a novel nowadays, but then, behind your own back so to speak, give birth to a whopper, a novel to end all novels. (17)

There are, indeed, any number of ways in which one can begin a story – and develop and conclude a story as well. In fact, by the time Oskar is assailed by such narratological considerations, his own narrative is already well under way: he has drawn attention to his status as a psychiatric patient, discussed the artistic tendencies of his keeper Bruno, described his white-painted hospital bed with the bars, the embarrassment of visiting days, the commissioned purchase of a sufficient quantity of paper by Bruno, and Bruno's account of the furious blushes of the salesgirl who filled Oskar's order for five hundred sheets of 'unschuldiges Papier' (10) / 'innocent paper' (16).

Oskar's reflections on how one *might* begin a narrative might very well distract the reader's attention not only from their overt spuriousness (in that he *has* already begun) but also from the fact that both the single most important thematic concern of *Die Blechtrommel* on the one hand and its central narrative strategy on the other have also already been clearly marked in the ostensibly peripheral reference to the salesgirl's blushes. The very buying of the paper for Oskar's narrative is already implicated in the dialectic of *Schuld* and *Unschuld*, guilt and innocence, that is the central theme of Grass's quasi-historical novel of all too successful *Vergangenheitsbewältigung*, 'mastery of the past,' as the German phrase has it – but the weightiness of such a theme finds expression by narrative means that are flauntedly inappropriate. Here the incipient theme of a nation's guilt, rather than being presented as the cataclysmic result of some national pact of mythic dimensions with the forces of evil, is reduced to its trivialized lowest common denominator, the entirely everyday guilty conscience of entirely everyday people who are no better than they should be. In the process it is demonstrated that what society defines as guilt or the lack of it is a constructed and freely assignable quality: we witness neither the salesgirl's implied lack of innocence nor even her blushes; neither, moreover, does Oskar, who simply reports Bruno's report. Unless, of course, he even more simply invents it, for we notice the suspiciously appropriate introduction at precisely this point of a colour symbolism that will pervade his entire account: the salesgirl's red blushes concerning white paper foreshadow the red flames with which Koljaiczek burns down white sawmills, the red and white of the Polish flag and of nurse's uniforms and of Oskar's tin drum that produces such artistic rearrangements of old favourites.[4]

The cumulative guilt of the nightmare years of German history is refracted and rearranged most overtly in Oskar's grotesquely distorted narrative of his own personal guilt and/or lack of it. Oskar's account, after all, is that of an insane killer, at least as far as the courts are concerned, which have found that he did indeed, though insane, kill one Sister Dorothea Köngetter – whom Oskar freely admits to having also unsuccessfully attempted to rape on an earlier occasion. In the closing pages of his narrative, however, Oskar's thirtieth birthday brings what his lawyer calls 'einen glücklichen Zufall' (484) / 'a happy coincidence' (578) with the discovery that the murder was 'in fact' the handiwork of a jealous fellow nurse instead. The case is to be reopened, Oskar will be set free, as Oskar claims – and Oskar, again as Oskar claims, is terrified at the prospect, much preferring the safety of his hospital bed to any freedom the outside world can offer him. The text offers considerable (though not conclusive) support for the case that Oskar did indeed kill Sister Dorothea (476–77/569); what is of more compelling interest to us here, however, is the suspiciously theatrical discovery, as the curtain falls, of his innocence all along. For Dorothea's death is by no means the first death in which Oskar, by his own account, is involved. Indeed Oskar achieves the unique distinction, always according to his own account, of being no less than a triple parricide, for he claims at various points to be responsible for the death of all 'three' of his parents. But 'involved' is a very slippery word, and the details invite – indeed demand – considerable further scrutiny.

The first of the three deaths to occur is that of Oskar's mother. We note that though Oskar makes much of his own grief on that occasion, his account of Agnes's grotesque death – she gorges herself to death on fish – makes no mention of any feelings of guilt on his part (132). He first accuses himself – or rather reports that others accuse him – of having been responsible for his mother's death only considerably later in an impassioned speech to the exotic Roswitha, when he claims that 'everybody' says that 'Der Gnom hat sie ins Grab getrommelt. Wegen Oskarchen wollte sie nicht mehr weiterleben, er hat sie umgebracht!' (138) / 'The gnome drummed her into her grave. Because of Oskar she didn't want to live any more; he killed her' (171). Immediately afterwards Oskar admits that he 'übertrieb reichlich, wollte womöglich Signora Roswitha beeindrucken' (138) / 'was exaggerating quite a bit, probably to impress Signora Roswitha' (171), since in fact most people blamed Matzerath and Bronski for her death. Only two or three pages later, however, Oskar abruptly reverses his story and informs the reader that he did indeed hear his grandmother saying that Agnes died 'wail se das Jetrommel nich mä hätt vertragen megen' (141) / 'because she couldn't stand the drumming any more' (174), and immediately begins his next paragraph with the admission 'Wenn schon schuldig am Tod meiner armen Mama ...' (141) / 'Even though guilty of my poor mama's death ...' (174).

Oskar, in other words, apparently expects the reader to take at face value the admission of guilt that he himself has just conceded was simply a ruse to make himself more interesting in Roswitha's Mediterranean eyes the last time he admitted (or claimed) it. Has Oskar had a change of heart in between, been granted the major insight that he was not, after all, exaggerating when he spun what he thought was a fancy tale for Roswitha's benefit? At any rate, Oskar seems to think so (or wants to make us think so): some sixty pages later he talks of his involvement in Jan Bronski's death as definitely 'meine zweite große Schuld' / 'my second great burden of guilt,' for

Ich kann es mir nie, selbst bei wehleidigster Stimmung nicht verschweigen: meine Trommel, nein, ich selbst, der Trommler Oskar, brachte zuerst meine arme Mama, dann den Jan Bronski, meinen Onkel und Vater, ins Grab. (201)

Even when I feel most sorry for myself, I cannot deny it: it was my drum, no, it was

I myself, Oskar the drummer, who dispatched first my poor mama, then Jan Bronski, my uncle and father, to their graves. (247)

The occasion of Bronski's death was the quixotically futile defence of the Polish Post Office in September 1939. As Oskar presents it, however, Bronski is no hero prepared to die for his beliefs, defending his homeland against the German oppressor. In fact, Jan had already fled the Post Office once and finds himself there again only because Oskar persuades him to take him there to ask the janitor Kobyella to repair one of his broken tin drums. And far from fighting for his country, Bronski is discovered after the battle in a back room, half dead with fear, dazedly attempting to play a three-handed card game with Kobyella, who is quietly bleeding to death, and Oskar, who reveals himself as an expert card player and has little patience with the sloppy play of the other two. Jan is duly taken away to be shot by the quickly victorious Germans, the Queen of Hearts still pathetically clutched in his hand as the condemned man waves a last goodbye to a grieving Oskar.

Or something like that, at any rate, for Oskar begins his next chapter by observing that he has just reread the account of Bronski's arrest and is not entirely satisfied. Moreover:

Wenn ich auch nicht zufrieden bin, sollte es um so mehr Oskars Feder sein, denn ihr ist es gelungen, knapp, zusammenfassend, dann und wann im Sinne einer bewußt knapp zusammenfassenden Abhandlung zu übertreiben, wenn nicht zu lügen. (200)

Even though I am not too well pleased, Oskar's pen ought to be, for writing tersely and succinctly, it has managed, as terse, succinct accounts so often do, to exaggerate and mislead, if not to lie. (246)

There are three separate points that need correction, in fact, for Oskar 'möchte bei der Wahrheit bleiben, Oskars Feder in den Rücken fallen und hier berichtigen' (200) / 'wishes to stick to the truth, to go behind Oskar's pen's back and make a few corrections' (246). First, Jan's final hand had been incorrectly described, for it was 'kein Grandhand, sondern ein Karo ohne Zwein' / 'not a grand hand but a diamond hand without twos.' Second, Oskar left not just with a new drum he had accidentally found, as previously reported, but with his old one as well, just in case. And third, 'ferner bleibt noch zu ergänzen' / 'a little omission that needs filling in,' when the soldiers led the defenders out of the Post Office,

stellte sich Oskar schutzsuchend zwischen zwei onkelhaft wirkende Heim-
wehrmänner, imitierte klägliches Weinen und wies auf Jan, seinen Vater, mit
anklagenden Gesten, die den Armen zum bösen Mann machten, der ein unschuldiges Kind in die Polnische Post geschleppt hatte, um es auf polnisch unmenschliche
Weise als Kugelfang zu benutzen. (200)

Oskar made up to two Home Guards who looked like good-natured uncles, pre-
tended he was looking for protection, put on an imitation of pathetic sniveling, and
pointed to Jan, his father, with accusing gestures that transformed the poor man
into a villain who had dragged off an innocent child into the Polish Post Office to
use him, with typically Polish inhumanity, as a buffer for enemy bullets. (246)

Oskar's ruse, he reports, saves his two drums, as he had planned it would,
from any possible damage – while Jan is conscientiously kicked and beaten
by the properly scandalized German soldiers before being led off to be
shot. Oskar's guilt still haunts him: 'Doch wie jedermann halte ich mir ...
meine Unwissenheit zugute, die damals in Mode kam und noch heute
manchem als flottes Hütchen zu Gesicht steht' (201) / 'But like everyone
else I make allowances for my ignorance, the ignorance that came into style
in those years and that even today is worn by so many like such a becoming little hat' (248).

As the Second World War, in Oskar's telling of it, opens with the Polish
Bronski's death, so it closes symmetrically with the death of the German
Matzerath, Oskar's 'other' father, who is cowering in a cellar with his family when Russian troops burst in, just as German troops had once burst
into the storage room where Jan was hiding. Matzerath had hurriedly
attempted to hide the damning evidence of his political colours by kicking
his Nazi party pin into a dark corner of the cellar, where Oskar retrieves it.
Under the eyes of the Russians, Oskar obligingly passes the pin back to
Matzerath, who, in desperation, foolishly tries to swallow it. 'Hätte er doch
zuvor ... die Nadel des Parteiabzeichens geschlossen' (327) / 'If only he had
first ... closed the pin' (394), Oskar observes in retrospect. As it is, the fran-
tically gagging Matzerath is saved from choking to death only because one
of the Russians equally obligingly 'ein ganzes Magazin leerschoß, schoß,
bevor Matzerath ersticken konnte' (327) / 'emptied a whole magazine into
him before Matzerath could suffocate' (394).

As in the case of Bronski's death, Oskar's complicity is again evident,
but the form of its presentation makes it read as though arising from a
childish lack of understanding at worst. Oskar admittedly claims he had in
fact first fought his 'son' Kurt for the discarded pin on the grounds that it

would be far too dangerous for Kurt to have if the Russians found it, yet he casually passes it (the pin thoughtfully opened) to his presumptive father allegedly because he needs free hands to pick a louse off the collar of one of the Russians – then promptly loses interest in the lice and goes back to watching a column of marching ants. Perhaps it was not the right thing to do, Oskar admits in retrospect: 'Man kann jetzt sagen, das hätte ich nicht tun sollen. Man kann aber auch sagen, Matzerath hätte nicht zuzugreifen brauchen' (327) / 'You may say I shouldn't have done that. But one could also say that Matzerath didn't have to take it' (393). One can, in fact, once again, say anything one wants, and this is a freedom Oskar exercises to the full.

In the deaths of all 'three' of his parents, Oskar's complicity is multiply presented. In Matzerath's case Oskar initially portrays himself as an innocently playing child, goes on to recognize some degree of guilt in admitting that some might say he shouldn't have done what he did, then rejects this suggestion by observing that Matzerath wasn't forced to act the way he did either. In Bronski's case Oskar first portrays himself as an innocent bystander, then reveals (or portrays) himself as having contributed to his death. Does the fact, however, that one version of the arrest follows the other necessarily make the second more true than the first? Or is it too no more than a temporarily convenient formulation that may also have to be revised at some appropriate point? In Agnes's case he first shows himself as the grief-stricken child (132/161), then as guilty of her death (138/171), then as merely exaggerating his guilt (138/171), then as guilty after all (141/ 174, 201/247).

Perhaps the most revealing example of Oskar's 'guilt' as narrated by himself, however, is his account of his grandfather's death. Joseph Koljaiczek is first said by Oskar to have drowned while on the run from the police, attempting to make good his escape by swimming out to a raft in the mouth of the Mottlau River. Apparently there are those who do not accept this story, however.

Man hat die Leiche meines Großvaters nie gefunden. Ich, der ich fest daran glaube, daß er unter dem Floß seinen Tod schaffte, muß mich, um glaubwürdig zu bleiben, hier dennoch bequemen, all die Versionen wunderbarer Rettungen wiederzugeben. (27)

My grandfather's body was never found. Though I have no doubt whatever that he met his death under the raft, I suppose if I am to retain my credibility I have to put down all of the variants in which he was miraculously rescued. (36)

In order to remain thus 'credible,' Oskar goes on to give these competing versions – other people's, not his own – of how Koljaiczek met his end. One of these is that Koljaiczek simply hid under the raft until it was dark, then escaped unscathed on a Greek tanker. Another is that Koljaiczek swam under water clear across the river, emerged undetected on the other side, and eventually left the country on a Greek tanker – 'hier trifft sich die erste mit der zweiten Rettungsversion' (27) / 'here the first two versions converge' (37). Only 'der Vollständigkeit halber' / 'for the sake of completeness' does Oskar mention 'die dritte unsinnige Fabel' / 'the third preposterous fable' that his grandfather is washed out to sea, picked up by Swedish sailors, escapes to Sweden, 'und so weiter, und so weiter' / 'and so on and so on' (27). Even more nonsensical than all this 'Unsinn und Fischergeschwätz' / 'nonsense and fishermen's fish stories' is the further fairy tale that his grandfather was seen five years or so later in Buffalo, New York, by now a highly successful businessman under the name of Joe Colchic (27/37).

Oskar tells Koljaiczek's story (or stories) to Bruno and his friends Klepp and Vittlar on one of the visiting days in the psychiatric hospital, when his two friends, to amuse him and each other, 'parodierten Szenen aus meinem Prozeß' (28) / 'parodied scenes from my trial' (38). Asked which version they prefer, Bruno finds death by drowning 'ein schöner Tod' (29) / 'a beautiful death' (38) and advises Oskar against belief in any of the competing versions, while Klepp merely shrugs off the question and claims to be too tired to choose. Vittlar, whose testimony had first alerted the police to Oskar's complicity in the death of Sister Dorothea, choosing first to believe in Koljaiczek's death by drowning, accuses Oskar with theatrical emphasis of (another) double parricide – of the murder not just of his grandfather, after all, but also and simultaneously of his grand uncle (through Jan Bronski, who is Agnes's cousin). Then, 'aus einem Pathos ins andere springend' (29) / 'with a quick transition from one brand of pathos to another' (39), Vittlar parodically prophesies that Oskar will some day be found innocent – and thus set free to find his vanished grandfather in America. Though Oskar claims he finds Vittlar's words both sardonic and offensive, he also claims they give him a 'Gewißheit,' a 'certainty' provided neither by Bruno (who accepts one story as the definitive one) nor by Klepp (who refuses to privilege any one of them). In Vittlar's deliberate refusal to treat any one of the narratives as superior to the others, and thus left still with at least two versions of the story to play with – with Koljaiczek neither definitively dead nor definitively alive; or rather, with Koljaiczek *either* dead or alive as needed – Oskar has exactly the 'certainty' he needs.

Da lobe ich mir doch Vittlars Großväter konservierendes Amerika, das angenommene Ziel, das Vorbild, an dem ich mich aufrichten kann, wenn ich europasatt die Trommel und Feder aus der Hand geben will: 'Schreib weiter, Oskar, tu es für deinen schwerreichen, aber müden, in Buffalo USA Holzhandel treibenden Großvater Koljaiczek, der im Inneren seines Wolkenkratzers mit Streichhölzern spielt!' (29–30)

God bless Vittlar's America, preserver of grandfathers, goal and ideal by which to rehabilitate myself when, weary of Europe, I decide to lay down my drum and pen: 'Write on, Oskar. Do it for your grandfather, the rich but weary Koljaiczek, the lumber king of Buffalo, USA, playing with matches in his skyscraper.' (40)

Oskar's function as narrator is likewise above all to play, to play with versions of a truth that is always essentially narrative rather than experiential – and consequently always plural rather than singular, generating multiple meanings rather than a single definitive meaning, denominating possibilities rather than actuality. It is hardly surprising that Oskar, sentenced to a lifetime in a hospital for the criminally insane, chooses to end his account by accepting Vittlar's 'prophecy' that he will be found innocent of Sister Dorothea's murder and set free again. It does not have to be true, for in Oskar's world narrativity is always more important than truth: Oskar's motto as maker of stories is certainly the apocryphal tag *Se non è vero, è ben trovato* 'It may not be true, but it's a beautiful story.'

We are at liberty as psychologically acute readers to interpret Oskar's evasiveness in matters of personal guilt as symptomatic of an obsessively guilty conscience, his conscious or unconscious desire to direct attention away from his real guilt in the death of Sister Dorothea leading to extravagantly exaggerated self-accusation in cases where he is either obviously innocent (Koljaiczek), very likely innocent (Agnes), or in all likelihood only peripherally involved as a possible minor contributing factor (Bronski would have been shot anyway, Matzerath might well have survived if he had not panicked so disastrously). But to indulge in such an eminently reasonable interpretation is to fall spectacularly into the hermeneutic mantrap that is the central characteristic of *Die Blechtrommel* as a whole, namely, that we take seriously stories that are quite literally entirely impossible to believe. For Oskar himself, like most of the stories he so flamboyantly tells, is a quite impossible invention – as Oskar himself is so repeatedly at extravagant pains to remind us. But because Oskar calls himself *ich* and tells us the story of his life, we diligently and even obsessively set about turning Oskar into a human being with all the psychological attributes we feel comfortable in assuming such a human being in such a set of circumstances would very likely possess or be possessed by. We believe because we want to believe – want perhaps above all to believe that however odd things may seem to be, there must surely be a rational explanation.

The satirical implications for Grass's German readership in 1959 are patent. *Die Blechtrommel*, however, does not neatly identify for us what is right and wrong and then call on us for our agreement. Its interest is not in answers but in questions – and the variety of possible answers and pseudo-answers that the right kinds of question might lead to. Oskar is generous with the number of possible answers he provides, so generous that we are evidently invited as readers to consider whether these quasi-answers might not better be regarded merely as restatements of the questions they ostensibly claim to answer.

Critics have indulged in vigorous debate as to which sides of Oskar's narrated personality represent the real Oskar, which of his narrated actions are real and which only fantasized. But in the end the only thing we can be sure of about Oskar is precisely that he *narrates*. Oskar is less the literary simulacrum of a human being than a disembodied narrative voice; an 'Ankleidepuppe' (76), a 'dressmaker's dummy' (95), who is less a character than a literary device; a 'realized contrivance,' in Ann Mason's phrase (1974: 28), for generating possible narratives inviting possible responses – including extratextual narratives that are implied rather than narrated, possible narratives implied by impossible narratives. *Die Blechtrommel* insistently exemplifies Shklovsky's dictum that literature is a device for making strange, for making us see things in a new light – or rather, for *allowing* us to see things in a new light if we choose to do so, for literature can never force the reader to do anything, only make it possible (or more attractive) to do certain things rather than (or as well as) others.

The narrative art of *Die Blechtrommel* is an art of indirection, allowing us to glimpse things not by making us stare straight at them but by directing our attention to something beside them or beyond them or where they should be but are missing or to something else entirely that might remind us of them, whether because of the existence of some more or less logical connection or, more often, because of an implied connection that is outrageously inappropriate.[5] Grass's brilliant use of disturbingly astigmatic objective correlatives has been noted by almost all critics. Agnes's long-drawn-out dying is introduced by a meticulous description of her vomited breakfast (121/150); the greengrocer Greff's suicide is counterpointed by a 'Waschschüssel mit der grauen Seifenlauge vom Vortage' / a 'washbasin with the grey soapsuds from the previous day' in a dingy room that needed

Greff's death 'um zu neuem, erschreckend kaltem Glanz zu kommen' (258) / 'to achieve a new, terrifyingly cold radiance' (313); Matzerath's death fails to disturb a column of marching ants, for the sugar they are salvaging from a burst sack 'hatte während der Besetzung der Stadt Danzig durch die Armee Marschall Rokossowskis nichts von seiner Süße verloren' (328) / 'had lost none of its sweetness while Marshal Rokossovski was occupying the city of Danzig' (395).[6]

Gaudily painted 'symbols' whose flaunted symbolicity invites scepticism likewise abound, the most relevant of them in our present context being that 'schwarze Köchin,' literally the 'Black Cook,' though Manheim prefers to call her the 'Black Witch' – 'Fragt Oskar nicht, wer sie ist! Er hat keine Worte mehr' (493) / 'Don't ask Oskar who she is! Words fail him' (589) – whose (alleged) omnipresence allows Oskar to conclude his account with a gratifying portrayal of abject existential terror. So overwhelming is this terror that the reader might well forget Oskar's previous claim that his fright was initially self-induced, so as to lend some realistic motivation to his flight – 'Ohne Furcht keine Flucht!' (486) / 'No fright, no flight' (580). The flight in turn was allegedly undertaken merely out of consideration for his friend Vittlar, who has just turned him in to the police; and Vittlar's denunciation, for its part, was 'in fact' at Oskar's generous suggestion, since Vittlar had always wished to see his name in the papers (482/576).

From this network of fictions and counterfictions one thing at least emerges clearly. Grass's text is certainly 'about' guilt and innocence, *Schuld* and *Unschuld*, as many critics have already observed, but to spend our time analysing Oskar's own putative guilt or innocence (as more than one critic has done) is to allow ourselves to be badly sidetracked. Lester Caltvedt has more usefully argued that the point of Oskar's discursive tergiversations is to draw attention to the *fact* of unacknowledged historical guilt itself (1978: 287). But while this may certainly be the main satiric thrust of Grass's text, it is evident that from the point of view of textual semiotics *Die Blechtrommel* is most centrally about the narrative processes by which the categories of guilt and innocence are discursively constructed and construed.

The reflexivity and unreliability of Oskar's account are underscored, paradoxically, by the fact that he allows parts of it to be narrated by two other narrators, whose independent testimony might perhaps be expected to serve as yardsticks against which Oskar's own account might be measured. The two narrators in question, however, are Vittlar and Bruno, and each of their narratives, while in some degree corrective of Oskar's own account, quickly reveals itself as equally untrustworthy – if not entirely Oskar's own invention. Vittlar, a window dresser by trade, is first discovered lying in the fork of an apple tree and takes the opportunity himself of drawing attention to inviting biblical parallels (470). 'Vittlar liebte es immer schon, mich zu verwirren' (484) / 'Vittlar always liked to confuse me' (578). His account (471–83/563–76) largely concerns Oskar's fantastic rescue of Viktor Weluhn, a one-time defender of the Polish Post Office, from the hands of the West German police in 1952 and hardly inspires confidence in Vittlar as an independent witness. Bruno Münsterberg, 'er hinter dem Guckloch, ich vor dem Guckloch' (11) / 'him on his side of the peephole, me on mine' (17), provides an account of Oskar's flight from Danzig (348–56/419–28) that is in a considerably more sober style, but, to say the least, is also rendered somewhat suspect by Bruno's own artistic leanings. For Bruno, like Oskar, is an artist, 'knotet ordinäre Bindfäden ... zu vielschichtig verknorpelten Gespenstern, taucht diese dann in Gips, läßt sie erstarren' (9) / 'knots ordinary pieces of string ... into elaborate contorted spooks, dips them in plaster, lets them harden' (15), discusses with Oskar whether they would be more effective if he added colour. Listening to Oskar's stories, Bruno reshapes them in string and plaster – but like Oskar he is frequently dissatisfied with the end result, and 'was ich rechts knüpfe, löse ich links auf, was meine Linke bildet, zertrümmert meine geballte Rechte' (352) / 'what I knot with my right hand, I undo with my left; what my left hand creates, my right fist shatters' (424).

Bruno and Vittlar alike are members of a series of quasi-artist figures that ghost through the pages of *Die Blechtrommel*. They include Oskar's friend Klepp, who assists Oskar in cutting up and reassembling passport photos of themselves, creating, they hope, new and happier combinations (40/52); Bebra, leader of a troupe of midget circus acrobats, whose most successful trick is knowing how always to be on the winning side; Roswitha Raguna, *femme fatale* and most famous somnambulist of all Italy; Schugger Leo, who is gloriously mad and conjures up glowing visions of redemption before he dies riddled with bullets; Meyn the SA man who plays the trumpet so beautifully when not otherwise engaged; and Corporal Lankes, who has a thing about nuns, casually machine-gunning a group of them during the war, equally casually raping another after the war, and subsequently establishing an artistic reputation as a painter of accomplished studies of nuns. Grass himself notes in an interview the extent to which all of these (quasi-)artist figures are hypothetical extensions of Oskar himself, 'Randfiguren als Fußnoten zu der Randfigur Oskar' / 'marginal figures as footnotes to the marginal figure Oskar,'[7] developing further possibilities of his character, synecdochic projections and reflections alike of the artist/historian's ability both to shape and to distort the reality on which he draws –

and in any event either to accept or to reject as he chooses any given degree of responsibility for the results of his labours.

III

In the end, *Die Blechtrommel*, by relentlessly urging the reader throughout to recognize the total unreliability of its narrator, invites the reader to confront the question of narrative unreliability itself, the question as to how reliable *any* discourse can ever be, since discourse is always a matter not just of presentation but of context-appropriate presentation, putting things in a particular perspective, a particular context – and your context is not necessarily mine, nor mine yours. What is true of literary narrative is equally true of historical narrative, even if one of the most enduring generic conventions of the latter has been the concealment of its own fictionality. The readiness with which Oskar admits to or even eagerly claims guilt for events which are clearly not his responsibility overtly implies the possible existence of other events for which certain readers in the Germany of 1959 were perhaps equally unwilling to accept responsibility. The implied author, as we might say, draws the reader's attention to what is omitted by allowing Oskar to exaggerate grotesquely what is not omitted. By unsettling the reader's reaction to Oskar, who is allowed to present himself now as an innocent and defenceless child, now as a complete monster, now as a freedom fighter, now as the very face of Nazism itself, the textual discourse pervasively and systemically implies the degree to which the line between such comfortingly black and white positions can be a shifting one – and the degree to which the determination of that line is and must always be a matter of discourse.

Die Blechtrommel is about many things, but perhaps most centrally it is about authority and its discursive implications – and it is consequently also about reading. For this reason if for no other it may be observed that the distinction between real authors and implied authors is not merely a narratological parlour trick for the amusement of professional literary critics. It in fact defines the boundary between the type of reader who wishes to be shown conclusive answers and the reader who would prefer to attempt to discover his or her own, however tentative and provisional they may have to remain. Real authors naturally intend their work to be read in particular ways, and this is entirely as it should be. Günter Grass himself, as politician and public figure, has repeatedly stated entirely unambiguous views on the German past, present, and future. Readers who carefully set as their exclusive interpretive goal the reconstruction of the real author's real meaning, however, are readers already trapped in a particular ideology, readers who want their thinking to be done for them by someone else – and quite clearly this is exactly the kind of thinking *Die Blechtrommel* most centrally rejects. Implied authors, on the other hand, are the reader's creation, the reader's attempt to discover what a particular textual discourse may most productively be *read* as meaning in a given set of hermeneutic circumstances. The implied author I may read as being at work in *Die Blechtrommel* today is certainly not the same as the one I constructed when I first read it thirty-odd years ago, and neither of them is the same as the one I might construct in a reading ten years from now. For not only do times change and readers with them, the implied authors they construct change with them too.

Die Blechtrommel is an enormously complex work of narrative art, and to limit oneself to a single aspect of it as we have done here is merely to tease out just one strand in a very densely textured pattern. Some strands, however, will always be more important than others in any pattern, however complex, and none can ever be more fundamentally important than the nature of the discourse by means of which we gain access to the story told. In the case of *Die Blechtrommel* the semiotics of discourse, as we have seen, is overtly a semiotics of unreliability – but perhaps the most centrally important point of Grass's text is precisely that this is so in the case of *any* narrative discourse, even (or especially) those lacking so very overt an unreliable narrator to remind us of that fact.

6

Two Views:
The Authority of Discourse
in Uwe Johnson's *Zwei Ansichten*

Uwe Johnson's *Zwei Ansichten* (1965), translated into English as *Two Views*, has to date fallen very definitely in the shadow of his longer narratives.[1] Published criticism of Johnson's work has overwhelmingly focused on his *Mutmaßungen über Jakob* (1959), on *Das dritte Buch über Achim* (1961), and, above all, on the massive four-volume *Jahrestage* (1970–83). From the writer of the highly sophisticated *Mutmaßungen über Jakob* – who had himself moreover moved from East Germany to West Berlin in 1959 – *Zwei Ansichten* even seemed to early readers to be almost embarrassingly simple-minded as to its plot: a selfish and irresponsible young West German feels confusedly obliged to help his conscientious and level-headed East German girlfriend escape to the West after the building of the Berlin Wall; increasingly discouraged by the situation in East Germany, she eventually does make a successful escape attempt, but is so disillusioned by her West German boyfriend that she will have nothing more to do with him. The fact that the young people are moreover called simply B. and D. seemed a quite sufficient indication to early readers that their full names were really BRD and DDR respectively, and although East German reviewers expressed their appreciation of the book, West German reviewers were far from amused.[2] Political concerns, however, are not the sole interest of any of Johnson's works, and the following reading of *Zwei Ansichten* will concentrate instead on what is clearly an at least equally central preoccupation, namely, the complexities, the conventions, and the implications of narrative itself as a form of discourse. Read from this perspective *Zwei Ansichten* reveals itself as an intriguingly complex text in its own terms, rich in those millimetre shifts of vision, to borrow Mark Boulby's phrase (1974: 70), which have been aptly characterized as marking the essence of Johnson's highly individual style of writing. In what follows we will examine not only how its textual strategies operate in the two parallel stories suggested by the title, but also the degree to which their operation can be said to constitute a third story, also parallel, namely, that of the reader – inducing the reader in the process to question the system of the text in the same way that the characters come to question the nature of the reality in which they find themselves. Their individual realities, however, are sufficiently different to warrant reading the three narratives as operating in three quite distinct typological modes, classifiable respectively as realism, modernism, and postmodernism.

I

The narrative – which carries no conventional generic descriptor such as *Roman*, *Novelle*, or *Erzählung* – is divided into ten chapters, focusing alternately on its two main characters, the young West German photographer B. and the East German nurse D., with whom he fancies himself in love. Nurse D. is not the only object of his desires, however, and in the opening chapter, which focuses on B., we become aware of her existence only gradually, while his love of expensive fast cars is immediately reported. 'Der junge Herr B. konnte die Hand auf großes Geld legen und kaufte einen Sportwagen' (7) / 'Young Herr B. managed to lay hold of a large sum, and bought a sports car' (3), the text begins, without preamble.[3] 'Young B.' – he is in fact twenty-five years old, but the formula 'der junge Herr B.' is employed consistently throughout – is a freelance photographer for the local newspaper of an unnamed small town in Holstein – and for anybody else who is willing to pay him. For B., as it very quickly emerges, is completely untroubled by unnecessary scruples when profits are at stake. His newly acquired riches come from reselling his last two years' work to the local tourist board. 'Leider war das Geschäft erst zustande gekommen,' the text reports in lapidary fashion, 'nachdem B. verzichtet hatte auf einige Bilder, die die städtischen Hilfen für Alte und Bedürftige zeigten wie sie waren. Tage danach noch beim Rasieren wandte er den Kopf, wenn er im Spiegel auf die eigenen Augen traf' (7) / 'Unfortunately, the deal had gone through only after B. had agreed to withdraw some pictures that showed the town's assistance program for the aged and needy as it was. For days afterwards, while shaving, B. turned his head whenever he met his own eyes in the mirror' (4). From the beginning the text is at pains to make clear B.'s status as a completely hollow man, opportunistic, casually venal, totally self-centred, and entirely immature. He believes himself to be in love with Nurse D. because he has learned from the cinema what being in love means

(26/18), and he casts himself in the role of her rescuer from East German captivity because he shares with 'die illustrierten Blätter' (152) / 'the illustrated magazines' (115) an unshakeable regard for the threatened sanctity of the individual. He has no compunctions at all, however, we notice in passing, about attempting to buy off the outgrown affections of a previous girlfriend with the gift of an old car, likewise outgrown, once he acquires the money to buy a better one.

This somewhat dubious knight in shining armour has to brave a very twentieth-century enchanted forest, namely, the now-divided metropolis of Berlin, in order to rescue his damsel in distress. B. takes up arms bravely, drives into West Berlin, 'den Rücken gesteift' (14) / 'well set up' (9), in the first flush of ownership of his new red sports car, 'glaubte sich mit gleichem Recht eingeordnet in die Kolonnen, die um den Raum zwischen den langen Hausblocks kämpften ... In Lokalen war der Autoschlüssel doch nicht lange in der Tasche geblieben, lag auf dem Tisch jedem Blick offen' (14) / 'felt just as entitled to take his place in the columns of cars that fought for room between the long rows of buildings ... In restaurants the car key did not remain in his pocket long; it soon appeared on the table, exposed to everyone's eyes' (9). B.'s unspoken challenge is quickly taken up, unfortunately for him, and during his very first night in West Berlin his prize possession, 'sein rotes Ding' (15) / 'his red thingy' (10), is quietly, efficiently, and irrevocably stolen from under his hotel room window.

This primal defeat characterizes the future course of all B.'s dealings with 'die fremde Stadt' (8) / 'the alien city' (4), where it now seems to him that 'alle einen Bescheid wußten, den er hätte kennen sollen' (18) / 'everybody knew what he should have known' (12). His major preoccupation, indeed, more important even than the shattering loss of his car, is not to give the appearance of being a mere 'Besuch aus einer unwissenden Provinz' (19), a 'visitor from the ignorant sticks' (13). For it is August 1961, and Berlin, dramatically split by its Wall, is not just any town. 'Sein Unglück schien ihm eigentlich blamabel. Er glaubte versagt zu haben vor der größeren Stadt, die seine Schulbücher und Zeitungen gefährlicher gemalt hatten als andere, beschämender für den, der da scheiterte' (24) / 'His misfortune really seemed shameful to him. He felt that he had failed in his encounter with the big city, which his school books and newspapers had painted as more dangerous than others; all the more humiliating for anyone who came to grief there' (17). Berlin, in fact, rapidly becomes a personal labyrinth for B. – as it did for many people after August 1961. In B.'s case, however, as we shall see, it is a personally *constructed* labyrinth – but that will not make it any easier to escape. Rather than escaping it, however, B.'s initial ambition emerges as being to become an indistinguishable part of it. After the theft of his car he turns increasingly to alcohol as an alternative provider of security, and occasionally, late at night in some tavern or other, 'da dachte B. es schon gefunden zu haben. Er war hier, um unter dem hellen Licht in Ruhe nachzudenken, da sollte mal einer kommen. Zweck seines Besuches in dieser Stadt war, leise mitzulachen in dem Gespräch, das ihn umstellte' (34) / 'then B. felt he had put his finger on it. He was here to think quietly under the bright light, no-one could fool him. The purpose of his visit in this city was to laugh softly along with others in the conversation that sur-rounded him' (24).

This alcoholic insight does not last, however, and B.'s indulgence in it is an early indication – to the reader, at any rate, if not to B. – of the degree to which he is already losing control of the situation and of himself. B.'s job, as a photographer, is precisely to retain clarity of vision, to compose reality, to control relationships, to work with ordered information; his turning to alcohol involves a concomitant blurring of outlines, an increasing loss of control, a trafficking precisely in disordered rather than ordered informa-tion – and Berlin, as far as B. is concerned, is precisely an informational labyrinth. 'Er glaubte sich angenommen in der Stadt, seit er sich nicht mehr verfuhr im unterirdischen Bahnnetz, seit er einem Einheimischen hatte eine Straße weisen können, er glaubte sich wunder wie vertraut und eingesessen, wenn er gängige Ausdrücke benutzte' (143) / 'He thought himself accepted by the city since he no longer took wrong trains in the underground net-work, since he had been able to give a native directions; he thought himself really familiar and established when he was able to use the latest slang' (109), as the narrator ironically observes, but clearly his belief is based on insufficient real as opposed to assumed information. 'Die fremde Stadt,' the 'alien city,' will remain alien for B., an information system beyond his capacity to process. Both his initial feeling of overwhelming inadequacy vis-à-vis the faceless powers that hold D. captive and his gradual horrified realization that he has trapped himself into actually doing something about it none the less – 'andere hatten es geschafft, er war nicht freizusprechen' (164) / 'others had done it; he could not be acquitted' (124) – are essentially a function of this overall failure.

This is evident in the frequent use of dislocation motifs in the presenta-tion of B. throughout. The relationship between sharply seen details and fuzzily focused wholes is striking, for example, as B. encounters a chance acquaintance:

Über der schwarzglasigen Brille die Augenbrauen nicht, die Lippen nicht, erst eine übers Ohr in die Haare greifende Handbewegung brachte ihn auf eine schnelle betrunkene Nacht und den Fahrstuhl, in dem er mit diesem Mädchen auf und nieder gefahren war, seine Handrücken auf den Schaltknöpfen und in den Händen ihren Rücken. (16)

Above dark glasses neither her eyebrows, nor her lips, but finally a movement of her hand as she smoothed her hair about her ear, reminded him of a fastmoving, drunken night and the elevator in which he had ridden up and down with this girl, the backs of his hands, clasped behind her back, pressed against the elevator buttons. (11)

Nurse D. is little clearer in his memory:

Er wußte nicht erheblich mehr, als sein Gedächtnis ihm aufbewahrt hatte, meist Anblicke, Lichtverteilungen, zum Beispiel Morgensonne unter der Vorhangkante, schlafkrumme Hand, schneeiges Waldstück mit kurzen Fußspuren; aber ihr Gesicht nur mit Mühe, und nicht oft. (37)

He did not know very much more than his memory had preserved for him, mostly glimpses, distributions of light, for example, morning sunlight under the edge of the curtain, hand curled in sleep, snowy patches of woods with small footprints; but her face only with effort, and not often. (26)

In each case here the photographer's eye searches out the pregnant detail – and in each case the whole is obscured or even erased by the obtrusion of the details which allegedly go to make it up. Individuals deconstruct into assemblages of constituent details of dubious overall relevance, essentially reflecting B.'s own disjointed perception – we notice the role of B.'s consciousness as manipulated object rather than shaping subject in each of these passages: 'erst eine ... Handbewegung brachte *ihn* auf eine schnelle betrunkene Nacht' / 'finally a movement of her hand ... reminded *him* of a fastmoving, drunken night'; 'er wußte nicht erheblich mahr, als *ihm* sein Gedächtnis aufbewahrt hatte' / 'he did not know very much more than his memory had preserved *for him*.'

The relationship of actions and reactions is frequently similar. Distraction and self-estrangement become the hallmarks of his increasingly disturbed behaviour. He obsessively tries to phone D. in East Berlin, even though he is vaguely aware that it may cost her her job: 'Er wußte nicht wozu, und versuchte sie zu erreichen' (27) / 'He did not know what for, and tried to reach her' (19). He is gripped by a sudden and irresistible necessity to fly back to Berlin, does so, and 'wußte aber nicht warum er unterwegs war' (30–1) / 'did not know why he had set out' (22). 'Auf der Fahrt zum Flughafen war er so verlegen um einen Grund für die Reise, er trieb den Taxichauffeur zur Eile an' (31) / 'On the ride to the airport he was so much at a loss for a reason for this trip that he urged the cab driver to hurry' (22). When somebody he was supposed to meet fails to appear, 'war er wütend über die versetzte Verabredung, da fiel ihm ein, daß der Sonntag ausgemacht war, nicht der Sonnabend, um den er früher gefahren war' (71) / 'he was furious over the missed appointment, then it occurred to him that Sunday had been agreed upon, not the Saturday he had come earlier for' (53). He spends an entire night travelling from Berlin to Hamburg and from Hamburg to Stuttgart in order to demand compensation from the wealthy family of the young man who turns out to have stolen his car, but the obvious expensiveness of the furniture in their entrance hall 'lenkte ihn ab, so daß er eher liebenswürdig die Hausherrin begrüßte, die ihn lange hatte warten lassen' (87) / 'so distracted him that he was quite amiable in his greeting to the mistress of the house, who had made him wait a good long time' (65). This episode strongly reinforces his profound 'Empfindung der Niederlage' (89), his 'sense of defeat' (67), which is once again exacerbated by his need, as he sees it, to return as urgently as possible to Berlin, and this in spite of his newly discovered terror of flying. Fear of flying, indeed, becomes a central metaphor for B.'s growing alienation, his pervasive and crippling disconnection, his perceived failure to belong and, above all, to be taken seriously: 'Je länger er auf die im Frühlicht verschatteten Ackerfarben starrte, die unter dem Überfliegen ihren Umriß geringfügig verzogen, erschreckte ihn sein Abstand zur Erde' (68) / 'The longer he stared at the colors of the tilled fields, misted by the early-morning light, which changed their outlines slightly down below, the more he was frightened by his distance from the ground' (51).

Flying is only one of a whole network of communication channels that traverse B.'s world, underlining his failure precisely to communicate, a failure which is thematically foreshadowed even in his original acquisition of the ill-fated red sports car – B. had bought it at a highly advantageous price from an unnamed foreign tourist who had gone astray in the streets of B.'s home town and driven into the canal – 'Der Mann hätte auch weniger genommen, um das Unglücksauto und die fremde Stadt rasch verlassen zu dürfen ... B. hielt sich nicht für abergläubisch' (8) / 'the man would have taken even less to be rid of the unlucky car and the alien town ... B. did not consider himself superstitious' (4). B. becomes a tourist astray himself in the other 'fremde Stadt,' the 'alien city' of Berlin, loses his car in turn, and

promptly becomes hopelessly enmeshed and disoriented – a latter-day
Theseus – in a labyrinthine network of streets, subway lines, border crossing points, airports, planes, cars, taxis, buses, letters, telegrams, and endless
telephone calls, all of which seem to hold out invitingly the promise of
some sort of eventual communication, but all of which in the end lead
merely to a blank wall – or, to invoke the central countersymbol to that of
the network of possible communication channels in the text, a blank Wall.
The Wall, symbol of the utter negation of all communication, is nowhere
more ironically paralleled in the text than by B.'s alcoholically induced loss
of memory at the very point where he makes his crucial decision, which is
in turn no less the result of alcoholically induced emotion: his letter to D.
assuring her of his love and urging her to flee East Berlin to be with him, an
invitation 'am nächsten Tag vergessen' (138) / 'forgotten the next day'
(105).

The Wall, indeed, is the ultimate symbol of B.'s failure and of the frustra-
tion to which he becomes increasingly prey. His reaction when D. eventually does start out on her highly dangerous flight from East Germany is
typical of his will to failure, the ambiguity of his relationship with D. reach-
ing an extreme as the growing possibility of contact seems to inspire B. to
increasingly panic-stricken flight himself. When told by his contact, the
unnamed barmaid in the bar he frequents, that he can expect to see D. the
day after next, B. 'glaubte ihr nicht, er hielt ein Entkommen für nicht
möglich. Er verbrachte den Tag damit, viele Aufnahmen von der D. zu so
großem Format zu vergrößern, wie seine Schalen irgend zuließen; die
fertigen Bilder zeigten eine fremde Person, die fragend blickte' (176–7) /
'did not believe her, thought an escape impossible. He spent the day enlarg-
ing many photographs of D., blowing them up as large as his trays permitted; the finished prints showed a strange person with a questioning look'
(133). His excitement at fever pitch, he 'versaß die Nacht in Bars. Von Morgen an fuhr er stundenlang in der Untergrundbahn kreuz und quer durch
die Stadt, um die Zeit zu vertreiben' (177) / 'sat up all night in bars. From
the morning on he rode for hours in the subway, back and forth across the
city, to kill time' (133). But when the time until their meeting can at last be
reckoned in hours rather than days, B.'s behaviour becomes entirely erratic:
rather than simply continuing his vigil, however impatiently, he abruptly
'flog am Nachmittag nach Hamburg und stieg da in eine Maschine nach
Stuttgart um. Nach langen Telefongesprächen hatte eine Kraftfahrzeugfab-
rik in Württemberg zugesagt, ihm am nächsten Morgen einen Sportwagen
außer der Reihe zu verkaufen' (178) / 'flew that afternoon to Hamburg, and
changed there to a plane for Stuttgart. After lengthy telephone calls an

automobile factory in Württemberg had agreed to sell him a sports car on an immediate delivery basis the next morning' (133–4).

B.'s purpose, as it emerges, is to drive as fast as possible not straight back to Berlin, as we might have expected, but rather to Hamburg, from where he will fly to Berlin, then fly back to Hamburg again with D., who then 'hatte aus dem Flughafen in sein Auto steigen sollen' (238) / 'was supposed to have stepped out of the plane into his car' (178). The hare-brained plan comes to grief – as it was supposed to? – since the sensitive engine of the new car has not yet been run in. D. is now long since in West Berlin, as B. determines in a series of increasingly frantic phone calls to the bar, but she refuses to speak to B., who hurtles through the night towards Hamburg in his failing machine, totally exhausted, 'versucht einzuschlafen, dem Wagen seinen Willen zu lassen, mit der donnernden Uhr gegen den nächsten Brückenpfeiler zu gehen' (239) / 'tempted to fall asleep, to let the car have its head, let the thundering clockwork slam into the next pylon' (179). D.'s silence is in one way only another version of the noisy silence of 'die fremde Stadt,' the 'alien city.' B. is so tired, so overwhelmed, that in the end he even sleeps through the flight from Hamburg to Berlin 'vor Gleichgültigkeit' (239) / 'out of sheer indifference' (179). The last scene of the frantic comedy in which B. by now seems to be trapped, its potentially nightmarish quality reminiscent both of vintage Chaplin and of the demise of Josef K., is his eventual aborted arrival at the bar where he is supposed finally to meet D.: 'An der Straßenkreuzung oberhalb der Kneipe lief er bei rotem Licht gegen ein langes übermächtiges Tier von Autobus, und hatte es um die Kurve schwenken sehen. Im Fallen war er ganz zufrieden' (239) / 'At the intersection above the bar he ran across on a red light against a long, overpowering beast of a bus, and had seen it coming around the curve. As he fell he was quite content' (179).

B.'s final (fortunate?) fall, happily – as is the nature of comedy – results not in his death but only in a mild concussion. The degree, indeed, to which B.'s adventures come to demand a comic rather than a tragic reading is striking: in the end, for example, the increasingly distraught B. is the victim not only of a traffic accident but also, we notice, of a narrative joke, now literally 'zerfahren' (155)[4] – and by a bus of all things, a parodic vehicle of that communication system he has never managed to decode. His undoing, of course, does not take place without quite a bit of help on his own part – always assuming, at any rate, that we can trust to the reliability of the narration. That assumption, however, may very well be quite unwarranted, as the reader by this point is increasingly coming to appreciate. We cannot be entirely sure, indeed, in view of the phrase 'und hatte es um die Kurve

schwenken sehen' / 'and had seen it coming around the curve' whether B.'s
fall is entirely accidental or some confused, perhaps semi-delirious suicide
attempt. By the end of B.'s adventure, indeed, B. is far from being the only
one who is confused,[5] but before examining the degree to which the reader
too is enmeshed in an informational labyrinth let us look at the second
story involved in *Zwei Ansichten*, the story of D.

II

The portrayal of Nurse D., in the five even-numbered chapters, is quite different in tone from that of the hapless and hopeless B. in the other five.
While the narrator's attitude towards B. might best be characterized as one
of satirical irony verging on something close to amused contempt, his attitude towards D. is more one of only slightly ironic affection and sympathy.
D. is characterized from the beginning as a down-to-earth, responsible,
orderly, and conscientious if somewhat unimaginative person, very conscious of her obligations to her patients, her profession, her family, and her
country – even though to a large extent, as gradually emerges, she is taken
entirely for granted by all of these. D. quickly enlists our sympathy as readers too, while by the time we are finished with B. we hardly care any more
what foolish exploit he will engage in next.

D. is an East German citizen, almost twenty-one years old, and we first
encounter her in a position that effectively dramatizes the relationship of
the individual and the authoritarian system:

Die Krankenschwester D. war noch nicht lange von einer großen Klinik in Ostberlin angenommen, da bot ihr die Verwaltung einen Platz im Personalhaus des
Kombinats an. Dem Mann hinter dem Schreibtisch wischte grünes Gartenlicht
hinter seinem Rücken das Gesicht dunkel, ein Platz in einem Zweibettenzimmer
galt als Vergünstigung, sie stand. (11)

Not long after Nurse D. had been granted employment by a large hospital in East
Berlin, the administration offered her lodging in the organization's staff house. The
face of the man behind the desk was darkened by green garden light from behind his
back; a place in a two-bed room counted as a privilege; she was standing. (6)

D. does not want the shared room, however, even if the offer does represent
some degree of recognition on the part of the faceless system. She has
already, a small illegality, rented herself a furnished room of her own in the
city without getting the necessary permit, a shabby room, but one that

'bedeutete für sie den ersten Versuch, nach Elternhaus und Schule allein zu leben' (12–13) / 'meant to her a first attempt, after home and school, to live alone' (8). One of her reasons for wanting a private room rather than shared accommodation, as it emerges, is that she 'brauchte die Adresse auch für die Briefe eines jungen Westdeutschen, mit dem sie etwas angefangen hatte im Januar, eine Liebschaft, eine Bändelei, eine Woche, ein Verhältnis, einen Anfang, sie wußte das Wort nicht und nicht warum' (13) / 'needed the address for the letters of a young West German with whom she had started something in January, an affair, a flirtation, a week, a relationship, a beginning; she didn't know what to call it, nor why' (8). Clearly, the relationship is of less than vital importance to her, while the room itself is a treasured possession and a symbol of her own ability to look out for herself. What the bright red sports car is to B., her room is to D.: 'Wenn sie nun die Zimmertür verschloß, hinter der sie nicht vermutet wurde, war sie noch lange nahezu stolz. Sie hatte etwas zu verteidigen, sie hatte sich zur Wehr gesetzt, mit Erfolg' (13) / 'When she closed the door behind her now, to the room where no one knew she lived, she felt something like pride. She had something to defend; she had stood up for it, and successfully' (8).

B.'s attitude towards life is essentially aggressive and predatory, though his native rapaciousness is effectively kept in check by a massive inferiority complex. D. also suffers occasionally from feelings of inferiority – in the company of people who have been to university, for example, since she herself was not permitted by the state to study (100/76) – but she has these feelings well under control, and her attitude towards life can be characterized as essentially one of protectiveness, protectiveness of her own (and her family's) privacy, of her right to lead a productive and useful life, of her right not to be interfered with unduly or unfairly by a system which has, as she sees it, arrogated to itself the role of parent and schoolteacher in one. Scrutinized by the faceless man behind the anonymous desk, D. 'begann, sich so blond, unverdorben, vertrauenswürdig zu geben, wie der andere glauben wollte. Sie fühlte sich überhaupt an die Schule erinnert' (13) / 'tried to look as blonde, unspoiled, and trustworthy as the man wanted to believe she was. Altogether, she felt reminded of school' (6). It would, of course, be wonderful to be quite so unspoiled as the anonymous functionary and the state he represents might wish her to be; she has to make do merely with being 'nicht über die Verhältnisse hinaus verlogen' (39) / 'not a liar beyond necessity' (29) in a system where petty deception is a necessary defence against the massive deception which she suspects to be practised by the state itself upon its own citizens.

The final blow to any trust she might have been able to have in that system comes on the fateful day when West Berlin is declared to be henceforth forbidden territory: 'Am nächsten Morgen erklärten die ostdeutschen Sender die Grenzen Westberlins für gesichert, und die Rundfunksender der verbotenen Stadt übersetzten: daß ihr Gebiet gesperrt war für alle gewöhnlichen Leute aus Ostberlin und Ostdeutschland' (45) / 'Next morning the East German radio declared the borders of West Berlin secured, and the radio stations of the forbidden city translated the message: that its territory was now inaccessible to all ordinary persons from East Berlin and East Germany' (34). The contrast here between the cold impersonality of the machine (in both applications of the word) and the living individuals who are intimately affected by this anonymous decision as a matter of meat-and-potatoes reality rather than the demands of political theory – the 'ordinary persons' for whom West Berlin is simply 'inaccessible' and 'forbidden' rather than 'secured' – is patent and is central to the dilemma in which D. now increasingly finds herself involved. The dilemma hinges on the ability to trust: she had been able to forgive economic and social inefficiency, bureaucratic arrogance and stupidity, even judicial arbitrariness; 'erst die Absperrung von der Welt trieb ihr kalte Wut ins Gehirn, wie in Kinderzeiten ein tückischer Wortbruch' (184) / 'the isolation from the world was what finally drove cold fury into her brain, as in childhood a mean breach of a promise' (139).

The decision to flee or not to flee depends for D. on a complex blend of private and public motivation, as we see on an earlier occasion when a sympathetic friend from West Berlin actually smuggles in false identity papers for her: 'Sie gab den Ausweis zurück. Ihre Angelegenheiten waren nicht in Ordnung. Sie war mit B. nicht im Reinen. Ihr jüngster Bruder war nicht versorgt. Sie bestand aber darauf, daß sie während der Schicht das Krankenhaus nicht verlassen konnte' (63) / 'She gave back the identification. Her affairs were not in order. Her youngest brother had still to be taken care of. But what she insisted on was that she could not leave the hospital in the middle of a shift' (47). When she eventually takes the crucial decision it is in a spirit less of hope or enthusiasm for what life in the West may bring than of sheer discouragement with life in the East. Ultimately – as far as we can judge, at any rate, and that is a major reservation, as we shall see – her flight appears to have much to do with personal motivation and very little to do with reasons of idealism or ideology. For all its failings, home is home, and the other side of the Wall is the essentially unknown, the other, the threat of difference, and for months before she finally takes the plunge, as thousands of others already flee to the West, 'Angst vor der Fremde verengte der D. den Hals, als ginge sie heute schon mit' (41) / 'fear of the strange new world tightened D.'s throat as if she were going along with them right now' (31). The dialogue of uncertainty and loss on the one hand and sought-for stability and order on the other is carried throughout D.'s story by the motif of a room of one's own. Her illicit room in East Berlin represents security, privacy – and also a small but satisfying personal statement against a repressive system from within the system itself. This personal symbol of individuality is quickly lost (paralleling B.'s similar loss on the other side of the Wall) when her younger brother takes the decisive step of open resistance and flees to West Germany, inadvertently betraying D.'s secret by an incautious telephone call that leads to her immediate eviction (95/72). After D. takes the step of fleeing to the West herself, she does not have to think twice about refusing young B.'s proposal of marriage, since to accept would involve leaving Berlin – and that she has no intention of doing, even if this Berlin is on the 'other' side of the Wall; in the last sentence of the text D. is busily underway with a newspaper, for 'da wollte sie sich ein Zimmer suchen' (243) / 'she wanted to look for a room' (183).

In her single-minded search for the reassuring sameness of the four walls that will entirely undramatically redefine her personal stability, D. is able to find the resources (even if this is made easier for her largely by a certain lack of imagination) to survive the single Wall so dramatically defining political difference on the larger stage of world history. D., though at home in the 'other' Berlin, is struck more by the similarities than by the differences of the two cities, 'befremdet von der Ähnlichkeit' / 'surprised at the similarity' of West and East, as the text phrases it, 'eigentlich darum verlegen, die Herkunft der Unterschiede zu begreifen' (39) / 'somewhat at a loss to grasp the source of the differences' (29). Ironically, it is the West German tourist B., free to come and go as he pleases, rather than the East German refugee D. who is finally incapable of adjusting to the subtleties of the 'alien city,' unable to read the samenesses and differences of the system.

III

There is a third story operating throughout *Zwei Ansichten*, however, in spite of the title, and for our present purposes it is the most interesting one, namely, the story of the reader. At a first reading, as early reviews of the text demonstrate (cf. Neumann 1978: 284–8), Johnson's narrative can easily give the impression of being a rather disappointing squib involving two frankly not very interesting people and operating with a surprisingly stereotyped picture of the Federal Republic and the Democratic Republic alike. The more closely one subsequently scrutinizes the text, however, the less rather than more accessible it becomes, and the more difficult the reader finds it either to accept the stereotyped social milieux at face value or, especially, to say with anything like certainty what precisely it is that *motivates* either one of the two main characters at any given point. The ostensibly straightforward account, in short, proves on closer examination to contain a number of what we might call narrative instabilities, the cumulative effect of which is to raise serious doubts as to the entire reliability of the account with which we are presented.

Our instinctive reaction as readers, for better or for worse, is to trust the narrative voice presenting the story we read, to regard it, in short, as the voice of authority. We also tend instinctively to subscribe to the traditional notion that this authoritative narrator will to some degree, in the interests of communication, attempt to make it easier for us to understand the point of the narrative. In the case of *Zwei Ansichten*, however, for all its surface simplicity of plot, neither of these assumptions proves particularly useful. By way of illustration let us examine first some aspects of the communication between text and reader in those chapters focused on the story of B. There are several episodes, for example, that offer ironic parallels or quasi-parallels to the main story-line. In the first of these, B.'s boasting of the extent of his intimacy with Berlin on both sides of the Wall encourages a young 'Bauernsohn' (66), a 'country lad' (50), to turn to him with the request to take along a letter to a girl in East Berlin since the young man 'könne die Trennung von dem Mädchen nicht aushalten' (67) / 'could not stand being separated from the girl' (50). Then there is the episode where B. discovers that his stolen car has been used by a young man from West Germany to get his fiancée out of East Berlin by trying (unsuccessfully) to run the low-slung vehicle under the barrier (83/63) – and B. must later listen, 'entwaffnet' / 'disarmed,' to the young man's parents recounting the story of their son's love for his girlfriend, 'von dem übrigens nur der Vorname bekannt war' (88) / 'of whom incidentally they knew only her first name' (67). In a third episode, a drunken evening with the couple from West Berlin in whose apartment B. first met D. allows him to play the 'Rolle des Unglücklichen' / 'role of unhappy lover' so convincingly that he eventually, 'bedauert wegen seiner Trennung von Gesicht und Geschlechtsteil' (93) / 'pitied for his separation from face and genitals' (70), ends up on the floor mechanically having sex with the wife to the accompaniment of the husband's snores, 'und hätte doch lieber allein gesessen beim Bier' / 'and would far rather have sat alone over a beer' and over his agreeably melancholy 'Erinnerungen an die D.' (94) / 'recollections of D.' (70). Finally, B. spends increasing amounts of his time in Berlin in the bar through which D.'s escape is eventually arranged, staring vacantly at the barmaid, who not only has the allure of coming from the big city but enjoys the dual advantages of being comfortably within arm's reach and a willing dispenser of comfort, even if the comfort is strictly of an alcoholic nature: 'so starrte er gedankenlos zu ihr hinüber, immer bereit, den Blick jählings wegzuschwenken, tastete blind nach dem Schnapsglas, trank tiefe Schlucke, konnte das leicht abgekehrte Profil Atemzüge lang für das der D. nehmen' (149) / 'and he would stare unthinkingly over at her, always ready to turn his glance precipitately away, reached out blindly for his glass of schnaps, drank long swallows, and for brief moments could confuse the slightly sideways profile with that of D.' (113).

These episodes (and others, including several casually anonymous sexual encounters which appear to be entirely without importance for B.) are employed by the text as a set of ironically angled narrative mirrors in which not only B.'s multiple inadequacies but also various possible interpretations of the relationship between D. and himself are obliquely reflected – and reflected upon. Narrative irony, indeed, is a highly obvious constant in the five chapters devoted to B. What is considerably less obvious, however, is the end to which this irony is employed. Sometimes the narrative voice clearly has an unambiguously satirical edge to it, as when the amount that B. is reluctantly prepared to contribute to the expenses of organizing D.'s escape is reckoned as 'den zehnten Teil der Summe, die damals einen mittleren Wagen wert war' (173) / 'the tenth part of the value of a compact car at that time' (130); when B. is described on another occasion as being 'mit aller Miene einer der solidarischen Westdeutschen, die zu jeder Hilfe bereit sind, gründlich erleichtert, daß Hilfe nicht anging' (81) / 'with all the dignity of West German solidarity, prepared to lend any assistance, thoroughly relieved that assistance was not in order' (61); or when he almost causes a last-minute disaster by forgetting what colour D.'s eyes are for her forged identity papers.

Politically minded readers, of course, have had little difficulty in seeing such references as clear evidence of Johnson's fundamentally critical attitude towards western capitalism and especially West Germany. Much of the narrative irony, however, is far less obviously edged with satire. B., for example, is directed by the police to a 'Büro für Befragungswesen' (84), an 'Inquiry Office' (63), for further information on what has happened to his car, but the purpose of the interview quickly emerges as being to question him rather than to allow him to ask questions. Is this merely a comment on the efficiency and ubiquity of the West German counterespionage network? If so, to what purpose? Why again is B. 'im Halbschlaf gehalten von

Erinnerungen an Nächte mit Geschlechtsverkehr' / 'kept in a doze by memories of nights of sexual intercourse' as he flies following one of his abrupt changes of plan from Berlin to Hamburg to Württemberg in a single night (86/65)? Is it merely for the sake of the punningly oblique reference to *Verkehr* ('traffic'), which plays so significant a role in B.'s undoing? Does the sentence 'B. stand nicht an, all seine Ungeschicklichkeiten für richtige Auskünfte über Berlin zu nehmen' (73), uttered with the apparent authority of an omniscient narrator, imply primarily that B. did not 'hesi-tate' or that it was 'inappropriate' for him 'to take the results of all his own blunderings for reliable information about Berlin' (55)? Why does the reader have to wait so long to be told that the Berlin bar frequented by B. 'nach einer Haltestelle der Untergrundbahn hieß' (146) / 'was named after a subway stop' (111)? Is the revelation at this late point of some particular significance? Or is it of no significance at all? And so on.

All of these unexpectedly unstable points in the text (and the examples could easily be multiplied), some conveying too little information and some conveying too much, actively invite doubt on the reader's part, actively contribute to the growing disorientation of the reader as the story of the growing disorientation of B. is unfolded. One of the most obvious of these difficulties throughout is constituted by the determined and striking awk-wardness of the narrator's language, which ensures that the text will be read either very slowly or very inaccurately or both. Another is the chronology of the text, which is clear enough in broad outline but the details of which – the crucial sequence of letters between B. and D., for example – readers must reconstruct for themselves with considerable difficulty and multiple marginal cross-references unless they choose simply to give up the struggle and just take the narrator's word for it. The reader's perception of what is happening both on the level of the story and on the level of the telling of the story, in other words, is consistently delayed, dislocated, and implicitly undermined by a systemic technique of narrative retardation and subtly inculcated doubt.[6] The most blatantly provocative example is the sudden and entirely unmotivated introduction of the narrator – whose voice to this point has been entirely that of an external and third-person observer – in first-person form and as a participant in the events narrated in the very last paragraph of the narrative concerning B.: 'Ich habe ihn aufheben helfen und bin mit dem heulenden Krankenwagen zur Unfallstation gefahren' (239) / 'I helped to pick him up and rode in the howling ambulance to the emer-gency station with him' (180). One chapter later, in the last paragraphs of the narrative concerning D., the first-person narrator reveals himself for the second and final time: 'Später nahm sie mir ein Versprechen ab. – Aber das müssen Sie alles erfinden, was Sie schreiben! sagte sie. Es ist erfunden' (242) / 'Later she made me promise. "But you must make up everything you write!" she said. It is made up' (183).

It is really only at this point, half a page from the end of the text, that readers finally have all the information they need to confirm that to a degree they have been the victim of a narrative confidence trick, though in retrospect it will be clear that the signs have been there all along. The character of the narrative as ostentatiously *invented* discourse has to some extent been evident throughout, if only in the various and multiple difficulties that are wantonly placed in the way of an uninterrupted reading, not to mention the manifest overall artificiality of interleaving the two narratives in alternate chapters. The text, in addition, through parodic intertextual reference, indulges in continual playful self-reflective manoeuvres concerning the relationship of allegedly 'true' stories and overtly fictional stories. The status of the narrative as an ironic twentieth-century rewriting of the tale of Romeo and Juliet – where it is not the lovers who die but rather their love (Boulby 1974: 90) – has routinely been noted by critics, including Johnson himself (cf. Neumann 1978: 270–8). The role of the Wall as intertextual reference to yet another pair of star-crossed lovers, Pyramus and Thisbe, is also evident, even if its immediate political implications tend naturally to obscure the fact. B.'s frustrated attempts to read his situation are consistently if parodically reminiscent of Kafka's frustrated searchers, his desire above all not to be stamped as 'Besuch aus einer unwissenden Provinz' (19) / 'a visitor from the ignorant sticks' (13) proclaiming him close kin to the 'Mann vom Lande,' the 'man from the country,' in *Der Prozeß* who sets out fruitlessly to gain entry to the law, even his attachment to the anonymous barmaid recalling similar proclivities on the part of Josef K. The parallel accounts of young men who succeed or fail in rescuing young women from the clutches of the East German state function also, as we have seen, as ironically tilted *mises en abyme* – and recall Kafka's similar practice in *Der Prozeß*. The portrayal of B. throughout, in short, suggestively hints that he is a creature more of words and ink than of flesh and blood, hovering consistently on the verge of caricature.

For most readers, however, I think it fair to say, this is not at all true of D. – and indeed this essentially unstable relationship between the two central characters is a constitutive strategy of *Zwei Ansichten*. While the narrator consistently presents B. from on high with overt ironic detachment, setting forth his erratic behaviour in a markedly lapidary fashion as if suggesting with a shrug that it is understandable neither to B. nor to the narrator, he tells the story of D. in a manner which is far more evidently sympathetic to her. As narrative theorists would put it, in D.'s case the narration is consonant rather than dissonant, and moreover it is predominantly focalized through D. herself – angled, that is to say, from her point of view rather than (as in B.'s case) from that of a predominantly detached and distanced narrator. The overall effect – as in any realist text – is that we tend to react to D. as if she were a real person and her story a 'true' story; we become sympathetically involved in her difficulties and we share her doubts and her anxiety before and during her flight from East to West.

For all that, however – and this is an important reservation – the narrator rarely allows us a completely unmediated insight into the privacy of D.'s thoughts and aspirations. We certainly feel that we approach more closely to her than we do to B., but we are none the less firmly kept at a definite distance – indeed, to put it another way, if the portrayal of B. is clearly overwritten, that of D. is equally clearly underwritten: where B. is a caricature, D. is a bas-relief. As in the case of B., moreover, there are occasional discreet but interesting deviations from this narrative norm in the presentation of D. also. 'Die ansehnliche Puppe fing an zu heulen, das verdarb ihnen den Spaß' (96) / 'The good-looking doll began to cry; that spoiled their fun' (73), we are told as D. is being interrogated by East German security police following her newly escaped brother's incautious telephone call from West Germany. The phrase 'die ansehnliche Puppe' here, 'the good-looking doll,' is clearly focalized through the police interrogators rather than through either D. herself or directly by the narrator, giving us a brief and unusual external perspective on her rather than the internal perspective to which we have become accustomed in her case.

Again, she is described in one episode as taking charge of the situation 'in ihrer manchmal vorlauten Art' (111) / 'in her sometimes pushy manner' (84) and talking 'naseweis und besserwisserisch' (112) / 'pertly and in a know-it-all tone' (85) to a fellow nurse. Here the focalization appears rather to be that of a more or less detached narrator, one whose attitude is characterized by the faintly censorious tone predominantly employed for the presentation of B. rather than the more sympathetic tone usually reserved for D.'s doings – but it could also be a realistic presentation of subsequent self-recrimination on D.'s part. Similarly, when the 'eigensüchtige Enttäuschung' (124), the 'selfish disappointment' (93), of D.'s fugitive younger brother is mentioned, the reader does not have enough unambiguous information to decide whether the phrase should be attributed to D.'s naïveté, D.'s irony, or the narrator's irony, all of which are possible options. In another episode we find the account of a patient's death in D.'s ward supported by a brief parenthetical passage of quoted monologue –

'Wir ham da Rotz un Wasser geweint' (118) / 'We bawled snot and water, I tell you' (89) – where the reader has no way of knowing to whom this remark should be attributed or why it is mentioned at this point at all. A page later we find a similar parenthetical passage, but with a clear attribution – 'Das warn Ringkämpfe, Mensch: sagt sie' (119) / ''It was like wrestling matches, I tell you,' she says' (90) – where it becomes apparent that D. is being quoted directly. What we still do not know, however, is whether the narrator is functioning as an old-fashioned omniscient narrator who is privy to everything a character thinks or says or as a participant in the action himself who is quoting what he has already heard D. say on some occasion. The narrative tone of the account of D.'s doings so far – with the exception of a few brief passages like those under discussion here – would lead us to assume the former; as it turns out, however, the introduction of a first-person narrator at the conclusion of the narrative shows us (or appears to show us) that we were dealing with the latter after all. Examples of this kind – which run counter to the presentational norm of the D. narrative, as we have seen – again illustrate the element of constant if subtly nuanced reflexive self-interrogation on the part of the text, which by such means continually questions its own ability to provide any single authoritative account of what really happened.

Every event, in other words, is potentially subject not only to the two views of the title but to multiple views, multiple constructions, multiple narrations, multiple readings. D.'s flight from the repressive political system of the East to the (relative) freedom of the West is no exception, in however self-righteously positive terms such a flight may subsequently be painted in the Western press. D.'s predecessor at the hospital had also fled the East for a lover in the West; D. wonders what she is supposed to think about such a nurse, 'die dem Dienstvertrag eine Liebschaft vorgezogen hatte' (117) / 'who had preferred a love affair to her job agreement' (88). This reflection of D.'s own plans can, of course, be read merely as a quite realistic portrayal of her own last-minute feelings of guilt and anxiety by a narrator whose primary interest is a psychologically convincing portrayal of an individual under stress. Later, however, when D. begins her escape only to find herself accompanied on the train by a well known East German actress whom she has previously helped treat for a breakdown after an affair with a West German, it is evident that readers are implicitly invited to construct some possible parallels of their own – which may or may not reflect positively or negatively or neutrally on D.'s flight, but will at any rate reflect.

The relationship of the reader to the text in *Zwei Ansichten*, indeed, is prefigured in the text itself by the separate relationships of both B. and D. to their respective systems. Like D., the reader is necessarily involved, 'trapped' within the constraints of an essentially untrustworthy system, in one case political, in the other textual; like B., the reader is necessarily an interpreter, with all the possibilities for failure that such a sense-making role carries with it. D.'s 'Angst vor der Fremde' (41) / 'fear of the strange new world' (30) and B.'s fear of 'die fremde Stadt' / 'the alien city' translate alike on the level of reading into the reader's anxiety to make sense – *authorized* sense – of the strenuously resisting text. D.'s world is a highly structured one, highly authority-oriented; B.'s world verges on the entropic, flagrantly devoid of authoritative norms, devoid of reliable orientation; both worlds, however, are ultimately concerned with precisely the question of authority. The role of the reader, in the textual world in which he or she in turn must operate, is likewise precisely to explore this same question of what we might call the *authority* of authority, focused especially on the increasingly complex process of authoritatively determining motivation, whether it be in the case of B. or that of D., whether it be in the case of the text itself or, ultimately, that of the reader.

IV

The reality of *Zwei Ansichten*, though firmly anchored in the very real world of Berlin in 1961, and in spite of the text's quasi-documentary aura (Neumann 1978: 218), is first and foremost a fictional one, whose primary characteristic is precisely (and increasingly overtly) its *inventedness*. A major part of this particular text's strategy, however, if only because of the immediacy and recentness of the political and social issues involved, is to steer the reader away from grasping this inventedness. Only in the final paragraphs of the respective narratives do we have it on the specific authority of the narrator, now made even more immediately authoritative by his recent assumption of first-person status, that we may finally admit the fact that the entire narration is fiction – a fact which is of course at the heart of all storytelling, all narrative (including, we need to remember, the self-narration of political and ideological systems),[7] but which we surprisingly often manage to ignore. Even the fact that we allow the (invented) authority of the (invented) narrator to influence us into accepting this deconstruction of his own fiction, of course, is part of the overall textual strategy.

Zwei Ansichten is certainly 'about' the political situation in Berlin in the early sixties; given Uwe Johnson's own biography, any assertion to the contrary would be ludicrous. But it is certainly also 'about' other matters as well, and most importantly in our present context it is about narrative and its authority on the one hand and about the role of the reader as evaluator and interpreter of that authority on the other. *Zwei Ansichten* consists not of two but of three narratives in one, each obliquely reflecting the others, and each can interestingly be read, without our becoming too fanciful, as concerned with an attempted escape from a labyrinth, insofar as the labyrinth provides an attractive symbol of both the necessity and the complexity of all sense-making activity. The argument can be taken an interesting step further, however, for the most significant feature of the three narratives from the point of view of overall textual strategy is that they work in quite different ways. Their interplay, indeed, constitutes a remarkable narrative structuration, for in terms of narrative attitude they correspond to typological modes of articulation classifiable respectively as essentially realist, modernist, and postmodernist.

The first of the three narratives, in these terms, relates the story of D., which is told in a manner very close to that of traditional realist narrative, ostensibly dealing with the real problems of a real person. Here the labyrinth involved is a political one, and the escape seems to be at least a qualified success, at least as far as concerns the eastern half of the labyrinth. The second narrative recounts the story of B., which is narrated in a manner *parodically* reminiscent of the concerns of historical modernism rather than of realism, with B. presented as a Chaplinesque marionette operating on the verge (at least) of quasi-Kafkan comedy. Here the labyrinth involved is defined by the uninterpretability of information – a quintessential modernist concern – rather than the authoritarianism of a political system, and the 'hero's' attempt to locate an escape seems to be an almost complete failure. The third 'narrative' is that of the reader, in which the narrative strategies involved correspond neither to those of realism nor to those of modernism but are essentially postmodernist in their emphasis. Here the labyrinth involved is one defined by textuality and hermeneutic play, and the possibility of interpretive 'escape,' as in the case of the other two labyrinths, lies very much in the reader's ability to play the particular kind of game involved. The reader of *Zwei Ansichten*, in other words, is parodically *challenged* by the text – in a metafictional gesture that is essentially postmodern – to become an *opponent* in a game played for the stakes of literary meaning, where all neatly packaged solutions are by definition suspect and interesting questions are always more appropriate than comfortable answers.

Zwei Ansichten, like many twentieth-century narratives, is vitally and overtly concerned with the ways in which narrative is produced and the ways in which it is received. Rather than any attempted narrative closure,

the reader is presented with – and invited to participate in – the play of relationship, the balancing of alternatives, the reinforced awareness that there
are always, at the very least, the two views of the title. Narrative, ultimately,
is always a form of persuasion, of intellectual coercion – but to a significant
degree also this is the case only as long as we allow it to be.[8] *Zwei Ansichten*
directs attention to its own weak spots as a discourse of representation by
means of discreetly understated narrative ploys and quietly provocative
textual play – but the word *play* here should certainly not be taken to
involve any lack of seriousness, any more than a theatrical play need necessarily be a comedy. In a parodic play with conventional expectations, social,
political, and literary alike, the reader is presented with the all too invitingly
suggestive pseudo-allegorical relationship of B(RD). and D(DR)., the characters handily pre-characterized by their stereotyped professions, their
stereotyped societies likewise all too appropriately characterized by way of
their respective stereotyped literary articulations, late-capitalist BRD modernism versus the realism espoused by socialist literary theory in the DDR.

The *two* views of the title, it becomes apparent, are on this level ultimately interrogative rather than prescriptive, ironically challenging the
reader to put a name to them. B.'s view versus D.'s, capitalist versus socialist, male versus female, the narrator's versus the reader's, modernist versus
realist, comic versus serious, 'fiction' versus 'reality': which pair is 'really'
at stake? The narrative leaves it up to the individual reader to decide – and
in the process to emulate the hapless B. in the attempt to sort out valid conclusions from those that are mere 'Ungeschicklichkeiten' (73) / 'blunderings' (55). The narrator's parodically unnecessary *double* intervention *ex
machina* as a fellow participant in the closing words of each account ostentatiously and significantly *relativizes* the strategy of each account: the
pseudo-modernist narrative of B.'s quasi-Kafkan disorientation with its
spurious resonances of modernist alienation is ironically brought down to
earth by an all too 'realistically' available eyewitness, while the pseudo-
realist narrative of D.'s 'true story' is by way of contrast offhandedly
declared, precisely on the authority of this same guarantor typical of realist
narrative, to be frankly fictional. The ironic intervention has one overriding
implication for the role of the reader, who is overtly invited to become in
turn – but always at his or her own risk – an active fellow participant in the
production of the narrative rather than a passive consumer of a discourse
too easily deemed to be authoritative merely because it speaks with the
voice of authority.

The Goalie's Anxiety:
Signs and Semiosis
in Peter Handke's *Die Angst*
des Tormanns beim Elfmeter

Like many of Peter Handke's texts, narrative or dramatic, *Die Angst des Tormanns beim Elfmeter* (1970) – translated into English as *The Goalie's Anxiety at the Penalty Kick* – is conspicuously short on plot in any traditional sense. Josef Bloch loses his job as a construction worker in Vienna, strikes up a chance acquaintance with a cinema cashier, and immediately takes her to bed. Next morning he abruptly strangles her and then takes a bus to a remote village on the southern Austrian border where an ex-girlfriend of his lives. There he rambles about aimlessly for several days, idly reading the newspapers that tell of the steady progress the police are making in tracking him down. The story ends – completely inconclusively – with Bloch, who was once a well-known soccer goalkeeper himself, critically watching a local goalie's performance and expatiating at some length on the almost insuperable difficulties involved in saving a penalty shot.

Bloch is clearly a very disturbed man, and Manfred Durzak speaks for one major thrust of *Tormann* criticism over the last twenty years (and no doubt for most ordinary readers) when he sees the text as being first and foremost a pathological case study, inspired by Handke's reading of Klaus Conrad's psychiatric work on incipient schizophrenia (Durzak 1982: 67) – a debt to which Handke himself had already drawn attention in a letter to the journal *Text und Kritik*. In the same letter, however, Handke also succeeded in muddying the critical waters considerably – and no doubt not without a certain degree of mischievous intent – by maintaining that *Tormann*, in spite of this, should not be read as a case study of a schizophrenic. Bloch, as Handke claimed, was in fact just a normal person disoriented by the sudden shock of the murder, even if the narrative perspective chosen for the text was admittedly modelled on the perspective typical of incipient schizophrenia ('Die Angst' 45). In the wake of this distinctly dubious advice, *Tormann* criticism has duly developed in two different (though certainly complementary) directions, the one more or less ignoring Handke's observation and treating the text as primarily a psychological investigation after all, the other concentrating rather on the semiotic implications of Bloch's vision of the world he lives in. In either event, however, critics have shown a marked tendency to focus solidly on Bloch and his problems.[1] Durzak, indeed, praises *Tormann* as the most important of Handke's early narratives (1982: 66) precisely because of what he takes to be Handke's decision, after the experimental pyrotechnics of *Die Hornissen* (1966) and *Der Hausierer* (1967), to concentrate on Bloch's disturbed perception of the world he lives in rather than on the techniques involved in the narrative portrayal of that world – an alleged decision, that is to say, to privilege *story* at the expense of *discourse*.

Such a reading of *Tormann* is certainly facilitated, indeed encouraged, by the fact that its narrator is markedly inconspicuous, apparently withdrawing almost completely into the disturbed perspective of the central character, allowing the story to 'tell itself' as experienced by Bloch (cf. Mixner 1977: 125; Renner 1985: 14). Thus Durzak, for example, emphatically sees the narrative perspective as the product of Bloch's diseased mind throughout (1982: 67). He is highly critical of Handke's attempt in *Text und Kritik* to suggest otherwise and thus generalize the descriptive reach of a diseased, abnormal perspective rather than employing the narrative perspective of a normal, healthy person who sees the world clearly and without distortion. Durzak's praise of *Tormann*, in fact, is essentially for what he sees as its primarily realist mode of expression, albeit coupled with a regrettable lingering tendency on Handke's part to slide towards an experimental modernism.

It can be argued, however, that *Tormann* is in fact read most productively neither as a realist text, focusing our attention primarily on the world of its characters, nor as a modernist text, directing our attention primarily to its mode of narrative production, but rather as an essentially postmodern text, challenging us to concentrate primarily on the nature of its constitution *as* a text in the first place. For the central narrative strategy of *Tormann* – though almost entirely ignored by Handke criticism so far – is precisely to place the *reader*, rather than the narrator, in the position of Bloch. Bloch's multiple confusions on the level of story are reflected in the multiple possibilities for confusion that are put in the way of the reader on the level of discourse. *Die Angst des Tormanns beim Elfmeter* occupies a significant place both in Handke's continuing investigation of narrative as a discursive system and in the international discourse of literary postmodernism, in that it constitutes first and foremost an interrogation of the act of reading itself – whether of the literary text at hand or of the world we live in, a world that is always, to echo Rilke, precisely a 'gedeutete Welt' (20), an 'interpreted world.'

I

As readers of Handke's text, we are immediately struck by Bloch's completely erratic and unpredictable behaviour (Durzak 1982: 71). Bloch, indeed, is a stranger to himself and to everyone else, prey to a number of interlocking obsessions that reflect the *Angst* of the eponymous goalkeeper, and obsessed, above all, by the relationship between effects and their causes, between details and the whole picture.[2] Bloch's world is one of potential order disrupted by ubiquitous evidence of palpable disorder in the scheme of things. Indicatively, he strikes up his brief acquaintance with the cinema cashier as the result less of any sexual or personal attraction than of his fascination with the 'Selbstverständlichkeit' (8), the 'naturalness' (6), of her behaviour: he is retrospectively intrigued 'daß die Kassiererin die Geste, mit der er das Geld, ohne etwas zu sagen, auf den drehbaren Teller gelegt hatte, mit einer anderen Geste wie selbstverständlich beantwortet hatte' (7) / 'that the cashier had responded to the wordless gesture with which he had put his money on the box-office turntable with another gesture, as if it were perfectly natural' (5).[3] It is precisely her sureness that initially appeals to Bloch and turns her into a (very temporary) guarantor of order. After that guarantee turns out to be untrustworthy, he simply disposes of her. Bloch's obsessive restlessness, which finds pervasive expression in his overwhelming need to communicate, by telephone, by taxi, by bus, by train, in endless (and often apparently pointless) conversations, is only another aspect of this almost frenzied search for 'meaning' – just as his frequent lapsing into deep sleep (reminiscent of Kafka's questers) can be read as an attempted escape from his failure to achieve this communication with some ultimate lodestone of meaning and order.

To put it another way, he is obsessed by signs and their interpretation. Bloch lives in a world full of signs, and he continually comes to grief as a result of his efforts to interpret them. This is evident even from the opening sentence, where Bloch, as he assumes, loses his job:

Dem Monteur Josef Bloch, der früher ein bekannter Tormann gewesen war, wurde, als er sich am Vormittag zur Arbeit meldete, mitgeteilt, daß er entlassen sei. Jedenfalls legte Bloch die Tatsache, daß bei seinem Erscheinen in der Tür der Bauhütte, wo sich die Arbeiter gerade aufhielten, nur der Polier von der Jause aufschaute, als eine solche Mitteilung aus und verließ das Baugelände. (7)

When Joseph Bloch, a construction worker who had once been a well-known soccer goalie, reported for work that morning, he was told that he was fired. At any rate, that was how he interpreted the fact that no one except the foreman looked up from his coffee break when he appeared at the door of the construction shack, where the workers happened to be at that moment, and Bloch left the building site. (5)

This particular misunderstanding – as it almost certainly is – may very well be the spark that leads to the murder of Gerda, the cinema cashier, which takes place three days later. But it is difficult to say with any certainty whether it is or not, for Bloch's questionable reading of the situation in this case is only one of many throughout the story – and may not necessarily have been the first or the decisive one. Indeed, almost all his readings are questionable. He sees the cashier standing outside the cinema, for example, and then stepping into a car. 'Bloch schaute zu ihr hin. Sie erwiderte, schon im Auto auf dem Beifahrersitz, seinen Blick, indem sie das Kleid unter sich auf dem Sitz zurechtzog; zumindest faßte Bloch das als Erwiderung auf' (13) / 'Bloch watched her. When she was in the car, in the seat next to the driver, she answered his look by adjusting her dress on the seat; at least Bloch took this to be a response' (10). Expecting a response, Bloch construes actions as reactions, establishes connections where no connections exist. 'Auf der Straße hob er den Arm, aber das Auto, das an ihm vorbeifuhr, war ... kein Taxi gewesen' (7) / 'On the street he raised his arm, but the car that drove past ... was not a cab' (5). The conventional signal for hailing a cab, in other words, inexplicably (for Bloch, at any rate), does not *produce* a taxi by virtue of its having been used. 'Schließlich hörte er vor sich ein Bremsgeräusch; Bloch drehte sich um: hinter ihm stand ein Taxi, der Taxifahrer schimpfte; Bloch drehte sich wieder um, stieg ein und ließ sich zum Naschmarkt fahren' (7) / 'Finally he heard the sound of brakes in front of him. Bloch turned around: behind him there was a cab; its driver started swearing. Bloch turned around again, got in, and told the driver to take him to the Naschmarkt' (5). It is all too much for Bloch: 'Alles, was er sah, störte ihn; er versuchte, möglichst wenig wahrzunehmen' (7) / 'Everything he saw bothered him. He tried to notice as little as possible' (5).

Like Bloch, we all live in a world of signs that demand, more or less overtly, continual interpretation and appropriate reaction. Mostly, of course, as 'normal' people, we can completely forget that we are in fact engaged in a labour of interpretation. Somebody smiles and we smile back, the light turns red and we stop, the sky darkens and we reach for our umbrellas – or a bird calls out urgently and we ignore it. We have learned, in short, to distinguish between what is important – which is to say, relevant to the particular context of reception – and what is not. We have, in other words, become competent readers of the semiotic text we live in.[4] Bloch, however, has essentially lost his semiotic innocence, lost his interpretive bearings, his sense of 'naturalness.'

Bloch, the outsider, frequently feels 'als sei er aus sich selber herausgefallen' (70) / 'as if he had fallen out of himself' (59), utterly defenceless, turned inside out, 'ekelhaft das Innere nach außen gestülpt' (71) / 'his insides sickeningly turned outwards' (60). Bloch's inability to play the monstrous game in which he feels himself to be trapped, continually to pretend to understand, leads to his repeatedly finding everything 'unerträglich ... mit einem Schlag alles unerträglich ... Ein heftiger Ekel packte ihn. Er erbrach sofort in das Waschbecken. Er erbrach einige Zeit, ohne Erleichterung ... Er war nicht schwindlig, sah im Gegenteil alles in einem unerträglichen Gleichgewicht' (51) / 'unbearable ... everything all at once unbearable ... A fierce nausea gripped him. He immediately vomited into the sink. He vomited for a while, with no relief ... He was not dizzy; on the contrary, he saw everything in a state of excruciating equilibrium' (43). Or again, 'es kam ihm vor, als hätte ihn ein Stemmeisen von dem, was er sah, abgestemmt, oder als seien vielmehr die Gegenstände ringsherum von ihm abgehoben worden. Der Schrank, das Waschbecken, die Reisetasche, die Tür: erst jetzt fiel ihm auf, daß er, wie in einem Zwang, zu jedem Gegenstand das Wort dazu dachte' (52) / 'it seemed to him as if a crowbar had pried him away from what he was seeing, or, rather, as though the things around him had all been pulled away from him. The wardrobe, the sink, the suitcase, the door: only now did he realize that he, as if compelled, was thinking of the word for each thing' (43), 'die Gegenstände so gesehen [habe], als ob sie gleichzeitig Reklame für sich selber seien' (52) / 'had been seeing the things as though they were, at the same time, advertisements for themselves' (43–44).[5]

Not that finding the right words is much help, for Bloch constantly and especially doubts the stability of language – as, for example, in a casual conversation with two policemen:

Die Gendarmen, die die vertrauten Bemerkungen machten, schienen dennoch damit etwas ganz andres zu meinen; jedenfalls betonten sie Wörter wie 'Geh weg!' und 'beherzigen' absichtlich falsch als 'Gehweg' und 'Becher-Ziegen' und ver-

sprachen sich ebenso absichtlich, indem sie 'zur rechten Zeit fertig' statt 'rechtferti-
gen' und 'ausweißen' statt 'ausweisen' sagten. (38)

The policemen, who made the usual remarks, nevertheless seemed to mean something completely different by them; at any rate, they purposely mispronounced
phrases like 'got to remember' and 'take off' as 'goats you remember' and 'take-off'
and, just as purposely, misspoke others, saying 'whitewash' instead of 'why watch?'
and 'closed, or' instead of 'close door.' (31)

Communication becomes an impossibility: 'Je länger er sprach, desto weniger natürlich kam Bloch vor, was er redete. Allmählich schien ihm gar jedes
Wort einer Erklärung zu bedürfen. Er mußte sich beherrschen, um nicht
mitten im Satz ins Stocken zu geraten' (59) / 'The longer he talked, the less
natural what he said seemed to Bloch. Gradually it began to seem that
every word needed an explanation. He had to watch himself so that he
didn't get stuck in the middle of a sentence' (49).

Faced with this proliferating meaninglessness, Bloch devises various
strategies for survival, mostly involving minutely logical consideration of
the causes motivating social behaviour – and above all linguistic behaviour.
Language, the means by which most of us instinctively make sense of the
world we live in, is no guarantor of semiotic order for Bloch, for its guarantee is valid only as long as you believe in it, and Bloch's faith has lapsed:
'es kam ihm nicht geheuer vor, wie man zu reden anfangen und dabei schon
wissen konnte, was man am Ende des Satzes sagen würde' (79) / 'it seemed
uncanny to him how someone could begin to speak and at the same time
know how the sentence would end' (67). An apparently innocuous phrase
such as 'Ich habe vergessen, einen Zettel zu hinterlegen' / 'I forgot to leave
a note' causes him to reflect immediately that in fact he has no idea 'was er
mit den Worten "Zettel" und "hinterlegen" eigentlich meinte' (12) / 'what
he actually meant by the words "note" and "leave"' (10). Language, taken
entirely for granted by normal people, becomes for Bloch the most obvious
component of a giant semiotic trap.

One of Bloch's central strategies in coping with this recalcitrant world
that refuses to make sense is to treat it as a joke. Unable to decide what an
untidy stack of fruit crates beside a market stall 'means,' he concludes that
it must be a joke of some sort: 'als ob die Kisten eine Art von Spaß seien,
nicht ernst gemeint. Wie Witze ohne Worte! dachte Bloch, der gern Witze
ohne Worte anschaute' (16) / 'as if the crates were a joke of some kind, not
meant seriously. Like cartoons, thought Bloch, who liked to look at cartoons with no words' (13). He meets an acquaintance who tells him that he

is on his way to referee a soccer game: 'Bloch faßte diese Auskunft als einen Witz auf und spielte mit, indem er meinte, dann könnte er ja gleich als Linienrichter mitfahren' (15) / 'Bloch thought this idea was a joke and played along with it by saying that he might as well come along too then, as the linesman' (12). When the acquaintance tries to prove that he is in earnest by showing him his referee's uniform and the lemons he has brought along for half-time, Bloch is merely all the more convinced that the whole thing is a particularly well prepared practical joke, a 'beiderseitige Verstellung' (15) / 'mutual pretense' (12), mere 'Verstellung und Getue' (16) / 'pretense and playing around' (13), like everything else.

But if Bloch is sometimes able to see himself as being the observer of a joke, and thus at least potentially in control of the situation, he more often feels as if he is caught up in one himself, a mere pawn in some impenetrable game operating by rules he can only guess at. The elaborate game – as far as Bloch is concerned at any rate – played by him with a waitress as unsuspecting opponent is a good example.

Bloch bestellte im Stehen ein Bier. Die Kellnerin hob einen Stuhl vom Tisch. Bloch nahm den zweiten Stuhl vom Tisch und setzte sich. Die Kellnerin ging hinter die Theke. Bloch legte die Hände auf den Tisch. Die Kellnerin bückte sich und öffnete die Flasche. Bloch schob den Aschenbecher weg. Die Kellnerin nahm im Vorbeigehen von einem anderen Tisch einen Bierdeckel. Bloch rückte mit dem Stuhl zurück. Die Kellnerin nahm das Glas von der Flasche, auf die sie es gestülpt hatte, legte den Bierdeckel auf den Tisch, stellte das Glas auf den Deckel, kippte die Flasche in das Glas, stellte die Flasche auf den Tisch und ging weg. Es fing schon wieder an! Bloch wußte nicht mehr, was er tun sollte. (33)

Bloch, still standing up, ordered a beer. The waitress lifted a chair off the table. Bloch took the second chair off the table and sat down. The waitress went behind the bar. Bloch put his hands on the table. The waitress bent down and opened the bottle. Bloch pushed the ashtray aside. The waitress took a beermat from another table as she passed it. Bloch pushed his chair back. The waitress took the glass, which had been slipped over the neck of the bottle, off the bottle, set the beermat on the table, put the glass on the beermat, tipped the beer into the glass, put the bottle on the table, and went away. It was starting up again. Bloch did not know what to do any more. (27)

Here Bloch, to begin with, confidently answers every 'move' of the waitress by a parallel 'move' of his own, even scoring some points in the early stages in countering her merely taking a chair from the table by taking another chair from the table himself *and* sitting down. The increasing complexity of the waitress's 'moves,' however, vainly countered by what one might call 'basic' moves on Bloch's part, soon proves too much for him, and his 'opponent' administers a crushing if totally unwitting *coup de grâce* with her final seven-part onslaught.

Bloch's response to this, as we notice, is to try to erase his defeat in this particular game by immediately beginning another:

Endlich erblickte er einen Tropfen, der außen am Glas herunterlief, und an der Wand eine Uhr, deren Zeiger durch zwei Streichhölzer gebildet wurden; ein Streichholz war abgebrochen und diente als Sekundenzeiger; er hatte nicht den herunterlaufenden Tropfen angeschaut, sondern die Stelle auf dem Deckel, auf die der Tropfen wohl treffen könnte. (33)

Finally he noticed a drop running down the outside of the glass and, on the wall, a clock whose hands were two matches; one match was broken off and served as the hour hand; he had not watched the descending drop but the spot on the beermat that the drop might hit. (27)

The attentive reader also notices that the strategy Bloch employs in this second game is one of his favourites. Idly watching a hawk hovering and then diving on its prey, 'fiel Bloch auf, daß er nicht das Flattern und Herabstoßen des Vogels beobachtet hatte, sondern die Stelle im Feld, auf die der Vogel wohl herabstoßen würde' (32) / 'Bloch realized that he had not been watching the hawk fluttering and diving but the spot in the field that the bird would presumably hit' (26); watching a dog running towards his master, 'bemerkte er, daß er nicht mehr den Hund beobachtete, sondern den Mann' (86) / 'he realized that he was not watching the dog any more but the man' (73); casually eavesdropping on a conversation, Bloch 'beobachtete nicht den, der gerade sprach, sondern jeweils den, der zuhörte' (111) / 'did not watch the one who happened to be speaking but always the one who was listening' (95); watching a soccer game, he attempts 'bei einem Angriff von Anfang an nicht die Stürmer zu beobachten, sondern den Tormann, auf dessen Tor die Stürmer mit dem Ball zuliefen' (111) / 'to look away from the forwards at the beginning of a rush and to watch the goalie whose goal the forwards were rushing toward with the ball' (95). The appeal of this strategy for Bloch – which even he himelf characterizes as 'etwas ganz und gar Unnatürliches' (111) / 'something completely unnatural' (95) – is clearly that it again theoretically places him in a position of control, in a position to forecast an answer before it happens. But this opportunity for potential triumph is, of course, equally an opportunity for failure, the potential failure faced by the eponymous goalkeeper who tries to read the situation as the penalty kicker runs to the ball – and the failure also faced, of course, and by no means incidentally, by those readers who try to forecast the next 'move' in the textual game in which *they* are involved.

II

Readers of *Die Angst des Tormanns beim Elfmeter*, indeed, are faced with this situation of being overtly challenged to provide a reading as soon as they see the very title, with its loaded suggestion of a privileged moment of threat, truth, or terror – even if balanced against the implicit suggestion that the whole is also merely part of a game scenario of some kind, and consequentlyperhaps not to be taken as 'seriously' as it otherwise might be. The epigraph initially appears to offer the helpful suggestion that failure will be the central theme, and that this will adequately explain the anxiety of the title: '"Der Tormann sah zu, wie der Ball über die Linie rollte ..."' (5) / '"The goalie watched as the ball rolled across the line ..."' (3). The reader who approaches the text for a second time, however, will have noted that the concluding words of the text are 'Der Tormann ... blieb völlig unbeweglich stehen, und der Elfmeterschütze schoß ihm den Ball in die Hände' (112) / 'The goalkeeper ... stood absolutely still, and the penalty kicker shot the ball into his hands' (97), thus effectively cancelling the epigraph – which, as duly cautioned readers may now note if they have not done so already, has been in quotation marks from the start anyway. The first-time reader may also wonder at the possible implications of the prepositional *beim* rather than the more normal *vorm* in the title and will in due course come to appreciate, in short, that the anxiety in question is not only the goalie's and the murderer's but also, potentially at least, the reader's.

The opening paragraph establishes the rules of the game the reader is going to be obliged to play, involving a constant tension between the story, which concerns Bloch's various aberrations, and the discourse, marked by a provocative superabundance of 'clues' and whole shoals of red herrings. The opening phrase, for example, casually identifies Josef Bloch as a 'Monteur,' which as far as the level of story is concerned simply provides the relatively unimportant fact that he is a builder's labourer; but on the level of discourse the fact that Bloch – like everybody else, of course, but most relevantly in this context like the reader of *Tormann* – is a 'construction

worker,' a constructor and manipulator precisely of *meanings*, is crucial to
the entire economy of the text.

Bloch, as we remember, concludes that he has been fired, and immediately afterwards he leaves the building site.

Auf der Straße hob er den Arm, aber das Auto, das an ihm vorbeifuhr, war – wenn
Bloch den Arm auch gar nicht um ein Taxi gehoben hatte – kein Taxi gewesen.
Schließlich hörte er vor sich ein Bremsgeräusch; Bloch drehte sich um: hinter ihm
stand ein Taxi, der Taxifahrer schimpfte; Bloch drehte sich wieder um, stieg ein und
ließ sich zum Naschmarkt fahren. (7)

On the street he raised his arm, but the car that drove past – even though Bloch had
not been hailing a cab – was not a cab; its driver started swearing. Finally he heard
the sound of brakes in front of him. Bloch turned around: behind him there was a
cab; its driver started swearing. Bloch turned around again, got in, and told the
driver to take him to the Naschmarkt. (5)

Bloch, that is to say, raises his arm, but the approaching car turns out not to
be a taxi. So far so good, the reader may well think: Bloch clearly thought
the car was a taxi, but he was mistaken. Our initial easy grasp of the situation in such terms is immediately challenged, however, for on rereading the
sentence, as we have little choice but to do, it emerges that in fact Bloch had
not raised his arm for a taxi in the first place. Bloch may or may not be confused, but by this time – eleven lines into the text! – the reader certainly is.
And there is more to come, for Bloch now hears the screech of brakes 'vor
sich' / 'in front of him'; turns around to find 'hinter ihm' / 'behind him' a
taxi (after all!); turns around again, climbs in, and is driven off. It should, in
other words, be quite evident to the punch-drunk reader by now that the
text, at this juncture at least, is obviously much less concerned with reporting Bloch's disorientation (on the level of story) than it is with
demonstrating (on the level of discourse) the reader's own capacity to be
misled. It should certainly be obvious to readers that they *are* involved in a
game, a game that will have to be played for the stakes of meaning, as much
against as *with* a text that clearly refuses to be that mere transparent pane
between reader and story demanded by readers schooled in the conventions of realist narrative.

Bloch, as we have observed, repeatedly sees himself as player in a series
of games, some ending in victory, some in defeat, and some in which he is
not sure what might constitute winning or losing in the first place. In the
game, or series of games, played between *Tormann* and the reader the latter

is clearly cast in Bloch's role.[6] It turns out, for example, that a schoolboy from the village has gone missing; this 'Schüler' is first described to Bloch as 'gehbehindert' (31), having 'trouble walking' (25), but shortly afterwards Bloch 'las, daß es sich nicht um einen verkrüppelten, sondern um einen sprechbehinderten Schüler handelte' (31) / 'read that the missing boy was not crippled but had trouble talking' (25). Readers may well find themselves wondering if this incapacitated learner – generally referred to merely as 'der stumme Schüler' (53) / 'the dumb schoolboy' (45) – should be thought of as some sort of parallel case to that of Bloch, a narrative *mise en abyme* or internal reduplication whereby one aspect of the text is parodically mirrored in another. They may even suspect a further ironic parallelism in operation here, where the internal mirror-relationship of 'der stumme Schüler' and Bloch mirrors the external mirror-relationship of Bloch and the reader.[7] But if so, is Bloch supposed to learn something from this parallel? Or is the reader? Or is the whole thing simply a coincidence after all? What is the reader to make of the fact that it is Bloch rather than anyone else who (without passing on the information to the police) subsequently finds first the missing schoolboy's bicycle and later his drowned body? Readers, in other words, find themselves in exactly the situation Bloch faces when he wonders whether a stack of crates beside a stall is supposed to mean something or not, and if so whether it should be taken seriously or treated as a joke.

III

A literary text, by definition, is one in which the reader is invited to expect every word, every sign, to be meaningful. In cases of difficulty, the reader will *make* recalcitrant details meaningful, will *read* them as meaningful. To this extent Bloch's ultimate problem is precisely the necessity he feels to read his reality as if it were a literary text rather than 'real life.' The competence of the unproblematically normal person in reading the reality he or she inhabits is based precisely on an instinctive ability to recognize at any given point what can safely afford to be *ignored*, what is mere *noise*, as an information theorist would put it. Bloch's heroic incompetence, by contrast, derives from the fact that he is, as one might say, a semiotic saint, treating his reality as if it should *always* make sense, as if *everything* were always relevant in a world without noise. Bloch's world is incomprehensible to him precisely because it is *too* meaningful: the 'examined life' advocated by Socrates degenerates into an informational entropy reminiscent less of Socrates than of his precursor Zeno.

And this allows one more turn of the hermeneutic screw. For in the literary game that is being played here, not only is the reader cast in the role of Bloch as a wanderer in an informational labyrinth vainly searching for reliable signposts. Bloch himself, as a completely unreliable reader of the world he inhabits, is also a parodic mirror of the real reader's attempted sense-making activity. Indeed, the essential narrative strategy of *Tormann* reveals itself as based on a doubled, self-reflective *mise en abyme*, for just as the reader is put in Bloch-like situations throughout, so Bloch's efforts to establish order by discovering an overall system of meaning puts him in a situation throughout that parodically mirrors that of the reader.

One constituent of (and result of) this game of mirrors is the prevalence in the text, first, of a flaunted parodic intertextuality and, second, of an entire gamut of self-deflating pseudo-symbols – signs, that is to say, that seductively offer far more than they subsequently prove capable of delivering.

Die Angst des Tormanns beim Elfmeter pullulates with (pseudo-)references to other texts centred on the existential crises of 'unaccommodated men.' Bloch as a character is firmly (if ambiguously) situated in a long literary tradition of displaced persons living on or near the border between the normal and the abnormal, from Büchner's Lenz and Woyzeck and Dostoevsky's Raskolnikov to Hofmannsthal's Chandos, Kafka's Josef K., Döblin's Biberkopf, Canetti's Peter Kien, Sartre's Roquentin, Camus's Meursault, and Robbe-Grillet's Mathias, several of whom, like Bloch, as we note, also turn to murder.[8] The reader is supplied by implication with a positive embarrassment of intertextual riches: the thematization of madness in Dostoevsky and Büchner, of the insufficiency of language in Hofmannsthal, of epistemological uncertainty in Kafka and Sartre, of the absurdity of interpretation in Camus, of the activity of reading itself in Robbe-Grillet. And so on. The basic ingredients of the plot – murder, flight, pursuit, imminent capture – are those of innumerable detective stories and crime stories of one kind or another. What is less common, of course, is Handke's decision to let the whole thing simply, even gratuitously, peter out unresolved, thus providing the assiduous reader with yet another interpretive problem to play with.

As to the invitingly 'significant' pseudo-symbols, their name is legion. Bloch at one point finds a broken mirror (43/36), and some time later a broken mirror (the same or another?) belonging to the missing schoolboy is also mentioned as having been found (60/50). Bloch, who had once split his tongue in a collision with a goalpost (58/49), is informed that the missing schoolboy also has a cleft tongue (58/49), and shortly thereafter he finds a weasel that has been run over lying squashed on the road, its tongue sticking far out of its mouth (61/51). Almost immediately after that, standing on a bridge, staring blindly at the surface of the stream, Bloch – 'sein ganzes Bewußtsein schien ein blinder Fleck zu sein' (62) / 'his whole consciousness seemed to be a blind spot' (52) – gradually becomes aware of something under the water, something that turns out to be the missing schoolboy's drowned body. Before the murder, Bloch visits a bar once run by a football player who is now 'verschollen' (11), has 'disappeared' (9), and reads a newspaper item in which an eyewitness testifies about a murder (17/14); later he talks to Gerda 'von einem Fußballer namens Stumm' (20) / 'about a soccer player named Stumm' (20) – whose name, of course, means 'dumb,' the epithet usually reserved for the missing schoolboy. Among other similarly 'helpful' clues – or rather, pseudo-clues – for the reader-detective are references to 'Münzen' / 'coins' in connection with first a telephone (8/6), then a jukebox (11/9), then the coins Bloch accidentally drops in a bus as he leaves Vienna (27/22) and which will later serve as a clue for the police in their search for the murderer (106/91).

All these 'clues' confront readers with the same problem, namely, just how seriously to take them, presenting them continually with the same hermeneutic dilemma that *everything* constitutes for Bloch. In a text dealing with the boundary separating the normal and the abnormal, for example, is it significant that Bloch's flight takes him towards the 'Grenze' (24), the 'border' (20), rather than in any other direction? Or that when he reaches it he is informed that the border is closed (32/26)? Why does his friend the landlady have a name, Hertha, that is quite so similar to that of the murdered Gerda? Is the hawk Bloch sees swooping on its prey (32/26) significant? Or the small child that falls out of bed in its sleep and doesn't know where it is (46/39)? Or the fly that falls off the mirror into the sink and is swept away (105/90)? What about the customs official, whose professional difficulties in catching offenders seem so similar to Bloch's concerns as a one-time soccer goalie? How is the reader to know?

'Eigentlich gibt es keine Regel', sagte der Zollwachebeamte. 'Man ist ja immer im Nachteil, weil der andere einen ebenso beobachtet und sieht, wie man auf ihn reagieren wird. Man kann immer nur reagieren. Und wenn er zu laufen anfängt, wird er schon nach dem ersten Schritt die Richtung ändern, und man hat selber auf dem falschen Fuß gestanden' (102).

'There aren't any rules, really,' said the guard. 'You're always at a disadvantage because the other guy also watches to see how you're reacting to him. All you can ever do is react. And when he starts to run, he'll change his direction after the first step and you're the one whose weight is on the wrong foot.' (87)

One bravura episode combining both flaunted intertextuality and an ostentatious display of pseudo-symbols is the description of the visit Bloch pays to the local castle, with its unmistakable echoes of Kafka's parable in *Der Prozeß*, where another Josef meets another gatekeeper 'vor dem Gesetz' / 'before the law':

Vor dem Schloß klopfte er an das Fenster des Pförtnerhauses. Er trat so nahe an die Scheibe heran, daß er hineinschauen konnte ... Der Pförtner, der auf dem Sofa lag, war gerade aufgewacht; er gab ihm Zeichen, von denen Bloch nicht wußte, wie er auf sie antworten sollte. Er nickte. Der Pförtner kam mit einem Schlüssel heraus, sperrte das Tor auf, drehte sich aber gleich wieder um und ging voraus. Ein Pförtner mit einem Schlüssel! dachte Bloch; wieder kam es ihm vor, als sollte er das alles nur im übertragenen Sinn sehen. Er bemerkte, daß der Pförtner vorhatte, ihn durch das Gebäude zu führen. Er nahm sich vor, das Mißverständnis aufzuklären; aber obwohl der Pförtner kaum redete, ergab sich keine Gelegenheit. Auf die Tür des Eingangs, durch den sie eintraten, waren überall Fischköpfe genagelt. Bloch hatte zu einer Erklärung angesetzt, aber er mußte den richtigen Augenblick wieder verpaßt haben. Sie waren schon eingetreten. (65)

Before the castle, he knocked on the window of the gatekeeper's lodge. He went up so close to the pane that he could see inside ... The gatekeeper, who was lying on the sofa, had just wakened; he made signs that Bloch did not know how to answer. He nodded. The gatekeeper came out with a key and opened the gate but immediately turned around again and walked ahead. 'A gatekeeper with a key!' thought Bloch; again it seemed to him as if he should be seeing all of this only in a figurative sense. He realized that the gatekeeper planned to show him through the building. He decided to clear up the confusion, but, even though the gatekeeper said very little, he never had the chance. There were fishheads nailed all over the entrance door. Bloch had started to explain, but he must have missed the right moment again. They were inside already. (55)

The fishheads in question are no doubt those of red herrings. Taking the text at face value, Bloch, the one-time 'Tor-mann' himself,[9] seems momentarily to forget who is the gatekeeper – Handke's 'Pförtner,' Kafka's 'Türhüter' – and 'had started to explain' only to discover like Kafka's Josef K. (and perhaps the reader) that 'he must have missed the right moment again.' Many more details pleading for explanation give him (and the reader) several other chances, however. The passage continues:

In der Bibliothek las der Pförtner ihm aus den Büchern vor, wie viele Teile der Ernte früher die Bauern dem Gutsherrn als Pachtzins abliefern mußten. Bloch kam nicht dazu, ihn an dieser Stelle zu unterbrechen, weil der Pförtner gerade eine lateinische Eintragung übersetzte, die von einem unbotmäßigen Bauern handelte. 'Er mußte den Hof verlassen', las der Pförtner, 'und einige Zeit darauf fand man ihn im Wald mit den Füßen an einem Ast hängen, den Kopf in einem Ameisenhaufen.' Das Zinsbuch war so dick, daß es der Pförtner mit beiden Händen zukippen mußte. Bloch fragte, ob das Haus bewohnt sei. Der Pförtner antwortete, der Zutritt zu den Privaträumen sei nicht gestattet. Bloch hörte ein Klicken, aber der Pförtner hatte nur das Buch wieder abgeschlossen. 'Die Dunkelheit in den Fichtenwäldern', zitierte der Pförtner aus dem Kopf, 'hatte ihn um den Verstand gebracht.' (65–6)

In the library the gatekeeper read to him from the estate books how many shares of the harvest the peasants used to have to turn over to the lord of the manor as rent. Bloch had no chance to interrupt him then, because the gatekeeper was just translating a Latin entry dealing with an insubordinate peasant. '"He had to leave the estate,"' the gatekeeper read, '"and some time later he was discovered in the forest, hanging by his feet from a branch, his head in an anthill."' The estate book was so thick that the gatekeeper had to use both hands to shut it. Bloch asked if the house was inhabited. The gatekeeper answered that visitors were not allowed into the private quarters. Bloch heard a clicking sound, but it was just the gatekeeper locking the estate book back up. '"The darkness in the fir forests,"' the gatekeeper recited from memory, '"had caused him to take leave of his senses."' (55–6)

The gatekeeper's grim little tale tells of an ordered social system where the peasants pay their masters a regulated amount of their harvest in return for the land on which to cultivate it. The insubordinate peasant's fate is that of one who refuses to acknowledge the validity of this system – only to die grotesquely with his head in the middle of another highly ordered social system, the anthill. 'He had to leave the estate,' just as Bloch, as he thinks, fired, has to leave the pseudo-symbolic construction site, likewise expelled from the paradise of order to the darkness in the deep forests, with its subsidiary echoes of Thomas Bernhard.

The intertextuality of such a passage is a literary joke: the role of the reader is certainly to make the connection with Kafka – but simultaneously to recognize it merely as teasing textual play, offering interpretive assistance that is much more apparent than real. The reader finds similar assistance in such brightly painted but parodic 'symbols' as the castle, the gatekeeper, the keys, the weighty tomes containing the narratives of both history and the law, even the quasi-biblical apple of (self-deconstructive) knowledge that turns up at the very end of the passage: 'Vor dem Fenster gab es ein Geräusch, als löse sich ein schwerer Apfel von einem Zweig. Der Aufprall blieb aber aus' (66) / 'Outside the window there was a sound like a heavy apple coming loose from a branch. But nothing hit the ground' (56). The parodic biblical echo here has, of course, been present all along in the sense that *Tormann* is the story of a fall from hermeneutic grace, an expulsion from a semiotic Eden. Bloch's 'original sin' in these terms is not the murder, but his failure to interpret correctly a message. The cinema cashier is killed because she asks the wrong question: 'Ob er heute zur Arbeit gehe?' (21) / 'Was he going to work today?' (17). Readers can hardly say they haven't been warned.

IV

Handke's narrative concludes with Bloch – momentarily become a narrator himself (Dixon 1972: 38) – watching a local soccer game, explaining to a fellow spectator at length, and with much greater coherence than we have come to expect from him, why it is almost impossible for a goalie to save a penalty shot: 'Ebensogut könnte der Tormann versuchen, mit einem Strohhalm eine Tür aufzumachen' (112) / 'The goalie might just as well try to pry open a door with a piece of straw' (97). On the level of story the episode provides just one more example of Bloch's neurosis. On the level of discourse the scene is a final narrative joke, a further parodic *mise en abyme* aimed at both Bloch and the reader. Bloch's explanations are directed to an anonymous listener who describes himself as a 'Vertreter' (110), a visiting sales 'representative' (95). What the *Vertreter* 'represents' in this reading, so to speak, is no less than the waning patience of the sorely tried reader, who has been doubly 'representative' and 'represented' all along. When Bloch describes his method of forcing himself to concentrate exclusively on the goalkeeper's reactions and completely ignore the penalty kicker, the *Vertreter* answers with robust common sense that all one is likely to gain from such an exercise is a headache.

In the very last sentence, moreover, as we have seen, the goalkeeper, all expectations to the contrary, *does* save the penalty shot (112/97). Readers, for their part, are overtly challenged to incorporate this Parthian shot as a final sign in their reading of the textual whole. We have been programmed, as we have also seen, to expect failure on the part of the goalie since the very epigraph, as well as by Bloch's gloomy and exhaustively calculated prognostications of inevitable failure. Why then should the moment of crisis that has even served as the title of the entire narrative result in such an unexpected success in the text's final words?

The hermeneutic imperative to find an explanation at all costs for the wholly unexpected harmony is almost irresistible. And the harmony *is* wholly unexpected, for Bloch has demonstrated no evidence of any development in any way since the opening of the narrative, as various critics have observed.[10] That will certainly not prevent us from trying to justify what looks like a happy ending, however. To this end, we may very well overlook the fact that this is a completely arbitrary place to end; we may even overlook the fact that it is not Bloch himself who makes the save, but rather a *Vertreter*. One tempting solution to the puzzle is to decide that the goalie's success is due to his ability to gauge instinctively – that is to say, pre-linguistically rather than as the result of conscious reflection – what the penalty kicker will do, and critics have duly pointed to Kleist's celebrated essay *Über das Marionettentheater* (*On the Marionette Theatre*) for the parallel with the fight Kleist describes between an expert fencer and a bear, in which the skill of the swordsman is thwarted every time by the bear's unerring and completely unconscious ability to react instinctively to each of his moves, precisely the quality Bloch was so obviously lacking (Heintz 1974: 110; Thuswaldner 1976). Schiller's classic dichotomy between naïve and sentimental (which is to say, reflexive) modes of thought likewise offers itself as a ready and inviting parallel.

Such beguiling intertextual parallels are spurious, however. For after all, if goalkeepers could react with unerring and unreflected instinct every time they faced a penalty kick, then the kicker could *never* score, and experience shows that they frequently do. Bloch's quasi-logical position is equally untenable, for according to his calculations no goalkeeper could *ever* save a penalty shot, and experience shows that conclusion to be equally fallacious. Indeed, by Bloch's logic, since the kicker has to make all the same calculations as the goalie, the kicker and the goalie together *share* an impossible and comic situation, in which it is impossible either to score *or* to make a save, a modern parallel to Zeno's pre-Socratic demonstrations of the impossibility of motion.

Saves and scores in the real world, however, result alike from an unstable and unpredictable combination of experience, skill, logic, and instinct and a healthy measure of good luck. The same is true of the reader's scores and saves in the particular game we are called upon to play in the encounter with Handke's text. The point of the goalie's final save is far less to offer some idealistically inspired demonstration of how a lost harmony can be restored *malgré tout* on the level of story than it is to function as the punch-line of a joke on the level of discourse, unrelentingly provoking the reader to renewed reflection even in that very last sentence, where we might reasonably have hoped for hermeneutic peace and semiotic order. Like others of Handke's texts, *Die Angst des Tormanns beim Elfmeter* finally invites us as readers not to any self-congratulatory admiration of the order of things, literary or otherwise, but to a continued reflection on our own always-questionable efforts to discover – and if need be invent – that wished-for order.

The Lime Works:
Narrative and Noise
in Thomas Bernhard's *Das Kalkwerk*

The inevitability of failure is central to Thomas Bernhard's novel *Das Kalkwerk* (1970) – translated into English as *The Lime Works* – from its opening sentences: Konrad, the aging and misanthropic owner of a disused lime works, hovering on the verge of mental collapse after decades of entirely fruitless attempts to complete a scientific study on the nature and mechanics of hearing, is arrested for the murder of his crippled wife, a brutal act that definitively terminates both a very unhappy marriage and the ill-fated treatise. The murder and arrest are described (to use the term, as we shall see, quite loosely) over the first three or four pages; the full obsessive importance for Konrad of the abortive study emerges only gradually over the more than two hundred remaining pages of the narrative, which are devoted to an almost grotesquely rambling, disjointed, frequently self-contradictory, and altogether highly confusing account of how Konrad's life and labours came to this final catastrophic pass. The extent of the possible confusion is well attested to by the fact that even the authoritative *Oxford Companion to German Literature* can state, quite erroneously, that Konrad himself relates the story of his own life (Garland 1986: 79). In fact, however, the relationship between Konrad and the unnamed narrator is one of the most fascinating and obscure aspects of this fascinating and obscure tour de force of a book. The narrator presents himself as an acquaintance of Konrad, piecing the story together from a few conversations he has had with Konrad himself and with some of Konrad's neighbours and from miscellaneous scraps of gossip picked up in various local taverns. Doubt as to the reliability of these reported accounts, however, is evident from the very beginning – both to the reader and to the narrator – for they frequently conflict even in crucial details.

Completely dependent as we are on the narrator's account of the accounts he himself reports, *Das Kalkwerk* presents us with a number of crucial interpretive difficulties concerning the events it ostensibly relates, for, as always, the story presented is entirely inextricable from the discourse that presents it. *Das Kalkwerk*, once again, has no claims to uniqueness in this particular regard, but it is certainly true that while a central discursive function of most narratives is to assist us in our readerly endeavours to reconstruct the story, in *Das Kalkwerk* we find a text that gains much of its distinctive and subversive fascination precisely from the way in which the discourse pervasively *hinders* us in determining what exactly the story it tells really is. In order to examine this relationship in more detail, let us turn first to what we seem to know about Konrad and his world, move then to a more detailed consideration of the narrator and his presentation, and conclude with some reflections on the centrally constitutive role of discourse in Bernhard's narrative.[1]

I

Konrad, whom the police discover after his wife's murder cowering half-frozen in a dried-up cesspit, is above all else an extremist. His most striking characteristic, as variously reported, is certainly his monomaniacal obsessiveness, which emerges with equal intensity and virulence in each of the four areas that dominate his thinking: a comprehensively scathing vision of human existence in general and Austria in particular; the scholarly monograph he desperately needs to write; his wife, with whose help, voluntary or otherwise, he intends to accomplish this; and the lime works of the title as the only possible location for doing so. Once the wealthy heir, by his own account, to a 'riesige weitverzweigte Erbschaft' (49), a 'huge, far-flung inheritance' (50), Konrad has succeeded in losing almost all the family fortune (193/220) because of his obsession with his book and holds the strongest, most uncompromising, and most devastatingly bleak views on almost everything.[2] Living in a 'Dauerzustand tödlicher Verzweiflung' (117), a 'constant state of mortal despair' (130), surrounded by disease, criminality, hypocrisy, corruption, and malice 'in diesem ihm mehr und mehr durch seine extreme Unmenschlichkeit und Unverantwortlichkeit unheimlichen Land' (97) / 'in this increasingly monstrous country, as he saw it, with its extremes of inhumanity and irresponsibility' (106), Konrad's fundamental article of faith is that there is absolutely no hope of any sort:

Manche glaubten, dadurch, daß sie ihren Kopf mit Phantasie bevölkerten, gerettet werden zu können, aber kein Mensch und also kein Kopf könne gerettet werden, da sei ein Kopf und dadurch, daß dieser Kopf da sei, sei er rettungslos verloren, lauter verlorene Köpfe bevölkerten lauter verlorene Körper auf lauter verlorenen Kontinenten, soll Konrad zu Fro gesagt haben. (135)

There are plenty of people who think they can save themselves by filling up their heads with fantasies, but no one (and consequently no head) can be saved, because where there is a head, it is already irredeemably lost, there are in fact none but lost heads on none but lost bodies populating none but lost continents, Konrad is supposed to have said to Fro. (151)

Konrad's sole purpose in life is to complete his 'sogenannte Studie,' his 'so-called study.' Indeed, the proposed study *is* his life: 'ist die Studie niedergeschrieben, ist alles andere ohne Bedeutung' (183) / 'once the book is finished, nothing else matters' (206). He has in fact had this book complete in every detail in his head for no less than 'zwei oder gar drei Jahrzehnte' (210) / 'two or even three decades' (239), and only the perfect time and place in which finally to write it down have been lacking, for to have attempted to do so too soon, as Konrad explains, would have been a fatal mistake, while to leave it too late, on the other hand, as seems increasingly possible, would be even more fatal (191/216).

Every morning, by his own account, Konrad rises with the intention of finally putting the book down on paper once and for all, and almost every day he decides to carry out just one or two further hearing experiments first. As Konrad explains it to Fro, a neighbour, these involve such exercises as calling out with great rapidity from across the room a series of alliterating but otherwise totally unrelated expressions, such as 'Ural, Urämie, Urteil, Urfahr, Unrecht, Ungeheuer, Unzucht, Unendlichkeit, Ununterbrochen, Uruguay, Uriel et cetera,' or 'Kastanie, Karte, Karthum, Karfreitag, Katastrophe, Katafalk, Kabbala, Kakanien, Kabul, Katharsis, Katarakte et cetera' (100/110), or a single word like 'Labyrinth' endlessly repeated (103/114), and demanding an instant and detailed description from his long-suffering wife of the after-effects of this on her hearing. Or she must distinguish between various possible shades of how exactly she has heard:

Über den genauen Unterschied zwischen Horchen und Hören rede er, er mache ihr zuerst Horchen, dann Hören klar, Zuhören, Zuhorchen, Aufhorchen, Abhorchen, dann Überhören, Mithören und so fort. Abhören, Aufhören, Anhören, plötzlich, sage er zu ihr mehrere Male das Wort weghören. Hinhören, sage er. (100)

He would talk about the difference between listening and hearing, starting with an explanation of listening, then of hearing, giving ear, hearkening, pricking up one's ears, auscultation, overhearing, jointly hearing, etc. Listening in, mishearing, lending an ear. Then suddenly he would say to her: Trying not to hear. Listening hard, he would say. (110)[3]

Since the study is allegedly already complete except for the actual writing, the reason for such endless complementary and supplementary exercises remains unclear. Unless, of course, their real purpose, conscious or unconscious, is to prevent rather than enable the final writing of the study. For the endless exercises have in fact alternated for decades with equally endless distractions. 'Immer habe ihn etwas anderes an der Niederschrift der Studie gehindert, in Paris, in London die Größe, in Berlin die Oberflächlichkeit, in Wien die Schwachsinnigkeit der Leute, in München der Föhn' (196) / 'There was always something to prevent him from writing his book, in Paris and London it was the huge size of the city, in Berlin it was the superficiality, in Vienna it was the feeblemindedness of the people, in Munich the foehn' (222), and even (or especially) in the lime works the distractions are endless, whether thinking about what to eat for lunch, worrying whether someone is going to disturb him by unexpectedly dropping in, planning how best to deal with years of unanswered letters, or obsessively greasing and regreasing his boots.

Konrad, in short, even by his own account, is completely hypnotized by his own lack of resolve, once admitting to the narrator that

ein verschwommenes, mit der Studie nur durch Angst vor der Studie zusammenhängendes Bild von der Studie lasse ihn verzweifelt versuchen, auf andere Gedanken zu kommen, weg von der Studie auf alles andere, was ihm größtenteils auch gelinge, worin er aber bald wieder verzweifeln müsse, denn alles andere als die Studie bringe ihn selbstverständlich in der allerkürzesten Zeit zur Verzweiflung. (112)

a hazy outline of the book which had nothing in common with the real book except for his fear of it would drive him in desperation to try to think of other things, anything else rather than the book, but when he succeeded in driving the book from his mind, as he usually did, it made him desperate all over again, for anything other than the book naturally drove him to despair at once. (125)

Only towards the end, according to another neighbour, Wieser (198/225), does Konrad finally begin to consider the long rejected possibility that he will never actually get the book down on paper, complete though it already is in every important detail. This tragic realization may well have led to the catastrophe with which the narrator opens his account. Thus, at any rate, one version of the story as propagated by Konrad. At other points, however, Konrad essentially abandons the claim that the study is already theoretically complete and dwells instead on the absolutely insuperable difficulties involved in ever completing such an undertaking in the first place. The two conflicting reasons for the uncompleted study coexist uneasily throughout, occasionally being mentioned, quite incongruously, even in the same sentence.

Konrad's particular choice of subject is determined by the fact that hearing, for him, is the most important of all the senses: 'Das Gehör sei das philosophischste aller Sinnesorgane, soll Konrad zum Baurat gesagt haben, so Wieser' (66) / 'hearing is the most philosophical of all the senses, Konrad is supposed to have said to the works inspector, according to Wieser' (69). His professional watchwords are 'Vernunft' (98) / 'reason' (108) and 'Verstand' (129) / 'common sense' (144), and his scientific program 'Ursachenforschung,' a Faustean search for prime causes. Such a program, however, Konrad also holds, is merely a comforting (self)delusion, for

die Ursache finde man nicht, werde niemals gefunden, immer nur eine Ersatzursache ... die ganze Welt, wie wir sie glauben oder ganz einfach tagtäglich wiederzuerkennen glauben, erkläre man (sich) aus nichts anderem als aus Ersatzursachen durch Ersatzursachenforschung. (136)

the real cause can never be found, only fake causes ... Our whole understanding of the world, or what we believe to be the whole world, or what we simply think we recognize as the world from one day to the next, is based on nothing else but fake causes arrived at by fake reserch. (151–2)

Indeed, to attempt to explain *anything* is entirely futile, as Konrad also holds, for language itself, the one absolutely indispensable tool of the 'Gehirnarbeiter' (113) or 'brain worker' (126), is ultimately entirely unreliable – in fact, to put it quite plainly, 'die Wörter seien dazu da, das Denken abzuschaffen' (115) / 'words exist in order to abolish thought' (128).

To try to explain what the study in particular was 'about' would therefore be 'barer Unsinn' (65) / 'totally absurd' (69). Its overall structure, however, is quite clear, at least to Konrad, according to Konrad: it is divided into nine parts – 'Die Zahl neun spiele auch in seiner Studie die größte Rolle, alles sei in Neun aufzulösen, aus Neun könne alles exportiert werden' (66) / 'the number nine, in fact, played a most important part in his book, everything in it was divisible by nine, everything could be extrapolated from nine' (69). The first of these parts is an introduction, the ninth a conclusion, the second, 'naturgemäß' / 'naturally,' deals with 'Gehirn und Gehör, Gehör und Gehirn und so fort' / 'the brain and the ear, the ear and the brain and so forth,' the sixth deals with 'Subgehör' / 'the sub-auditory sense,' the seventh with 'Hören und Sehen' / 'hearing and seeing,' while the fifth, the central part, is the most difficult of them all and the only one that still has no title (66/69–70). Of the third, fourth, and eighth, however, the reader remains uninformed – as he or she does, indeed, of any further details of Konrad's apparent belief in the relationship of numerology and audiology.

Having laboured practically all his life on the same project, Konrad continually discovers new reasons why it has become more difficult rather than less difficult to complete. If nothing else, the deteriorating memory of old age now ensures that the occasional new insight that might still occur is invariably forgotten by the time he reaches his desk to record it, leaving him again and again 'in grenzenloser Gedankenlosigkeitsverzweiflung' (113) / 'in limitless despair at being so drained of all thought' (126). Not that this despair is anything new, for Konrad also tells the narrator at great length of his entirely similar despair at his total and entirely similar inability to think even as long as twenty-two years ago (118–26/132–40).

Whatever the other obstacles, however, 'schließlich und endlich hätte ihm aber immer wieder seine eigene Frau die Niederschrift der Studie unmöglich gemacht' (196) / 'finally and always his own wife had made it impossible for him ever to get the book written' (223). Konrad's total ruthlessness as far as his work is concerned is most obviously apparent in his treatment of his wife, who, confined to a wheelchair for many years, leads a truly 'fürchterliche Existenz' (16), a 'terrible existence' (13) at his hands. It emerges that she was already incurably ill and physically crippled when Konrad married her some thirty years before (208/237), and at one point Konrad even admits to having married her primarily in order to have a permanently available subject on whom to carry out his linguistic experiments. He also admits that he is – of necessity, as he sees it – experimenting her 'zu Tode' (91) / 'to death' (99). For all that, however, in a sense Konrad is just as much her victim as she is his.

The Konrads live in what one might call a mutually antagonistic support system, a world of ritualized obsessions meticulously respected by each of them. While he desperately tries (or persuades himself he is trying) to get his book written and brutalizes his wife in that cause, she continually forces him to undertake such maddeningly distracting and entirely pointless activities as trying on mittens she is allegedly knitting for him but invariably unravels and knits again in a different colour rather than finishing (139/158), or continually has him fetch her drinks that she then leaves untouched (151/171), or has him search the attic for long-forgotten dresses that she now wants to try on again. Konrad accedes to these demands just as meekly as she submits to his relentless experiments. Their leisure activities are equally scrupulously balanced: Konrad is permitted to read aloud to her from his favourite authors, usually Kropotkin (103/114), occasionally Wittgenstein (153/173), or talk about his favourite painter, Francis Bacon (44/45), all of whom she cordially hates, only if he follows this by reading aloud for exactly the same length of time from her favourite author, Novalis, or listening to her favourite composer, Mozart, both of whom he, naturally, hates with equal cordiality.[4]

Konrad's wife, in short, comes to symbolize for him everything that prevents him from achieving his goal, her physical paralysis a mocking mirror of his intellectual paralysis. About a year before the murder Konrad reportedly has a nightmare in which he finally manages to get the entire study down on paper, only to have to watch helplessly while his wife destroys it (149/167). By the end the Konrads have lost almost everything, rarely bother to eat or wash or even sleep any more, staying up all night staring at each other instead (185/209), torture each other with their inane and paralysing rituals.

Dann soll er, Konrad, gesagt haben, wir beide wissen, daß wir am Ende sind, machen uns aber jeden Tag vor, wir seien noch nicht am Ende, schließlich hätten sie, Konrad und seine Frau, aber sogar an der Tatsache, am Ende zu sein, Gefallen gefunden, weil an nichts anderem mehr. (144)

Later Konrad is supposed to have said: My wife and I both know that we are done for, but we keep pretending, day after day, that we are not done for yet. They had in fact come to take a certain satisfaction in feeling that they were done for, there being nothing else left to take satisfaction in. (161)

During her last days she suddenly, after years of submission, takes to taunting Konrad that his supposed study is nothing but a 'Hirngespinst' (146), a 'delusion' (164), and that he himself is not only a madman but a criminal as well. 'Ihrer beider Zusammensein wäre von Anfang an falsch gewesen, aber, ehrlich gesagt, soll Konrad zu Fro gesagt haben, welches Zusammensein ist nicht ein falsches ... ?' (144) / 'Their life together had been all wrong from the beginning, but which couple's life together, after all, is not all wrong, Konrad is supposed to have said to Fro' (162). One simply proceeds 'aus der Vorhölle des Alleinseins in die Hölle des Zusammenseins' (145) / 'from the purgatory of loneliness into the hell of togetherness' (162).

As for the lime works of the title, it has always been the one absolutely indispensable prerequisite for completing the study, because of its almost total and thus, for Konrad's purposes, ideal isolation. One of his first acts as owner is to intensify that isolation by having heavy bars installed on all the windows. By the time of the murder he has in fact already been living there for more than five years, but only after spending 'an die drei oder gar vier Jahrzehnte' (15) / 'three or even four decades' (11), trying with increasingly single-minded desperation to buy back, at any cost, the disused lime works, which had in fact once belonged to his own family, and where he had dreamed of living 'von frühester Jugend an' (15) / 'from his earliest years' (11). Not that the lime works is any idyll: Konrad's childhood memories of it are of 'Feuchtigkeit, Kälte, Finsternis, Verletzungsmöglichkeiten' (40) / 'damp, chill, darkness, getting hurt' (40), the last of these an expression he will, much later, apply also to the study itself (191/217). His expectations of what it will provide are hardly any more cheering: for at least two decades before he eventually bought it 'sei ihm das Kalkwerk durchaus schon als Verfinsterungsort erschienen, ideal für seine Studie' (40–1) / 'the lime works had meant to him a place of eclipse, an ideal retreat for working on his book' (40). The yearned-for isolation for the sake of his work will be its (and his) destruction, however. A 'place of eclipse' is exactly what the lime works turns out to be, from without and from within alike. The depravity of the world in general (and Konrad's Austria in particular) seems to be at its deepest and darkest in its immediate vicinity: 'in hundert Jahren etwa seien allein im Kalkwerk elf Morde, von welchen man Kenntnis habe, begangen worden' (36) / 'at the lime works alone eleven murders were known to have been committed over the last hundred years' (35). The lime works, Konrad's 'frühester Kinderspielplatz' (40) / 'first childhood playground' (40) and long the sole focus of his hopes, the only possible place that might conceivably still constitute a refuge from an impossible world, becomes in the end an intensified *mise en abyme* of that world.[5]

Konrad acknowledges towards the end, according to Wieser, that he probably should have listened to his wife's pleas and gone anywhere else in the world other than the fatal lime works, instead of which he quite deliberately chose to destroy her happiness and indeed her entire life in the interests of his book (171/194). And all to no end, for his efforts to avoid distraction have led only to ever-greater distraction (173/195). Rather than the best possible place, his choice turns out to have been the very worst possible place for the study: 'eine solche Unsinnigkeit wie in das Kalkwerk zu gehen ... bedeute Selbstmord' (176) / 'the senselessness of moving into the lime works ... was suicidal' (199). The long sought-for haven reveals itself as the locus of ultimate despair, inevitable from the beginning, the inescapable destination of all roads taken, the site not only of self-confrontation but of final failure and extinction: 'Unser Ziel ist das Kalkwerk gewesen, unser Ziel ist der Tod gewesen durch das Kalkwerk' (176) / 'Our destination was the lime works, our destination was to be done to death by the lime works' (198–9).

II

All this we know (or think we know) only from the account of a narrator whose radical unreliability has been evident from the very first pages, who never reveals his own name, or what his particular interest in Konrad and his affairs may have been, or his motivation for putting the story together in the first place. References to his own activities are minimal. He appears to be an insurance salesman, reporting the sale of life insurance policies both to Fro (117/130, 210/239) and to Wieser (188/213). His personal acquaintance with Konrad is only slight: 'Ich selbst bin Konrad mehrere Male auf der Straße nach Lambach, mehrere Male auch auf der Straße nach Kirchham begegnet, zweimal im Hochwald' (8) / 'I myself ran into him a few times on the road to Lambach, or Kirchham, and a couple of times walking through the high timber forest' (4). Their first meeting, 'im Hochwald' (96–9) / 'in the timber forest' (106), a 'Begegnung III' (110–15) / 'Encounter III' (123), and a 'Begegnung IV' (118–25) / 'Encounter IV' (132) are reported, and Konrad's obsessive soliloquies on each occasion recorded in detail (as far as we can tell, of course, for we have no conclusive means of checking either the narrator's accuracy or his veracity). Why the details of their other meetings are excluded is not revealed. As to his presentation, the most salient characteristics of the narrative are, first, its flaunted status as multiply compound discourse; second, its overt lack of linearity; and third, its complete obsessiveness.

The narrative opens with eleven paragraphs ranging in length from two lines to three pages, each, including the first, preceded and concluded by suspended periods (7–14/3–11). The remainder of the account, some two hundred pages in length, constitutes a single uninterrupted paragraph, also introduced by suspended periods (14–211/11–241). The opening paragraph already stresses the flaunted mediatedness, the overt constructedness, of the narrator's account, makes it clear that what we are reading is less a single account than a collation of disparate accounts picked up from a number of informants:

... wie Konrad vor fünfeinhalb Jahren das Kalkwerk gekauft hat, sei das erste die Anschaffung eines Klaviers gewesen, das er in seinem im ersten Stock gelegenen Zimmer habe aufstellen lassen, heißt es im Laska, nicht aus Vorliebe für die Kunst, so Wieser, der Verwalter der mußnerschen Liegenschaft, sondern zur Beruhigung seiner durch jahrzehntelange Geistesarbeit überanstrengten Nerven, so Fro, der Verwalter der trattnerschen Liegenschaft, mit Kunst, die er, Konrad, hasse, habe sein Klavierspiel nicht das Geringste zu tun gehabt, er improvisierte, so Fro, und habe, so Wieser, an jedem Tag eine sehr frühe und eine sehr späte Stunde bei geöffneten Fenstern und bei eingeschaltetem Metronom auf dem Instrument dilettiert ... (7; ellipses in original)

... when Konrad bought the lime works, about five and a half years ago, the first thing he moved in was a piano he set up in his room on the first floor, according to the gossip at the Laska tavern, not because of any artistic leanings, says Wieser, the manager of the Mussner estate, but for relaxation, to ease the nervous strain caused by decades of unremitting brain work, says Fro, the man in charge of the Trattner estate, agreeing that Konrad's piano playing had nothing to do with art, which Konrad hates, but was just improvisation, for an hour first thing early in the morning and another late at night, every day, spent at the keyboard, as Wieser says, with the metronome ticking away and the windows open ... (3)

From the beginning the narrator thus establishes his role as a collector and collator of accounts towards an 'explanation' of Konrad's murder of his wife, which is reported, again at second hand, in the third paragraph. Collecting various versions of the story to be welded into a single coherent narrative is, of course, not at all unusual; it is, after all, the standard practice of biographers. Our narrator never takes that final integrative step, but rather presents all the various versions collected, as if perhaps intending to sort the whole thing out later once *all* the conflicting voices have been heard:

... im Lanner heißt es, Konrad habe seine Frau *mit zwei* Schüssen, im Stiegler *mit einem einzigen* Schuß, im Gmachl *mit drei* und im Laska *mit mehreren* Schüssen getötet. Klar ist, daß bis jetzt außer den Gerichtssachverständigen, wie man annehmen muß, kein Mensch weiß, mit wie vielen Schüssen Konrad seine Frau umgebracht hat ... (8; emphasis and ellipses in original)

... at Lanner's the word is that Konrad killed his wife with *two shots*; at the Stiegler place, with *a single shot*; at the Inglenook, with *three*; and at Laska's with *several* shots. Obviously nobody really knows except, presumably, the police experts, how many shots Konrad took to kill his wife ... (5)

The reader is consistently kept at at least two discursive removes throughout by the narrator's report of accounts heard from Fro (whose versions are mainly unfavourable to Konrad), Wieser (whose versions are mainly favourable to Konrad), occasional others such as the building inspector, miscellaneous gossip picked up in the local bars, and Konrad himself on the three occasions when he speaks directly to the narrator. Quite frequently, however, the distance between what allegedly happened and the account we hear of it is much greater – as when we read of the accidental death of a sawmill worker at no fewer than five discursive removes from the events presented, first described by his wife to the one-time overseer of the lime works, Höller, who in turn tells Konrad, who tells Fro, who tells the narrator, who tells us (163/183).

The entire narrative is thus a metanarrative of variable complexity, a narrative about other narratives, a tour de force of compound discourse, relying heavily on the subjunctives of reported speech as well as on openly conflicting versions, highly involved syntax, and enormously rambling sentences, often of several pages in length. From the beginning the entire report thus emerges as suspect, an ostensibly objective collation of eyewitness reports that obviously leaves a great deal of room for entirely subjective rearranging. The degree to which the narrator is aware of this manipulation, however, is by no means clear. Individual sentences can suddenly change direction in a way that throws a distinctly dubious light not only on Konrad's thought processes but on those of the narrator as well. To take just one example: Konrad tells Wieser he could never explain why he married his crippled wife, so completely unsuitable for his scientific career, *or rather* he knew exactly why he married her, namely, in order to have a completely captive experimental subject, we are told within a single sentence (208/237).

The reader may have to wait a hundred pages or more before picking up a hint that may or may not retrospectively explain a (possibly) casual reference. Some intriguing suggested lines of enquiry are blocked off almost immediately. Thus Konrad's wife, we are told in passing, is in fact not only his wife, she is also 'in Wahrheit Konrads Halbschwester' (16) / 'in reality his half sister' (13), or indeed 'seine Schwester' (29) / 'his sister' (27) – but there the matter rests, and whether this is the same younger sister whose good health is contrasted to Konrad's sickliness (46/47) and who prefers as a child to play with his younger brother Franz rather than him, though likely, is never made entirely clear, almost as if the narrator had forgotten the whole business of incest. Why Franz, who plays absolutely no further part in the story, is dignified with a first name no less than twice on a single page (47/47–8), while all other characters, including Konrad and his wife/sister, have to make do throughout with only a last name or even just an occupational designation, is likewise, like much else, left unexplained. Strictly speaking, indeed, the narrator never tells us unambiguously that *any* of the events of the story, including Konrad's murder of his wife, actually takes place. What he describes in every case, including the murder, is not the event itself but descriptions of the event. The overall result, not surprisingly, is an entirely unreliable composite account of the events in question.

Narrators may be unreliable in a variety of ways, of course, whether consciously or unconsciously. There is no real indication that the narrator of *Das Kalkwerk* consciously attempts to mislead the reader, if only because of the pervasive evidence he provides of his own comprehensive confusion.[6] His essential unreliability stems, paradoxically, not from any ignorance of the facts on his part but precisely because he knows *all* the facts of the matter. Facts in fiction, after all, to turn a phrase, become facts only because they are fictions: we become aware of events only because they are narrated, we apprehend the story only because of the discourse. Bernhard's narrator unconsciously misleads the reader throughout not because he withholds information, but precisely because he presents the reader with *all* the facts (the *reported* facts) he has at his disposal, with little or no attempt to make sense of them, as if hypnotized by their very narratability. Unable to distinguish one fictional fact from another, he is at once well aware of his own unreliability – as his account of the number of shots allegedly fired shows, for example (8/4) – and chooses essentially to disregard it rather than attempting to rationalize the narrative contradictions involved. As a result, *Das Kalkwerk* is in the end far less about the story it purports to tell than about the discourse that ostensibly tells it – or fails to tell it.

The narrator's confusion – or deliberate disregard of contradictions – is especially evident in his treatment of chronology. As will already have become apparent, even the basic interpretive work of collecting the biographical details of the Konrads' lives and establishing more or less accurately the chronology of the story related presents considerable difficulty in the case of *Das Kalkwerk*. The narrator's account is pieced together mainly from individual conversations his two main informants, Fro and

Wieser, have had with Konrad over at least the last three years, but little sense of any development in Konrad's character can be gleaned from these accounts (each of which occasionally contradicts either itself or the other or both), since none of the conversations seems to be reported in full. Rather the narrator draws on them, more or less at random, to support individual points, attributions frequently consisting merely of a laconic 'so Fro' / 'according to Fro' or 'so Wieser,' with relatively few indications of any meaningful sequence of events. The result, accentuated by the very lengthy sentences and the complete lack of paragraphing for some two hundred pages, is a picture of Konrad's life as essentially static rather than progressive, a portrait of a man always on the brink of catastrophe.

Confusing the chronological sequence of the story is one thing, however; confusing the chronology of the discourse is quite another. Perhaps the best indication of this confusion occurs when the narrator at one point refers apparently casually to having sold Fro a new life insurance policy 'gestern' (117) / 'yesterday' (130), some thirty pages later expresses doubts that Fro will ever buy this same policy (149/167), and a further sixty pages or so later refers to having sold Fro the policy just 'heute' (210) / 'today' (239). Encounters dated by events in the natural sequence of expected future, present happening, and recollected past, in other words, are reported in the entirely illogical sequence past-future-present. A single identifiable example of this kind naturally predisposes the reader to wonder on the one hand if this is merely an isolated case and on the other how and why such a thing could have occurred. Has the order of pages become confused? Are we being deliberately manipulated by the narrator – and if so, to what end? Or has the narrator simply confused past, present, and future in his own mind? The last of these possibilities is supported by occasional glimpses of an overtly aleatory element in the narrator's presentation, as when a new episode is introduced by a phrase such as 'Dazu fällt mir ein' (177) / 'Which reminds me' (200).

Konrad's obsessiveness is scrupulously recorded by the narrator throughout. To take just one example, when Konrad buys the lime works, one of his first acts, 'so Konrad zu Wieser,' is to have all decorative elements removed from the building:

Zu einem Großteil habe er diese Schnörkel mit seinen eigenen Händen aus den Wänden heraus- und von den Wänden heruntergerissen, herausgebrochen und herausgeschlagen und herausgerissen und heruntergeschlagen und heruntergebrochen und heruntergerissen und er habe all diese heraus- und heruntergerissenen Schnörkel durch keine neuen Schnörkel ersetzt. (19)

Most of these ornaments he had torn out of and off the walls with his own hands, broken them off and knocked them off and broken them down and knocked them down and torn them down and ripped them out, and never replaced a single one of these broken off and knocked down ornaments with any new ornaments. (15–16).

The obsessiveness of the actions described here is entirely typical of Konrad, and it is possible that the language describing them is also Konrad's, recorded with scrupulous accuracy first by Wieser, then by the narrator. There are other occasions when the obsessively repetitive diction is certainly not Konrad's, however, as when the narrator mentions the few occasions on which he met Konrad personally and was engaged

jedesmal augenblicklich in ein mehr oder weniger rücksichtsloses medizinisches oder politisches oder ganz einfach naturwissenschaftliches oder medizinisch-politisches oder naturwissenschaftlich-politisches oder medizinisch-politisch-naturwissenschaftliches Gespräch. (8)

on the spot each time in a more or less ruthless discussion of some topic of a medical or a political or simply of a generally scientific nature or of a medico-political or a scientifico-political or a medico-politico-scientific nature. (4–5)

While the compulsiveness of the actions described here is once again attributable to Konrad, however, it is clear that the obsessiveness of the discourse describing them is the narrator's. To speak of a possible ironic imitation of Konrad's style by the narrator would be entirely inappropriate, for a central characteristic of *Das Kalkwerk* is the consistent lack of any such ironic distance on the part of the narrator. Most of the time the obsessiveness of the story and that of the discourse are indistinguishable.

One of the most intriguing questions concerning *Das Kalkwerk* is the implied mode of its presentation and the reason for its (fictional) existence in the first place. Why does the narrator, who by his own admission is only very casually acquainted with Konrad, attempt to assemble the story of his failure in the first place? Why, in short, is the narrator narrating? And how? And what, indeed, is our own implied role as receivers of that narration? Are we to assume that we are reading what the unnamed narrator considers to be a finished product of some sort, whether intended as the biography of an unusual man or as an amateur psychological case study – or perhaps even as a work of literature? Or are we reading just a collection of jumbled notes for such an undertaking? Or are we listening rather than reading, listening, say, to a lengthy and rambling tape recording as in

Beckett's *Krapp's Last Tape*? Or are we reading a stream-of-consciousness presentation à la Molly Bloom of the more or less randomly organized musings of a narrator who, for whatever reasons, is just as obsessed with Konrad as Konrad was with his 'so-called study'?

The fundamental reason for the narrator's interest in Konrad, clearly, is that Konrad is his own mirror image. The story of *Das Kalkwerk*, to the extent that the discourse allows us to make it out, is a story of failure, Konrad's failure as a writer and as a human being. But the story of the discourse is just as much a story of failure. Commenting in his very last sentence on Konrad's inability to complete his monograph, the narrator quotes Konrad as having admitted towards the end that

das Wichtige habe ihm gefehlt: Furchtlosigkeit vor Realisierung, vor Verwirklichung, Furchtlosigkeit einfach davor, seinen Kopf urplötzlich von einem Augenblick auf den andern auf das rücksichtsloseste um- und also die Studie auf das Papier zu kippen. (211)

he had lacked what was perhaps the most important quality of all: fearlessness in the face of realization, of concretization, fearlessness, simply, when it came to flipping his head over, suddenly, from one moment to the next, ruthlessly flipping it over and dumping his book onto the paper, all in one motion. (241)

Unlike Konrad, the narrator actually succeeds in putting his work down on paper. But in one major sense he none the less lacks precisely that same 'fearlessness in the face of realization' he claims Konrad lacks, for in the end, like Konrad, he too fails to complete his particular project, which essentially survives only as a collection of jumbled notes, reminiscences, and largely unevaluated second-hand reports that frequently contradict and undermine one another. In the end, the narrator's discourse results not in a story told but in a story *untold*, little more than a tissue of mutually deconstructive suppositions and metasuppositions about Konrad and 'die sich mit der Zeit merkwürdigerweise immer mehr verfinsternde Finsternis' (9) / 'the darkness that, strangely, only gets darker as time goes on' (5) surrounding his activities and motivations, an indecisive and incomplete collection of prolegomena, preliminary 'Mutmaßungen über Mutmaßungen über Konrad,' to adapt the title of Uwe Johnson's *Mutmaßungen über Jakob (Speculations about Jacob)*. The reader's efforts merely to discover what allegedly happened in the first place are continually thwarted on the one hand by the blanket-coverage pseudo-completeness of the evidence presented, as in the totally unreconciled contradictory accounts of the number of shots fired (8/4, 147/165), and on the other by the narrator's obdurate refusal to interpret rather than merely repeat the information he purveys.[7]

The narrator, like Konrad, is obsessed by failure, as we continually see in the gloomily thorough relish with which he minutely and repeatedly details the absolute contradictoriness of the respective characters of Konrad and his wife or the variety of distractions by which Konrad allows himself to postpone a final closure. The final catastrophe, known from the very first pages, throws its shadow over all that succeeds it in the discourse, all that precedes it in the story. The narrator's verbal labyrinth becomes the stylistic correlative of an existential labyrinth. The sheer amount of information provided (all of it of entirely questionable reliability) in the end simply overwhelms the narrator as it overwhelms the reader, converting narrative into noise – just as Konrad's attempted study has become noise for him. 'Anstatt daß ich aber während des Aufundabgehens an die Studie denke, soll er zu Wieser gesagt haben, zähle ich die Schritte und werde dadurch halb verrückt,' the narrator quotes Konrad at one point (195) / 'But instead of thinking about my book as I go pacing the floor, I fall to counting my footsteps instead until I am about to go half mad' (221). Not for nothing are these the exact words that also function as the epigraph to his own account (5/i). The narrator's discourse, in its obsessiveness, its compulsive repetitiveness and redundancy, its apparent exactness that only superficially conceals a fundamental indeterminacy, ultimately becomes independent, asserting its priority over the story it ostensibly sets out to relate.

III

Bernhard's portrayal of Konrad as a failed scholar, a writer *manqué*, brilliantly develops a familiar, even hackneyed, theme of German writing from Grillparzer's *Der arme Spielmann* to Thomas Mann's Christian Buddenbrooks and Canetti's Peter Kien, that of the failed artist or *Künstlernatur*.[8] His quite remarkable innovation in *Das Kalkwerk* is the use of an overtly doubled, reflexive presentation. An adequate reading of *Das Kalkwerk*, indeed, requires us once again to recognize the distinction between narratorial discourse and implied authorial discourse. While we have been using the term *discourse* so far as referring only to the narrator's account of Konrad's doings, in other words, there is – as indeed there always is, though usually only implicitly rather than explicitly – another and superior level of discourse simultaneously present, namely, that of the implied author, whose role, as the narrative theorists tell us, is precisely the contextual *positioning* of the narrator's account, the presentation of the narrator's presentation. Narrators narrate; implied authors suggest how the narrator's narration should be taken.[9] Konrad's failure, as we have seen, is presented through the entirely non-ironic lens of another failure, the narrator himself, whose presentation, however, is itself ironically presented (by virtue of the juxtaposition of failures) by an implied author whose central concern is not just *one* failed text (as it is for the narrator) but the relationship of *two* failed texts, failure reflected in failure.

Bernhard's narrative thus centres ultimately on the relationship of two complementary and mutually reflective entropic texts: Konrad's unwritten text (on the nature of hearing) remains completely silent, nothing is said; in the narrator's text (made up of accounts *heard* from others) much is said, but what information theorists call the signal-to-noise ratio is heavily weighted towards meaningless noise rather than meaningful signal. The act of hearing involves constantly receiving both communicative information and random noise and having to decide which is which. Just as Konrad, theoretically an expert on such communicative strategies, fails disastrously to communicate with his own wife, so the narrator fails as sender to communicate adequately with his potential reader, just as he fails as receiver to read adequately the relationship between the communications of Fro and Wieser, communications that are both mutually contradictory and self-contradictory. The narrator's ostensible desire for comprehensive understanding leads not to clarity but rather to a randomized logorrhoea that is simply another version of Konrad's mesmerized silence. Konrad's wife/sister, always referred to merely as 'die Konrad,' is portrayed by the narrator as a sort of female anti-Konrad, a mirror in which he can observe his own paralysis. Konrad serves the same purpose for the narrator.[10]

This element of reflexivity is only one aspect of a desperate hilarity pervading *Das Kalkwerk*. The sheer unrelenting gloom of Konrad's world, indeed, has something irresistibly comic about it, as one inevitable disaster is equally inevitably followed by another even worse. Despair and alienation are the very air Konrad breathes, the complete inevitability of failure is guaranteed, all would-be solutions are equally futile, and entropy is total and irreversible. Konrad's retreat from the world is a threefold one: an emotional flight from isolation into matrimony, an intellectual flight into the study, a physical flight into the lime works. All three are doomed to disaster, all three are not just bad solutions but the worst possible solutions in this worst of all possible worlds. Even if he were to complete the study, Konrad is well aware, the final results would just be 'lächerlich, wie ja

überhaupt alles, was man ausspreche, lächerlich sei, soll er gesagt haben'
(65) / 'ridiculous, just as anything one can say is ridiculous, he is supposed
to have said' (68).

The world of *Das Kalkwerk* is grounded not only in inescapable and
irrevocable catastrophe but also in the comedy of a Beckettean endgame:
'dadurch, soll er gesagt haben, ist ja alles erträglich, weil es so komisch ist'
(70) / 'that, he is supposed to have said, is why everything is still bearable
after all, because it is so comic' (74).[11] Konrad's personal endgame is drawing to a rapid close, his eyes failing (93/102), his memory unreliable (112/
126); he is increasingly subject to sudden weaknesses (112/125), occasional
loss of voice (206/235), and finally the dreaded hearing loss (210/239) that
makes his entire scientific project impossible – not that it was ever possible
anyway. In Bernhard's hands, as in Beckett's, the inevitability of disintegration becomes a comedy of entropy, at once appalling and hilarious. The
compulsive violence of its language and the single-minded extremity of its
misanthropy are the main vehicles of this comedy in *Das Kalkwerk*, but
there are also such comic set pieces à la Beckett as the mindless brutality of
the drunken policemen who arrest Konrad (10–11/6–7) and Konrad's desperately comic and futile attempts to dispose of his murdered wife's body
(12–13/8–9). The central paradox of the narrative – Konrad's life-long
inability to complete a book that is already complete – is, of course, also an
essentially comic situation, a comedy of stasis, reminiscent not only of the
necessity to wait for Godot *because* he will never come but also of Kafka's
man from the country who spends his entire life unable to pass through a
door intended only for him.[12]

All four of Bernhard's major narratives – *Frost, Verstörung, Das Kalkwerk, Korrektur* – have main characters on (or beyond) the verge of mental
collapse observed by narrators who do not seem to be far behind.[13] As in
the case of Kafka, indeed, each of Bernhard's novels can be read as just one
chapter in a continuing macronarrative of disintegration and catastrophe.
The Austria Bernhard portrays in these fictions, the post-imperial, post-
war, post-occupation Austria of the 1960s, is a gigantic penal institution for
the criminally insane, characterized by coldness, darkness, decay, and pervasive disintegration. Bernhard's world as portrayed in these texts, like
Konrad's, is a world of physical entropy and social anomie, where criminality, violence, and disease are rampant, isolation and incipient insanity
are pervasive, and random hostility and malice are the order of the day. The
casual brutality of an inimical society is matched by the brutal impassivity
of a hostile nature. Konrad's study is an inevitably foredoomed attempt to
establish some kind of limited order in this chaos – or at least to assert the

possible existence of such order, even if only entirely local. Naturally – 'naturgemäß' – it has no possibility of success, and it is this impossibility that exerts a hypnotic, even paralytic fascination on Konrad, doomed like Kafka's man from the country to continue trying and continue failing, to relive the myth of Sisyphus without any compensatory Camusean determination to make the best of a very bad existential job.

Bernhard's characters notoriously bear a marked resemblance to their author.[14] Like Konrad, Bernhard made absolutely no bones, in a large number of public utterances, about his personal disgust with Austria (*his* Austria) as a totally hopeless den of corruption and hypocrisy. Bernhard's own style, like Konrad's and the narrator's, to the degree that we can distinguish them, is completely uncompromising in its obsessive violence – and not by any means just in *Das Kalkwerk*. Like Konrad, Bernhard was a deeply disturbed man: his psychiatrist of the time was quoted as stating that for Bernhard writing was essentially a substitute for suicide (Graf 1971: 343). Whatever the biographical context to which it owes its origin, however, *Das Kalkwerk*, precisely because of the unrelenting consistency and desperate intensity with which it demonstrates the complete inevitability of failure, in the end paradoxically disproves its own entropic thesis. For *Das Kalkwerk* is not only a brilliantly successful text about the relationship of two failed texts, but also an extraordinary investigation of the relationship of discourse and story, narrative and noise.

Conclusion

Since the eight texts chosen for analysis here span most of the twentieth century, it is conceivable that there are readers who might expect some attempt at a historical summary at this point, showing the larger patterns I see as governing the development of German narrative across the century. Since the focus throughout the book has been analytical rather than historical, however, foregrounding individual texts rather than the relationships among them, let me conclude not with any foreshortened attempt at literary history but rather with a brief reflection on the chosen methodology and on the relationship between formalism and historicism in literary studies.

The purpose of this book, as formulated in the introduction, has been to apply the principles of semiotic narratology to a selection of twentieth-century narratives written in German, in order to generate readings that (I hope) have something to say to a dual audience: those who are primarily interested in the practical critical application of narrative theory and those whose primary interest is in modern German literature. Evidently, it is my belief that the eight individual readings proposed here demonstrate to at least some degree the advantages of employing a narratologically inspired approach as a reader. Evidently, other readers might well have chosen partially or even completely different sets of examples to make similar points. While I hope the selection of texts analysed was a reasonable one, it should be clear that ultimately it was also an arbitrary one, inspired certainly by my personal conviction that this particular approach has interesting things to say about these particular texts but inspired to at least an equally important degree by the fact that I particularly *like* these texts and *want* to say what I hope are interesting things about them. My pleasure in reading these particular narratives, in other words, has been so constant over the years that I wish in a certain sense not just to reread them one more time, but to *rewrite* them, to recast them in the terms of my own particular critical concerns.

The degree to which the critical engagement with a literary text is in one sense both a commentary on and, simultaneously, a *part* of that text, an extension or continuation of it, has been well expressed by Derek Attridge in the *Cambridge Companion to James Joyce* (1990). Noting that the already huge bulk of scholarly and critical books on Joyce continues to grow exponentially, Attridge observes that it is very possible to see the Joyce industry, like the similar Shakespeare, Proust, and Kafka industries, as an ever-greater obstacle between the text and its readers. Alternatively, however, he observes, it is also possible to regard it a good deal more positively as essentially an extension of Joyce's work rather than an occlusion of it. For 'this metatextual mountain is not in any simple way *outside* Joyce's own writing at all: it could be seen as continuous with the text it surrounds, extending that text to something much larger and richer than it was when Joyce first wrote it; and there is also a sense in which it is *inside* Joyce's original text, interleaving and interlineating it, dilating it to many times its original size' (Attridge 1990: 24).

Attridge's comments, in their context, are by no means restricted to purely formalist approaches to the literary text, but the metaphors of extension, interleaving, and interlineating he employs are particularly relevant to the formalist endeavour. Literary texts are texts that distinguish themselves from other related forms of social discourse by drawing attention, implicitly or explicitly, to their own particular modes of discursive functioning. The role of the reader who wishes to read literary texts *as* literary texts is therefore essentially to *extend* them in Attridge's sense, to observe and illustrate and exercise their particular modes of textual functioning – in short, to open up rather than curtail their particular capacities for textual play. Literary texts can, of course, be read (and frequently *are* read) for entirely different ends, whether as documentary evidence for historical or sociological or political purposes or as cultural or moral or intellectual monuments. While such critical activities are of vital social importance in their proper context – and are currently in vigorous ascendancy – that context is certainly *not* the study of literary texts specifically as literary texts.

Let me therefore conclude this book, as I began it, with an emphatic (if currently somewhat unfashionable) reaffirmation of the central necessity of formalist criticism as an intellectual activity, even (or especially) in so highly politicized and historicized an age as our own, when critical formalism has increasingly come to be seen in many quarters as close to self-indulgent if not openly escapist. Historicism *and* formalism, however, to repeat a point, are equally indispensable to the critical endeavour, complementary ways of reading literary texts, each displaying its own areas of blindness and insight. Historicism, whether of the old or of the new theoretical dispensation (as discussed in my introduction), has shown itself and will certainly continue to show itself to be a powerful and entirely indispensable scholarly and critical tool, but its fundamental weakness as a tool for the analysis of literary phenomena is quite clearly that it is incapable, by definition, of dealing with the specific literariness of literary texts. That task is the proper domain of the formalist critic, whether of the old or of the new dispensation, and as long as literature and the study of literature *as* literature continue to be regarded as worthwhile forms of social discourse, the central need for formalist criticism will also continue to exist.

Formalism, however, as already observed, has had both an aesthetic and a semiotic face in twentieth-century criticism. The quasi-religious certainties of the once-powerful aesthetic formalism of more innocent days find little resonance in our much less bibliocentric and far more sceptical times. The semiotic formalism espoused in the readings I have attempted here certainly shares with the aesthetic formalism of earlier days a fundamental concern for the literariness of literary texts – but that literariness is no longer located on the basis of a priori definitional criteria but rather in the play of textual strategies, the systemic intersection of particular ways of writing *and* particular ways of reading.

Reading, of course, has always been as much an art as a science, and no amount of earnest application of the impressive taxonomical and terminological resources of semiotics and/or narratology to a literary text is going to turn one ipso facto into an expert or even into a moderately interesting reader. As Robert Scholes puts it, with eminent good sense: 'My feeling is that the great usefulness of semiotics to literary studies will not be found in its elaborate analytical taxonomies, but rather is to be derived from a small number of its most basic and powerful concepts, ingeniously applied' (1982: xi). The applications attempted here have been undertaken in this spirit of readerly exploration in the semiotics of discourse – whether successfully or not will have been for my own reader to judge.

Notes

Introduction

1 This paragraph is borrowed with some modification from *Fictions of Discourse* (O'Neill 1994: 13), to which the interested reader is referred for further discussion.

2 Succinct and accessible introductions to the intellectual tradition of formalism, structuralism, and semiotics, with valuable bibliographical references, are variously provided by Scholes (1974), Culler (1975), and Hawkes (1977).

3 Of these, Rimmon-Kenan's excellent book, published in the New Accents series, is both the most accessible and the most systematic introduction to the field. Gerald Prince's *A Dictionary of Narratology* (1989) is an invaluable work of reference. For a comprehensive discussion of the range of twentieth-century theories of narrative, see Martin (1986). All three of these contain useful bibliographies. See also Prince (1982), Cohan /Shires (1988), and Toolan (1988).

4 See Adams (1971: 51–2, 62).

5 On the systemic relationship of controllers and controlled in the literary transaction, see O'Neill (1994: 107–31).

6 For further discussion of the relationship of realism, modernism, and postmodernism in these terms see O'Neill (1990: 59–65). My distinction between modernism and postmodernism in the present context draws on English-language rather than German-language models: for a useful discussion of the differences between the two models see Hoesterey (1988: 130–96); for the current state of discussion in the English-speaking world see Hutcheon (1988) and McHale (1987).

7 For a succinct and informed introduction to the development of modern German criticism, see the entry 'German Theory and Criticism' in Groden/ Kreiswirth (1994: 336–55).

8 For informed discussions of relativism in interpretation, see Fish (1980) and Armstrong (1990).

9 I have attempted to develop this position in both *The Comedy of Entropy* and *Fictions of Discourse* (O'Neill 1990, 1994).

Chapter 1: *Death in Venice*

1 I have argued this position at some length in *Fictions of Discourse* (1994), to which the interested reader is referred for further discussion.

2 Quotations in German are taken from *Der Tod in Venedig und andere Erzählungen* (Frankfurt: Fischer Taschenbuch Verlag, 1973), 7–68; English versions are taken, and silently modified where necessary, from David Luke's translation in *Death in Venice and Other Stories by Thomas Mann* (Toronto, New York: Bantam, 1988), 193–263.

3 For a survey of the enormous range of studies on *Der Tod in Venedig*, see especially Vaget (1984: 170–200; also 1990) and Kurzke (1985: 118–28).

4 For the terminology, see Lyons (1975: 70–81); for a wide-ranging application of these concepts to the classification of literary texts, see Lodge (1977: 73–81).

5 Another obvious example of this particular discursive strategy is Conrad's *Heart of Darkness*, which consequently displays a number of interesting parallels with *Der Tod in Venedig*; see McIntyre (1975). The primacy of setting in Luchino Visconti's film *Death in Venice* (1971) has likewise frequently been noted; for references, see Vaget (1984: 200).

6 On the interaction of character and setting, see Chatman (1978: 139–40), also O'Neill (1994: 53–4).

7 Since it is precisely the details and the sequence of their presentation that concern us here, it will be necessary to quote from the text at unusual length in this section.

8 *Odyssey* 8.249. Aschenbach quotes Johann Heinrich Voss's translation of 1781 (Dierks 1972: 237n38).

9 As Mieke Bal points out, the power relationship between a presenting narrator and a presented character is always such that a single negative word on the part of the narrator would, in principle, be enough to alter entirely the world of the character (1985: 149). See also O'Neill (1994: 41, 109).

10 Aschenbach's journey to Venice, down to such details as the Munich stranger, the gondolier, the street singer, the aborted trip to an Adriatic island, the outbreak of cholera, and the presence of a beautiful Polish boy, is closely based on a visit to Venice by Mann and his wife in the summer of 1911 (cf. Vaget 1990: 582–3). Aschenbach's family name probably derives from the nineteenth-century painter Andreas Aschenbach, whose paintings Mann would have seen

in the Munich Pinakothek; his first name, by Mann's own account, is a tribute to Gustav Mahler, with whom Mann was acquainted and news of whose death reached him on the Adriatic island of Brioni, en route to Venice, in 1911 (Vaget 1984: 170).

Chapter 2: *The Trial*

1 For preliminary orientation through the labyrinth of Kafka scholarship, see especially Binder (1979) and Dietz (1990), also Cohn (1978). For *Der Prozeß*, see especially Binder (1982), Elm (1979), and Nicolai (1986).
2 References to chapter order and the sequence of narrative events are to the long-familiar edition of Max Brod (*Der Prozeß*) rather than the more recent critical edition of Malcolm Pasley (*Der Proceß*). Quotations in German are taken from the easily accessible 1982 Fischer Taschenbuch Verlag edition; translations quoted are those of Willa and Edwin Muir's *The Trial*, silently amended where necessary.
3 The following treatment of Kafka's text returns to the discussion of *Der Prozeß* in my book *The Comedy of Entropy* (1990) in the new light of the theoretical position developed in my later book *Fictions of Discourse* (1994).
4 The example is taken from O'Neill (1994: 92–3), where it forms part of an extended treatment of narrative focalization.
5 On the concept of structural 'levels' in narrative, see Rimmon-Kenan (1983: 86–105), also O'Neill (1990: 87–102; 1994: 19–25, 110–16).
6 For a summary of the various arguments, see Binder (1982: 160–78).
7 Indicatively, Pasley observes in the critical edition of *Der Proceß* that while Kafka usually composed his narratives in strictly linear fashion, in the case of *Der Prozeß* he began by completing the first and last chapters, then typically worked on several of the intervening chapters simultaneously rather than following the story chronology (*Der Proceß* 2: 122–3).

Chapter 3: *Steppenwolf*

1 The most striking exception is Ziolkowski's classic essay on the use of sonata form in the novel (1965: 178–228).
2 For collections of responses to the novel see Hsia (1975), Schwarz (1980), and Voit (1992).
3 Quotations in German are from the Bibliothek Suhrkamp edition of *Der Steppenwolf* (Frankfurt: Suhrkamp, 1973); quotations in English are from *Steppenwolf*, trans. Basil Creighton, updated by Joseph Mileck, and here silently amended where necessary (New York: Bantam, 1971).

4 For more detailed consideration of the argumentation of the 'treatise,' see Ziolkowski (1965: 186–9).

5 Ziolkowski's position is shared, in varying degrees, by Field (1970: 106), Mileck (1978: 193), and Boulby (1967: 202); Dhority's is shared by Cohn (1969: 130) and Esselborn-Krummbiegel (1988: 106).

6 As Mileck, following Cohn, puts it, this lends Haller's tale 'a gripping immediacy despite its prevailing past tense. Past tense, in essence, becomes present tense. This immediacy is reinforced by Haller's usual retention in his reported interior monologues of the time indicators of direct interior monologue, and by his frequent use of these pointers to the present even when engaged in simple narration (today, now, yesterday, tomorrow, rather than that day, then, the previous day, the next day), and also by his numerous present tense asides' (1978: 197).

7 Hesse's debt to Romantic writers, especially Novalis, Jean Paul, and Hoffmann, is well established.

8 To my knowledge, Neuswanger is the only critic for whom Haller, as narrator, has learned to laugh at himself and his own one-time travails and pretensions, 'drawing a self-portrait in clown costume' (1980: 234), subjecting an ironically narrated Haller to improbable adventures in a parodic *Märchenwelt*.

9 On the central role of mirrors as illustrating the refraction of Haller's ego into its myriad components, see Freedman (1973), Artiss (1971), and Voit (1992: 28).

10 The relationship of the (nameless) editor and the protagonist in Hesse's novel is interestingly similar to that of the (nameless) editor and the protagonist in Sartre's *La nausée* (1938). See O'Neill (1990: 228–30).

11 Hesse, as Voit notes (1992: 22), went to some pains to make its physical otherness apparent by having it printed on different paper and in a different font.

12 For a collection of relevant extracts from Hesse's letters and other writings during the composition of the novel, see Michels (1972). See also Mileck (1978: 174–82) and Pfeifer (1980: 182–92). Haller's two poems first appeared in the collection 'Krisis: Ein Stück Tagebuch von Hermann Hesse' in the *Neue Rundschau* in November 1926.

13 The degree to which critics can fail to respond to its ludic structuration, however, is well demonstrated in Esselborn-Krummbiegel's contention that while Haller's crisis is adequately reflected in the theoretical sophistication of the treatise, it essentially remains without significance for the narrative structure (1988: 91–2), which she elsewhere classifies as unimaginatively traditional (113).

Chapter 4: *Auto da fé*

1 Quotations in German are taken from *Die Blendung* (Frankfurt am Main: Fischer Taschenbuch Verlag, 1965); quotations in English, silently modified

where necessary, are taken from *Auto da fé*, trans. C.V. Wedgwood (Harmondsworth, UK: Penguin, 1965).

2 That Canetti's reading of *Don Quijote* shapes the writing of *Die Blendung* has been noted by various critics, while Canetti himself enthusiastically acknowledges his admiration of Gogol (cf. Thomas 1991), and Barnouw compares the caricatural quality of his characters to the work of George Grosz (1979: 18).

3 The unnamed city bears numerous general resemblances to the real Vienna – and is significantly different in points of detail. Dissinger speaks of the setting as a caricatured Vienna, corresponding to its caricatured inhabitants (1971: 54).

4 Canetti's translators have opted for other resonances. C.V. Wedgwood's translation was called *Auto da fé* (London: Jonathan Cape, 1946) in England, *The Tower of Babel* (New York: Knopf, 1947) in the United States. Paule Arhex's French translation was also called *La tour de Babel* (Grenoble: Arthaud, 1949).

5 The contention that *Die Blendung* is a novel about reading is ironically reflected in the history of its reception: largely ignored when it first appeared in 1935 (Wien: Reichner), it was greeted with enthusiasm by foreign readers in both its English translation (1946) and its French translation (1949), was still largely ignored by German readers in its second edition of 1948 (München: Weismann), and advanced to the rank of modern classic only with its third German edition in 1963 (München: Hanser) and a subsequent pocketbook edition in 1965 (Frankfurt: Fischer).

6 Roberts (1975: 55–62) notes a number of other suggestive points of connection between Kien and Fischerle.

7 Barnouw (1979: 23–9). See also Roberts (1975: 118), Moser (1983: 56), and Thomas (1991: 126–7). Critics have differed radically on the question of Georg's sanity. For a summary of conflicting critical positions see Darby (1992: 142n41).

8 Franz Metzger, a budding scholar with an interest in things Chinese, is the only single character in the book who is not portrayed as suffering from a delusion of some sort, as Dissinger observes (1971: 96), though whether we should interpret this as some potential gleam of hope – a fourth face of the intellectual, perhaps? – or just as delusion postponed is left up to us.

9 Noting that Georg re-adopts the original German form of his name for his encounter with Peter, Darby (1992: 139) suggests that this may render suspect all of the passages dealing with him under the name 'Georges' – and also notes the intriguing parallel that Canetti's autobiography *Die gerettete Zunge* (1977) refers several times to the author's younger brother 'Georg,' who had settled in Paris, while the volume is dedicated to 'Georges' Canetti.

Chapter 5: *The Tin Drum*

1 For general introductions to recent Grass scholarship see Brode (1979) and Neuhaus (1979); for recent listings of general studies on *Die Blechtrommel* see Hermes (1988) and Neuhaus (1988); for further discussion of Oskar as narrator see Just (1972), Schnell (1975), Caltvedt (1978), Beyersdorf (1980), and Gerstenberg (1980).

2 Parenthetical page references to *Die Blechtrommel* are to the readily accessible Fischer Bücherei edition (Frankfurt: Fischer, 1962); English translations are taken from *The Tin Drum*, trans. Ralph Manheim (New York: Vintage, 1964), silently amended where necessary.

3 The term *implied author* was first suggested by Wayne Booth (1961: 70–1) and has been usefully developed by Chatman (1978: 147–51; 1990: 74–108). See also Rimmon-Kenan (1983: 86–9, 101–4) and O'Neill (1994: 66–71, 95–100).

4 In Ralph Manheim's translation, 'unschuldiges Papier,' literally 'innocent paper,' is more pointedly (but less suggestively than the play of *Schuld* and *Unschuld*) translated as 'virgin paper' (*The Tin Drum* 16). On colour symbolism in *Die Blechtrommel* see Willson (1966).

5 The most extended example of such flaunted discursive inappropriateness is the entire chapter 'Glaube Hoffnung Liebe' / 'Faith, Hope, Love'; see O'Neill (1974).

6 A very few examples may do duty for many here. The limitation, however, necessarily fails to convey the extent to which the practice is entirely typical of the narrative strategy of Grass's text throughout.

7 Cepl-Kaufmann (1975: 299); see also Neuhaus (1988: 45).

Chapter 6: *Two Views*

1 To my knowledge, the only extended treatments to date are the relevant chapters in Boulby (1974: 67–93), Fickert (1987: 75–94), and, especially, Neumann (1978: 217–88).

2 For concise surveys of early reactions see Schwarz (1970: 75–85) and Neumann (1978: 284–8); for a selection see Baumgart (1970: 139–62). Johnson subsequently protested the too facile equation of B. and D. with West Germany (BRD) and East Germany (DDR) respectively, and in his volume of lectures *Begleitumstände* (407) he ironically renames them *D*ietbert *B*(allhusen) and *B*eate *D*usenschön. (They are thus also called Dietbert and Beate in the English translation by Richard and Clara Winston cited here – but in order to avoid undue confusion I have reversed this change and continued to call them B. and D. in both languages throughout.)

3 *Zwei Ansichten* is quoted from the 1976 Suhrkamp Taschenbuch edition; quotations in English, silently amended where necessary, are taken from *Two Views*, trans. Richard and Clara Winston (New York: Harcourt, Brace and World, 1966).

4 *Zerfahren* is both 'distracted, restless' and (as here, punningly) 'run down.'

5 It is perhaps indicative that critics find it difficult to remember what exactly happens to B. in the end: Boulby has him 'run down by a truck' (1974: 81), while Fickert has him involved in an accident 'in his newly acquired car' (1987: 84).

6 I am not arguing that this is evidence of a technique previously unheard of in Johnson's oeuvre; such strategies are clearly in evidence already in *Mutmaßungen über Jakob* (1959).

7 See, for example, Lyotard's reflections on what he calls 'narratives of the legitimation of knowledge' (1984: 31).

8 For a balanced account of the game played between every reader and every writer for the stakes of textual authority see Culler (1982: 64–83).

Chapter 7: *The Goalie's Anxiety*

1 The case for a primarily psychological reading is argued, for example, by Durzak (1982), Heintz (1974), Summerfield (1979), Mixner (1977), and Renner (1985), while Lenzen (1976) adds a sociological dimension. A primarily semiotic orientation is adopted by Dixon (1972), White (1974), Falkenstein (1974), Schlueter (1981), and Bohnen (1976) – who is also a notable exception to the tendency to confine the investigation to Bloch's consciousness rather than its portrayal by a narrator. For a selection of early reviews see Scharang (1972: 64–78).

2 Bloch's 'camera-like' perception of reality as a series of discrete details has been discussed by Summerfield (1979); see also Renner (1985: 17–18) and Nägele/Voris (1978: 47). The filmic character of the text as a whole and its relationship to Wim Wenders's 1971 film adaptation of the same name are discussed by Brunette (1981).

3 Quotations from *Tormann* throughout are from the 1978 Suhrkamp Taschenbuch edition; quotations in English, silently amended where necessary, are taken from Michael Roloff's translation, *The Goalie's Anxiety at the Penalty Kick*, in *Three by Peter Handke* (New York: Bard/Avon, 1977): 1–97.

4 In the terms of reference of semiotics, all of the reality we inhabit is a text, and we as readers (simultaneously *in* and *of* that text), are necessarily engaged in a lifelong process of semiosis, i.e., the production, reception, interpretation, and evaluation of both linguistic and non-linguistic signs. For further discussion see Scholes (1982) and Eco (1979).

5 Here the similarity to both Sartre's Roquentin and Camus's 'stranger,' Meursault, is immediately striking. Handke himself pointed in an interview (qtd Durzak 1982: 75) to the similarity of the world-view of *Tormann* and *L'étranger* as far as the level of story is concerned, but, indicatively, he also drew attention to the difference between them on the level of discourse – 'weil die Sätze nämlich ganz anders sind' / 'because the sentences used are quite different' (qtd Durzak 1982: 76). To put it in a nutshell: where Meursault's (and Roquentin's) estrangement is epistemological, Bloch's is semiotic; cf. O'Neill (1990: 186–200, 216–33).

6 The gamelike relationship of author and reader obtains in a sense with respect to all literary texts, of course: the author constructs, the reader construes. The single most important quality of the postmodern text is the insistence with which it draws attention to its own gamelike qualities. By this definition the status of *Tormann* as a postmodern text is hardly debatable. The same is true, for example, of *Die Hornissen*, for which see Darby (1987), also O'Neill (1990: 271–83).

7 On *mise en abyme* in general see Dällenbach (1989).

8 Critics have pointed variously to the intertextual relationship with, e.g., Büchner (Bohnen 1976: 392–3), Hofmannsthal (Heintz 1974: 105), Kafka (Bohnen 1976: 391–2; Fingerhut 1980), Sartre (Schlueter 1981: 80–2), and Camus (Durzak 1982: 75–6). For the most part, however, the *parodic* nature of these echoes has tended to be ignored. Notable exceptions to this are Pütz (1975), who discusses the text's parodic relationship to detective fiction, and Bohnen – who also observes that while Josef Bloch's first name will clearly evoke Kafka for most readers, his surname also offers a tempting link with Thomas Bernhard's *Verstörung* (1967), which both impressed Handke and has a character called Bloch (1976: 398).

9 *Tor* is a usefully polyvalent word: *das Tor* means 'gate,' 'door,' or 'goal'; *der Tor* means 'fool.'

10 See especially Lenzen (1976); also Summerfield (1979: 105) and Brunette (1981: 192).

Chapter 8: *The Lime Works*

1 For studies of *Das Kalkwerk* from other perspectives, see Bohnert (1976), Leventhal (1988), Lindenmayr (1982). For general introductions to Bernhard's work, see Arnold (1991), Botond (1970), Dowden (1991), Jurgensen (1981), Meyerhofer (1985).

2 Parenthetical page references in German are to the 1976 Suhrkamp Taschenbuch edition of *Das Kalkwerk*; the English translations quoted, silently modified where necessary, are taken from *The Lime Works* (1973), trans. Sophie Wilkins.

3 Konrad's 'experiments' have been discovered to be based on a real audiological treatise by Victor Urbantschitsch, 'Über methodische Hörübungen und deren Bedeutungen für Schwerhörige' (Vienna, 1899) – whose therapeutic thrust, however, is entirely perverted by Konrad. See Mittermayer (1988: 222).

4 Ironically, Konrad's favourite author, Kropotkin, though certainly an anarchist, spent thirty years developing his very non-Konradean theory that cooperation and mutual aid are the norms in both nature and society.

5 On the lime works, with its echoing chambers and barred windows, as a metaphor for Konrad's own head, see König (1977).

6 There is, of course, always the hypothetical possibility that his confusion is only apparent, but the weight of evidence is against this.

7 Only very rarely does the narrator make any evaluation of an account, as when he disapproves of what he apparently sees to be Fro's disloyalty to Konrad (148/166) or characterizes Fro's financially motivated interest in the supposed study after Konrad's arrest as 'auf einmal plötzlich umschwenkend' (210) / 'a sudden complete about-face' (240).

8 The figure of the failed artist/scientist appears in Bernhard's earlier narratives *Frost* (1963) and *Verstörung* (1967) and recurs in *Korrektur* (1975). On parallels between Konrad and Canetti's Peter Kien, see Dissinger (1975).

9 For theoretical considerations of the role of the implied author, see Chatman (1978: 147–51), Rimmon-Kenan (1983: 86–9, 101–4), and O'Neill (1994: 66–71, 95–100).

10 On the importance of reflexivity in Bernhard's work in general, see Schweikert (1974) and Huntemann (1990).

11 The parallels with Beckett have been noted by many critics: see Ehrig (1979) and Esslin (1985).

12 See Huntemann (1990: 36); for further parallels with Kafka, see Fetz (1988); on the relationship of entropy and comedy, see O'Neill (1990).

13 After *Korrektur* (1975) Bernhard turned to more overtly autobiographical writing and to theatre.

14 One notes, for example, that Bernhard bought and renovated a run-down farmhouse in Ohlsdorf, near Wels in Upper Austria, in 1965, about the same time (7/3) that Konrad fictionally purchased the disused lime works in the same area (10/6).

Bibliography

This bibliography is made up of two separate listings, the first consisting of literary texts, the second of theoretical and critical texts. Items from the first list are cited in my own text by author and title, items from the second by author and date of the edition cited.

1 Literary Texts

Beckett, Samuel. *Krapp's Last Tape*. 1958. *Collected Shorter Plays of Samuel Beckett*. London: Faber, 1984. 53–63.

Bernhard, Thomas. *Frost*. Frankfurt am Main: Insel, 1963.

– *Das Kalkwerk*. Frankfurt am Main: Suhrkamp, 1970; Suhrkamp Taschenbuch Verlag, 1976.

– *Korrektur*. Frankfurt am Main: Suhrkamp, 1975.

– *The Lime Works*. Trans. Sophie Wilkins. Chicago: University of Chicago Press, 1973.

– *Verstörung*. Frankfurt am Main: Insel, 1967.

Borges, Jorge Luis. 'The Library of Babel.' *Labyrinths: Selected Stories and Other Writings*. Ed. Donald A. Yates and James E. Irby. New York: New Directions, 1964. 51–8.

Büchner, Georg. 'Lenz.' 1839. *Werke und Briefe*. Ed. Fritz Bergemann. dtv-Gesamtausgabe. München: Deutscher Taschenbuch Verlag, 1967. 65–84.

– 'Woyzeck.' 1879. *Werke und Briefe*. Ed. Fritz Bergemann. dtv-Gesamtausgabe. München: Deutscher Taschenbuch Verlag, 1967. 113–32.

Camus, Albert. *L'étranger*. 1942. Paris: Gallimard, 1957.

– *Le mythe de Sisyphe*. Paris: Gallimard, 1942.

Canetti, Elias. *Auto da fé*. Trans. C.V. Wedgwood. London: Jonathan Cape, 1946; Harmondsworth, UK: Penguin, 1965.

– *Die Blendung.* 1935. Frankfurt am Main: Fischer Taschenbuch Verlag, 1965.

– *Masse und Macht.* Hamburg: Claassen, 1960.

Conrad, Joseph. *Heart of Darkness.* 1902. Ed. Robert Kimbrough. Norton Critical Edition. New York: Norton, 1963.

Döblin, Alfred. *Berlin Alexanderplatz.* 1929. Olten, Freiburg im Breisgau: Walter, 1967.

Dostoevsky, Feodor. *Crime and Punishment.* Originally pub. in Russian, 1866. Trans. Jessie Coulson. Ed. George Gibian. Norton Critical Edition. New York: Norton, 1964.

Grass, Günter. *Die Blechtrommel.* 1959. Fischer Bücherei. Frankfurt: Fischer, 1962.

– *The Tin Drum.* Trans. Ralph Manheim. 1961. New York: Vintage, 1964.

Grillparzer, Franz. *Der arme Spielmann.* 1848. Wien: Schroll, 1930.

Handke, Peter. *Die Angst des Tormanns beim Elfmeter. Erzählung.* Frankfurt am Main: Suhrkamp, 1970; 1978 (Suhrkamp Taschenbuch 27).

– 'Die Angst des Tormanns beim Elfmeter.' *Text und Kritik* 24/24a (1971): 45.

– *The Goalie's Anxiety at the Penalty Kick.* Trans. Michael Roloff. New York: Farrar, Straus and Giroux, 1972. Repr. in Peter Handke, *Three by Peter Handke.* New York: Bard/Avon, 1977. 1–97.

– *Der Hausierer. Roman.* Frankfurt am Main: Suhrkamp, 1967.

– *Die Hornissen. Roman.* Frankfurt am Main: Suhrkamp, 1966.

Hesse, Hermann. *Der Steppenwolf.* 1927. Bibliothek Suhrkamp 226. Frankfurt am Main: Suhrkamp, 1973.

– *Steppenwolf.* Trans. Basil Creighton. 1929. Updated by Joseph Mileck. 1963. New York: Bantam, 1971.

Hofmannsthal, Hugo von. 'Ein Brief.' 1902. *Ausgewählte Werke in zwei Bänden.* Ed. Rudolf Hirsch. Stuttgart: Deutscher Bücherbund, 1966. 2: 337–48.

Johnson, Uwe. *Begleitumstände: Frankfurter Vorlesungen.* Frankfurt am Main: Suhrkamp, 1980.

– *Das dritte Buch über Achim.* Frankfurt am Main: Suhrkamp, 1961.

– *Jahrestage: Aus dem Leben von Gesine Cresspahl.* 4 vols. Frankfurt am Main: Suhrkamp, 1970–83.

– *Mutmaßungen über Jakob.* Frankfurt am Main: Suhrkamp, 1959.

– *Two Views.* Trans. Richard and Clara Winston. New York: Harcourt, Brace and World, 1966.

– *Zwei Ansichten.* Frankfurt am Main: Suhrkamp, 1965. Frankfurt am Main: Suhrkamp, 1976 (Suhrkamp Taschenbuch 326).

Joyce, James. *Finnegans Wake.* 1939. New York: Viking, 1971.

Kafka, Franz. *Der Proceß.* 1925. Ed. Malcolm Pasley. 2 vols. Frankfurt am Main: Fischer, 1990.

– *Der Prozeß.* 1925. Ed. Max Brod. Frankfurt am Main: Fischer Taschenbuch Verlag, 1982.
– *Das Schloß.* 1926. Frankfurt am Main: Fischer Taschenbuch Verlag, 1981.
– *The Trial.* Trans. Willa and Edwin Muir. 1937. New York: Schocken, 1968.
Kleist, Heinrich von. 'Über das Marionettentheater.' 1810. *Anekdoten. Kleine Schriften.* dtv-Gesamtausgabe 5. Ed. Helmut Sembdner. München: Deutscher Taschenbuch Verlag, 1964. 71–84.
Mann, Thomas. *Buddenbrooks.* 1901. Frankfurt am Main: Fischer, 1960.
– *Death in Venice and Other Stories by Thomas Mann.* Trans. David Luke. Toronto, New York: Bantam, 1988.
– *Der Tod in Venedig und andere Erzählungen.* Frankfurt am Main: Fischer Taschenbuch Verlag, 1954, 1973.
Rilke, Rainer Maria. *Duino Elegies.* 1923. German text with English trans. by J.B. Leishman and Stephen Spender. New York: Norton, 1963.
Robbe-Grillet, Alain. *Le voyeur.* Paris: Les Editions de Minuit, 1955.
Sartre, Jean-Paul. *La nausée.* Paris: Gallimard, 1938.

2 Theoretical and Critical Texts

Adams, Hazard, ed. 1971. *Critical Theory since Plato.* San Diego: Harcourt Brace Jovanovich.
Allemann, Beda. 1965. 'Franz Kafka: *Der Prozeß.*' *Der deutsche Roman.* 2 vols. Ed. Benno von Wiese. Düsseldorf: Bagel. 2: 234–90.
Armstrong, Paul B. 1990. *Conflicting Readings: Variety and Validity in Interpretation.* Chapel Hill, London: University of North Carolina Press.
Arnold, Heinz Ludwig, ed. 1991. *Thomas Bernhard.* Text und Kritik 43. 3rd, rev. ed. München: Text und Kritik.
Artiss, David. 1971. 'Key Symbols in Hesse's *Steppenwolf.*' *Seminar* 7 (1971): 85–101.
Attridge, Derek, ed. 1990. *The Cambridge Companion to James Joyce.* Cambridge: Cambridge University Press.
Auer, Annemarie. 1983. 'Ein Genie und sein Sonderling – Elias Canetti und *Die Blendung.*' Durzak 1983: 31–53.
Bakhtin, M.M. 1981. *The Dialogic Imagination: Four Essays.* Originally pub. in Russian, 1975. Ed. Michael Holquist. Trans. Caryl Emerson and Michael Holquist. Austin: University of Texas Press.
Bal, Mieke. 1985. *Narratology: Introduction to the Theory of Narrative.* Originally pub. in Dutch, 1980. Trans. Christine van Boheemen. Toronto: University of Toronto Press.

Barnouw, Dagmar. 1979. *Elias Canetti*. Sammlung Metzler 180. Stuttgart: Metzler.

Barthes, Roland. 1974. *S/Z*. Originally pub. in French, 1970. Trans. Richard Miller. New York: Hill and Wang.

Baumgart, Reinhard, ed. 1970. *Über Uwe Johnson*. Frankfurt am Main: Suhrkamp.

Beyersdorf, H.E. 1980. 'The Narrator as Artful Deceiver: Aspects of Narrative Perspective in *Die Blechtrommel*.' *Germanic Review* 55.4 (1980): 129–38.

Binder, Hartmut, ed. 1979. *Kafka-Handbuch in zwei Bänden*. Stuttgart: Kröner.

– 1982. '*Der Prozeß*.' *Kafka-Kommentar*. 2nd ed. München: Winkler. 2: 160–261.

Bloom, Harold. 1973. *The Anxiety of Influence: A Theory of Poetry*. London: Oxford University Press.

Bohnen, Klaus. 1976. 'Kommunikationsproblematik und Vermittlungsmethode in Handkes *Die Angst des Tormanns beim Elfmeter*.' *Wirkendes Wort* 26 (1976): 387–400.

Bohnert, Karin. 1976. *Ein Modell der Entfremdung: Eine Interpretation des Romans* Das Kalkwerk *von Th. Bernhard*. Wien: VWGÖ.

Booth, Wayne. 1961. *The Rhetoric of Fiction*. Chicago: University of Chicago Press.

Botond, Anneliese, ed. 1970. *Über Thomas Bernhard*. Frankfurt am Main: Suhrkamp.

Boulby, Mark. 1967. *Hermann Hesse: His Mind and Art*. Ithaca, London: Cornell University Press.

– 1974. *Uwe Johnson*. New York: Ungar.

Bradbury, Malcolm. 1993. *The Modern British Novel*. London: Secker and Warburg.

Brode, Hanspeter. 1976. 'Die Zeitgeschichte in der *Blechtrommel* von Günter Grass. Entwurf eines textinternen Kommunikationsmodells.' *Günter Grass: Ein Materialienbuch*. Ed. Rolf Geißler. Darmstadt: Luchterhand.

– 1979. *Günter Grass*. Autorenbücher 17. München: Beck; München: Edition Text + Kritik.

Brunette, Peter. 1981. 'Filming Words: Wenders's *The Goalie's Anxiety at the Penalty Kick* (1971).' *Modern European Filmmakers and the Art of Adaptation*. Ed. Andrew Horton and Joan Magretta. New York: Ungar, 1981. 188–202.

Busch, Günther. 1975. 'Der Roman des großen Erschreckens, *Die Blendung*.' Originally pub. 1963. Göpfert 1975: 31–4.

Caltvedt, Lester. 1978. 'Oskar's Account of Himself: Narrative "Guilt" and the Relationship of Fiction to History in *Die Blechtrommel*.' *Seminar* 14 (1978): 285–94.

Canetti, Elias. 1975. 'Das erste Buch: *Die Blendung*.' Originally pub. 1974. Göpfert 1975: 124–35.

Cepl-Kaufmann, Gertrude. 1975. *Günter Grass: Eine Analyse des Gesamtwerks unter dem Aspekt von Literatur und Politik.* Kronberg im Taunus: Scriptor Verlag.

Chatman, Seymour. 1978. *Story and Discourse: Narrative Structure in Fiction and Film.* Ithaca, NY: Cornell University Press.

– 1990. *Coming to Terms: The Rhetoric of Narrative in Fiction and Film.* Ithaca, NY: Cornell University Press.

Cohan, Steven, and Linda M. Shires. 1988. *Telling Stories: A Theoretical Analysis of Narrative Fiction.* New Accents. New York, London: Routledge.

Cohn, Dorrit. 1969. 'Narration of Consciousness in *Der Steppenwolf.*' *Germanic Review* 44 (1969): 121–31.

– 1978. 'Trends in Literary Criticism: Some Structuralist Approaches to Kafka.' *German Quarterly* 51 (1978): 182–8.

Conrad, Klaus. 1966. *Die beginnende Schizophrenie: Versuch einer Gestaltanalyse des Wahns.* Originally pub. 1958. Stuttgart: Thieme.

Craig, D.A. 1972. 'The Novels of Thomas Bernhard: A Report.' *German Life & Letters* 25 (1972): 343–53.

Culler, Jonathan. 1975. *Structuralist Poetics: Structuralism, Linguistics and the Study of Literature.* London: Routledge and Kegan Paul.

– 1981. *The Pursuit of Signs: Semiotics, Literature, Deconstruction.* Ithaca, NY: Cornell University Press.

– 1982. *On Deconstruction: Theory and Criticism after Structuralism.* Ithaca, NY: Cornell University Press.

Dällenbach, Lucien. 1989. *The Mirror in the Text.* Originally pub. in French, 1977. Trans. Jeremy Whiteley with Emma Hughes. Chicago: University of Chicago Press.

Darby, David. 1987. 'The Narrative Text as Palimpsest: Levels of Discourse in Peter Handke's *Die Hornissen.*' *Seminar* 23 (1987): 251–64.

– 1992. *Structures of Disintegration: Narrative Strategies in Elias Canetti's* Die Blendung. Riverside, CA: Ariadne Press.

Dhority, Lynn. 1974. 'Who Wrote the *Tractat vom Steppenwolf?*' *German Life & Letters* 27 (1974): 59–66.

Dierks, Manfred. 1972. *Studien zu Mythos und Psychologie bei Thomas Mann.* Thomas-Mann-Studien 2. Bern, München: Francke.

Dietz, Ludwig. 1990. *Franz Kafka.* Sammlung Metzler 138. 2nd ed. Stuttgart: Metzler.

Dissinger, Dieter. 1971. *Vereinzelung und Massenwahn: Elias Canettis Roman* Die Blendung. Studien zur Germanistik, Anglistik und Komparatistik 11. Bonn: Bouvier Verlag Herbert Grundmann.

– 1975. 'Alptraum und Gegentraum: Zur Romanstruktur bei Canetti und Bernhard.' *Literatur und Kritik* 10 (1975): 168–75.

- 1982. 'Der Roman *Die Blendung.*' *Text + Kritik* 28 (1982): 33–42.

Dixon, Christa K. 1972. 'Peter Handkes *Die Angst des Tormanns beim Elfmeter:* Ein Beitrag zur Interpretation.' *Sprachkunst* 3 (1972): 75–97.

Dowden, Stephen D. 1991. *Understanding Thomas Bernhard.* Columbus, SC: University of South Carolina Press.

Durzak, Manfred. 1982. *Peter Handke und die deutsche Gegenwartsliteratur: Narziss auf Abwegen.* Sprache und Literatur 108. Stuttgart: Kohlhammer.

- ed. 1983. *Zu Elias Canetti.* LGW-Interpretationen 63. Stuttgart: Klett.

Eco, Umberto. 1979. *A Theory of Semiotics.* Originally pub. 1976. Bloomington, London: Indiana University Press.

Ehrig, Heinz. 1979. 'Probleme des Absurden: Vergleichende Bemerkungen zu Thomas Bernhard und Samuel Beckett.' *Wirkendes Wort* 29 (1979): 44–64.

Ellis, John M. 1974. *Narration in the German Novelle: Theory and Interpretation.* Cambridge: Cambridge University Press.

Elm, Theo. 1979. '*Der Prozeß.*' *Kafka-Handbuch in zwei Bänden.* Ed. Hartmut Binder. Stuttgart: Kröner. 2: 420–41.

Esselborn-Krummbiegel, Helga. 1988. *Hermann Hesse:* Der Steppenwolf. Oldenbourg-Interpretationen. München: Oldenbourg.

Esslin, Martin. 1985. 'Beckett and Bernhard: A Comparison.' *Modern Austrian Literature* 18.2 (1985): 67–78.

Falkenstein, Henning. 1974. *Peter Handke.* Köpfe des XX. Jahrhunderts. Berlin: Colloquium.

Fetz, Gerald A. 1988. 'Kafka and Bernhard: Reflections on Affinity and Influence.' *Modern Austrian Literature* 21.3/4 (1988): 217–41.

Fickert, Kurt. 1987. *Neither Left nor Right: The Politics of Individualism in Uwe Johnson's Work.* New York: Lang.

Field, George Wallis. 1970. *Hermann Hesse.* Twayne's World Authors Series. New York: Twayne.

Fingerhut, Karlheinz. 1980. 'Drei erwachsene Söhne Kafkas: Zur produktiven Kafka-Rezeption bei Walser, Weiss und Peter Handke.' *Wirkendes Wort* 30 (1980): 384–403.

Fish, Stanley. 1980. *Is There a Text in This Class? The Authority of Interpretive Communities.* Cambridge, MA; London: Harvard University Press.

Freedman, Ralph. 1973. 'Person and Persona: The Magic Mirrors of *Steppenwolf.*' *Hermann Hesse.* Ed. Theodore Ziolkowski. Englewood Cliffs, NJ: Prentice-Hall. 153–79.

Garland, Henry and Mary. 1986. *The Oxford Companion to German Literature.* 2nd ed. Oxford: Oxford University Press.

Genette, Gérard. 1980. *Narrative Discourse: An Essay in Method.* Originally pub.

as 'Discours du récit' in *Figures III*, 1972. Trans. Jane E. Lewin. Ithaca, NY: Cornell University Press.

Gerstenberg, Renate. 1980. *Zur Erzähltechnik von Günter Grass*. Heidelberg: Winter.

Göpfert, Herbert G. 1975. *Canetti lesen: Erfahrungen mit seinen Büchern*. München: Hanser.

Graf, Hansjörg. 1971. 'Letzte Geschichten: Mutmaßungen über Thomas Bernhard.' *Neue Rundschau* 82 (1971): 343–53.

Groden, Michael, and Martin Kreiswirth, ed. 1994. *The Johns Hopkins Guide to Literary Theory and Criticism*. Baltimore, London: Johns Hopkins University Press.

Hawkes, Terence. 1977. *Structuralism and Semiotics*. Berkeley: University of California Press.

Heintz, Günter. 1974. *Peter Handke*. München: Oldenbourg.

Heller, Erich. 1961. *The Ironic German*. Meridian Books. Cleveland, New York: World.

– 1974. *Franz Kafka*. Fontana Modern Masters. London: Fontana/Collins.

Hermes, Daniela. 1988. 'Auswahl-Bibliographie.' *Text + Kritik* (München) Heft 1: Günter Grass. Sechste Auflage: Neufassung. 139–61.

Hoesterey, Ingeborg. 1988. *Verschlungene Schriftzeichen: Intertextualität von Literatur und Kunst in der Moderne/Postmoderne*. Frankfurt am Main: Athenäum.

Hsia, Adrian, ed. 1975. *Hermann Hesse im Spiegel der zeitgenössischen Kritik*. Bern und München: Francke Verlag.

Huntemann, Willi. 1990. *Artistik und Rollenspiel: Das System Thomas Bernhard*. Würzburg: Königshausen und Neumann.

Hutcheon, Linda. 1988. *A Poetics of Postmodernism: History, Theory, Fiction*. New York, London: Routledge.

Jurgensen, Manfred. 1981. *Thomas Bernhard: Der Kegel im Wald oder die Geometrie der Verneinung*. Bern: Lang.

Just, Georg. 1972. *Darstellung und Appell in der* Blechtrommel *von Günter Grass. Darstellungsästhetik versus Wirkungsästhetik*. Frankfurt: Athenäum.

Koelb, Clayton. 1983. 'Kafka's Rhetorical Moment.' *PMLA* 98 (1983): 37–46.

König, Josef. 1977. 'Schöpfung und Vernichtung: Über die Kopf-Metaphorik in Thomas Bernhards Roman *Das Kalkwerk*.' *Sprache im technischen Zeitalter* 63 (1977): 231–41.

Kurzke, Hermann. 1985. *Thomas Mann. Epoche – Werk – Wirkung*. München: Beck.

Laemmle, Peter. 1974. 'Stimmt die "partielle Wahrheit" noch?' *Text + Kritik* 43 (1974): 45–9.

Lämmert, Eberhard. 1955. *Bauformen des Erzählens*. Stuttgart: Metzler.

Lenzen, Arnulf. 1976. 'Gesellschaft und Umgebung in Handke: *Die Angst des Tormanns beim Elfmeter*.' *Wirkendes Wort* 26 (1976): 401–6.

Leventhal, Robert S. 1988. 'The Rhetoric of Anarcho-Nihilistic Murder: Thomas Bernhard's *Das Kalkwerk*.' *Modern Austrian Literature* 21.3/4 (1988): 19–38.

Lindenmayr, Heinrich. 1982. *Totalität und Beschränkung: Eine Untersuchung zu Thomas Bernhards Roman* Das Kalkwerk. Königstein: Athenäum.

Lodge, David. 1977. *The Modes of Modern Writing: Metaphor, Metonymy, and the Typology of Modern Literature*. Chicago: University of Chicago Press.

Lyons, John. 1975. *Introduction to Theoretical Linguistics*. Cambridge: Cambridge University Press.

Lyotard, Jean-François. 1984. *The Postmodern Condition: A Report on Knowledge*. Trans. Geoff Bennington and Brian Massumi. Minneapolis: University of Minnesota Press.

McHale, Brian. 1987. *Postmodernist Fiction*. New York, London: Methuen.

McIntyre, Allan J. 1975. 'Psychology and Symbol: Correspondences between *Heart of Darkness* and *Death in Venice*.' *Hartford Studies in Literature* 7 (1975): 216–35.

Mann, Thomas. 1937. 'Dem sechzigjährigen Hermann Hesse.' *Neue Zürcher Zeitung*, 2 July 1937. Repr. as 'Hermann Hesse: Einleitung zu einer amerikanischen *Demian*-Ausgabe.' *Neue Rundschau* 58 (1947): 248.

Martin, Wallace. 1986. *Recent Theories of Narrative*. Ithaca, NY: Cornell University Press.

Mason, Ann L. 1974. *The Skeptical Muse: A Study of Günter Grass' Conception of the Artist*. Bern: Lang.

Meyerhofer, Nicholas J. 1985. *Thomas Bernhard*. Berlin: Colloquium.

Michels, Volker. 1972. *Materialien zu Hermann Hesses Der Steppenwolf*. Suhrkamp Taschenbuch 53. Frankfurt am Main: Suhrkamp.

Michelsen, Peter. 1972. 'Oskar oder Das Monstrum. Reflexionen über *Die Blechtrommel* von Günter Grass.' *Neue Rundschau* 83 (1972): 722–40.

Mileck, Joseph. 1978. *Hermann Hesse: Life and Art*. Berkeley: University of California Press.

Mittermayer, Manfred. 1988. *Ich werden: Versuch einer Thomas-Bernhard-Lektüre*. Stuttgart: Heinz.

Mixner, Manfred. 1977. *Peter Handke*. Kronberg/Ts.: Athenäum.

Moser, Manfred. 1983. 'Zu Canettis *Blendung*.' Durzak 1983: 54–71.

Nägele, Rainer, and Renate Voris. 1978. *Peter Handke*. München: Beck.

Neuhaus, Volker. 1979. *Günter Grass*. Sammlung Metzler 179. Stuttgart: Metzler.

– 1988. *Günter Grass:* Die Blechtrommel. Oldenbourg-Interpretationen 16. München: Oldenbourg.

Neumann, Bernd. 1978. *Utopie und Mimesis: Zum Verhältnis von Ästhetik, Gesell-schaftsphilosophie und Politik in den Romanen Uwe Johnsons*. Kronberg/Ts.: Athenäum.

Neuswanger, R. Russell. 1980. 'The Autonomy of the Narrator and the Function of Humor in *Der Steppenwolf.*' *Hermann Hesse heute*. Ed. Adrian Hsia. Bonn: Bouvier Verlag Herbert Grundmann. 233–41.

Nicolai, Ralf R. 1986. *Kafkas* Prozess: *Motive und Gestalten*. Würzburg: Königs-hausen und Neumann.

O'Neill, Patrick. 1974. 'Musical Form and the Pauline Message in a Key Chapter of Grass's *Blechtrommel.*' *Seminar* 10 (1974): 298–307.

– 1990. *The Comedy of Entropy: Humour, Narrative, Reading*. Toronto: Univer-sity of Toronto Press.

– 1994. *Fictions of Discourse: Reading Narrative Theory*. Toronto, Buffalo, Lon-don: University of Toronto Press.

Pascal, Roy. 1982. *Kafka's Narrators: A Study of His Stories and Sketches*. Anglica Germanica Series 2. Cambridge: Cambridge University Press.

Pfeifer, Martin. 1980. *Hesse-Kommentar zu sämtlichen Werken*. München: Winkler Verlag.

Piel, Edgar. 1984. *Elias Canetti*. Autorenbücher 38. München: C.H. Beck/Text + Kritik.

Politzer, Heinz. 1966. *Franz Kafka: Parable and Paradox*. Originally pub. 1962. Ithaca, NY: Cornell University Press.

Prince, Gerald. 1982. *Narratology: The Form and Functioning of Narrative*. Berlin: Mouton.

– 1989. *A Dictionary of Narratology*. Originally pub. 1987. Lincoln, London: Uni-versity of Nebraska Press.

Pütz, Peter. 1975. 'Peter Handke *Die Angst des Tormanns beim Elfmeter.*' *Deutsche Bestseller – Deutsche Ideologie. Ansätze zu einer Verbraucherpoetik*. Ed. Heinz Ludwig Arnold. Stuttgart: Klett.

Reddick, John. 1974. *The 'Danzig Trilogy' of Günter Grass: A Study of* The Tin Drum, Cat and Mouse *and* Dog Years. New York: Harcourt.

Reed, T.J. 1974. *Thomas Mann: The Uses of Tradition*. London: Oxford University Press. 144–78.

Renner, Rolf Günter. 1985. *Peter Handke*. Sammlung Metzler 218. Stuttgart: Metzler.

Rimmon-Kenan, Shlomith. 1983. *Narrative Fiction: Contemporary Poetics*. New Accents. London: Methuen.

Roberts, David. 1975. *Kopf und Welt: Elias Canettis Roman* Die Blendung. München: Hanser.

Scharang, Michael. 1972. *Über Peter Handke*. Frankfurt am Main: Suhrkamp.

Schlueter, June. 1981. *The Plays and Novels of Peter Handke*. Pittsburgh: University of Pittsburgh Press.

Schnell, Josef. 1975. 'Irritation der Wirklichkeitserfahrung. Die Funktion des Erzählers in Günter Grass' *Die Blechtrommel*.' *Der Deutschunterricht* 27.3 (1975): 33–43.

Scholes, Robert. 1974. *Structuralism in Literature: An Introduction*. New Haven, London: Yale University Press.

– 1982. *Semiotics and Interpretation*. New Haven, London: Yale University Press.

Schor, Naomi. 1980. 'Fiction as Interpretation / Interpretation as Fiction.' *The Reader in the Text: Essays on Audience and Interpretation*. Ed. Susan R. Suleiman and Inge Crosman. Princeton: Princeton University Press. 165–82.

Schwarz, Egon, ed. 1980. *Hermann Hesses* Steppenwolf. Königstein: Athenäum.

Schwarz, Wilhelm Johannes. 1970. *Der Erzähler Uwe Johnson*. Bern: Francke.

Schweikert, Uwe. 1974. '"Im Grunde ist alles, was gesagt wird, zitiert": Zum Problem von Identifikation und Distanz in der Rollenprosa Thomas Bernhards.' *Text + Kritik* 43 (1974): 1–8.

Shklovsky, Victor. 1965. 'Sterne's *Tristram Shandy*: Stylistic Commentary.' Originally pub. in Russian, 1921. *Russian Formalist Criticism: Four Essays*. Trans. Lee T. Lemon and Marion J. Reis. Lincoln, London: University of Nebraska Press. 25–57.

Stanzel, Franz. 1955. *Die typischen Erzählsituationen im Roman: Dargestellt an Tom Jones, Moby Dick, The Ambassadors, Ulysses u.a.* Wiener Beiträge zur englischen Philologie 63. Wien: Braumüller.

Stevens, Adrian. 1991. 'Creating Figures: Narrative, Discourse and Character in *Die Blendung*.' Stevens/Wagner 1991: 105–17.

– and Fred Wagner. 1991. *Elias Canetti: Londoner Symposium*. Stuttgarter Arbeiten zur Germanistik 245. Stuttgart: Verlag Hans-Dieter Heinz, Akademischer Verlag.

Summerfield, Ellen. 1979. 'Die Kamera als literarisches Mittel. Zu Peter Handkes *Die Angst des Tormanns beim Elfmeter*.' *Modern Austrian Literature* 12.1 (1979): 95–112.

Sussman, Henry. 1977. 'The Court as Text: Inversion, Supplanting, and Derangement in Kafka's *Der Prozeß*.' *PMLA* 92 (1977): 41–55.

Thomas, Noel. 1991. '"My Great Russian": Reflections on Reality and Unreality in Canetti's *Die Blendung* and Gogol's *The Overcoat*.' Stevens/Wagner 1991: 119–30.

Thuswaldner, Werner. 1976. *Sprach- und Gattungsexperiment bei Peter Handke*. Salzburg: Alfred Winter.

Todorov, Tzvetan. 1969. *Grammaire du Décaméron*. The Hague: Mouton.

Toolan, Michael J. 1988. *Narrative: A Critical Linguistic Introduction.* London: Routledge.

Vaget, Hans Rudolf. 1984. *Thomas Mann – Kommentar zu sämtlichen Erzählungen.* München: Winkler.

– 1990. 'Die Erzählungen.' *Thomas-Mann-Handbuch.* Ed. Helmut Koopmann. Stuttgart: Kröner. 534–622.

Voit, Friedrich, ed. 1992. *Hermann Hesse* Der Steppenwolf. Erläuterungen und Dokumente. Stuttgart: Reclam.

White, J.J. 1974. 'Signs of Disturbance: The Semiological Import of Some Recent Fiction by Michel Tournier and Peter Handke.' *Journal of European Studies* 4 (1974): 233–54.

Willson, A. Leslie. 1966. 'The Grotesque Everyman in Günter Grass's *Die Blechtrommel.*' *Monatshefte* 58 (1966): 131–8.

Ziolkowski, Theodore. 1965. *The Novels of Hermann Hesse: A Study in Theme and Structure.* Princeton: Princeton University Press.

Index